Buying and Selling Business Opportunities
A Sales Transaction Handbook

Wilfred F. Tetreault, C.B.O.A., C.B.C.

President
American Business Consultants, Inc.

In association with
Robert W. Clements, C.B.O.A.

Addison-Wesley Publishing Company
Reading, Massachusetts · Menlo Park, California
London · Amsterdam · Don Mills, Ontario · Sydney

Library of Congress Cataloging in Publication Data

Tetreault, Wilfred, 1927-
   Buying and sellling business opportunities.

   Bibliography: p.
   1.   Small business—Law and legislation—United
States. 2.   Small business—United States—Purchasing.
3.   Business enterprises, Sale of—United States.
4.   Bulk sales—United States. I. Title.
KF1659.T47   346.73'0652   80-18771
ISBN 0-201-07711-6

ISBN 0-201-07711-6
ABCDEFGHIJ-AL-8987654321

Preface

"The American Dream"—owning your own business—has become the overwhelming drive for millions of American and foreign investors. Many people feel the need to escape the 8-to-5 syndrome, nonidentity in the corporate maze, and stagnation in bureaucracy.

In 1978, two and one-half million businesses changed hands and four hundred thousand new ones started up. The 11 million or so businesses in the United States cover a wide spectrum, from the "Mom and Pop" corner store to large national manufacturing corporations. These businesses offer many opportunities to 25 million investors. Thus a heavy demand for professional knowledge on the part of business owners and buyers has been created. So far little has been offered in the way of books on buying, listing, selling, and closing escrows in business opportunities. The author and his associates hope that the material herein will be an important contribution to normal business activity.

This book provides real estate brokers/agents, business owners, appraisers, buyers, certified public accountants, accountants, attorneys, escrow agents, assessors, planning engineers, bankers, financial consultants, acquisition and relocation agents, and consumers with knowledge and protection against litigation that will be necessary in the completion of all aspects of appraising, buying, and selling a business under the legal requirements of uniform commercial code—bulk sale transfer.

This book has been especially designed and developed with everything needed to perform a complete "turnkey" bulk sale transfer with "step-by-step" double initiative checklists with the assistance of practicing specialists in business opportunity, training specialists, real estate brokers and salespersons, accountants, attorneys, and business owners. Both the principles and concepts have been validated in practice during the past several years.

For the businessperson who is contemplating buying or selling a business, it would be a wise investment to purchase *Starting Right in Your New Business* (Addison-Wesley (1981)). The book covers an honest and realistic approach for self elevation beyond the emotional levels of decision. A decision to buy or sell a business must be one that concerns not only yourself but your family as well, since there can be a great impact on your future.

If you feel you need further instructions, you can attend either of two seminars. One concentrates on the entire bulk sale transfer and the other covers business opportunity appraising. These seminars are presented by the co-authors (under American Business Consultants, Inc., 1540 Nuthatch Lane, Sunnyvale, CA 94087) at many colleges and cities throughout the United States.

We would like to express special appreciation to the following people, whose experience, comments, and support have been invaluable aids in the preparation of this publication: Phillip Adleson, attorney at law; Larry R. Christenson, special agent, business and personal insurance; William H. Dunn, attorney at law; Axel K. Funke, business and tax consultant, enrolled agent practicing before the IRS; Tom L. Hall, CPA, real estate agent, and business owner; Bill Henry, attorney at law; Warren Hofstar, business consultant and financial specialist; John Leonard, financial consultant and loan specialist; Reg Lormon, attorney at law; Frank N. Mena, CPA and real estate broker; Fred Morello, banker and commercial loan consultant; Charles P. Spring, real estate broker, income investment and business opportunities; Paul Wilkins, attorney at law; P. Brien Wilson, attorney at law; and our wives, Catherine and Pamela.

Sunnyvale, California   W.F.T.
March 1980   R.W.C.

Contents

Chapter **1** Objectives

After reading this book you should be able to do the following:

1. Complete the business-opportunity buyer's authorization form, listing agreement, purchase (deposit/receipt) agreement, and escrow instructions. In addition to these, there may be other forms and form letters to complete in a legal, moral, and ethical manner in accordance with the following (as well as others):

   • Uniform commercial code—bulk sale transfer, consumer protection-consumer service, real estate department, building, zoning, local or county government, Internal Revenue Service, health department, alcoholic beverage control laws, codes, ordinances, rules and regulations.

   (The material given herein is based on California State Laws and Regulations. Our intention is to show all available options. However, all options do not necessarily apply to any one transaction.)

2. Identify and apply specific ethical principles in business-opportunities transactions.

3. Evaluate broker's and client's responsibilities.

4. Use two unique business opportunity appraisal forms for determining the true value of any business, including a bar, a cafe, a market, a restaurant, a service, a manufacturing plant, or a wholesale or a retail shop.

5. Identify, analyze, and interpret owner's books and records: accurately evaluate the business profit/loss status, rip-offs, frauds, and tax and legal problems.

6. Develop a personal strategy for establishing proper relations in the business community.
7. Practice negotiation techniques with clients in the owner's establishment with follow-up analysis.
8. Identify all parties and their responsibilities and functions in business-opportunities transactions, and procedures in negotiating. (Negotiation is both an art and a science. This book will teach you what to ask, who to ask, and how to negotiate to get commitments from buyers, sellers, landlords, note holders, equipment lease holders, unions, franchisers, attorneys, and accountants.)
9. Develop the proper procedures for professionals, buyers, sellers, and escrow holders. Using our double checklist system ensures that everything needed to perform a complete bulk-sale transaction has been covered.

This book has been written from the viewpoint that a real-estate salesperson is already involved in a transaction or is learning the business-opportunity brokerage operations. However, if you are planning to buy or sell a business and not use an agent or professional assistance, you will have to assume their duties as well as your own.

The greatest prestige in real estate specialties comes from a business-opportunity brokerage. This field is wide open to anyone who will take the time and effort to acquire the education needed to effectively list, sell, buy, and close business-opportunity transactions.

Ninety percent of all real estate salespersons pass up the enormous profit to be made because they lack the business-opportunity knowledge. Those who are presently enacting business-opportunity transactions without adequate knowledge are risking personal liability and loss of their real estate license; they are also performing a disservice to their clients.

To be successful in business opportunities one must have specialized knowledge. Specialists in business opportunities today must be aware of all laws and regulations in order to protect the seller, the buyer, and themselves. The bottom line when you face a judge and jury is not what was done in good faith, but what should have been done by you as a professional.

This book will save the business-opportunities specialist months of frustration. He or she will learn the "real world" step by step, including the fundamentals of successfully listing, buying, selling, and closing escrows. It is the goal of the author and his associates to show the reader how to complete transactions in a legal, moral, and ethical manner.

Some people feel that many businesses fail because of poor management or lack of funds, or both. In reality businesses fail because the operators do not understand how to run them. They fail to ask enough questions about how the business operates and how it is financed.

Let us now study some of the basics, step by step, and go through a complete business-sale transaction.

Chapter **2** Government Regulations

We live by and are affected by government regulations. In business opportunities we live by eight major codes:

> Administration code
> Civil code
> Commercial code
> Business and professional code
> Revenue and taxation code
> Government code
> Unemployment insurance code
> Internal Revenue code

Under these codes are numerous federal, state, county, and city codes, laws, ordinances, and rules and regulations by which we must abide. There are times that different rules and regulations conflict within the different codes. For example, the commercial code says it is legal to have a buy-back (option) contract; that is, the seller sells his business with a small downpayment and has a "buy-back clause" in the sales agreement. This clause means that should the buyers default on their payments, the sellers have the right to buy back the business. However, if the sale includes an alcoholic beverage control license, it is against the business and professional code to have any such buy-back option or lien on the license. It must be free and clear at all times.

Most people do not realize the many rules and regulations and the number of agencies that can affect business, even to the point of closing down the operation. The following is a list of some of the agencies involved:

- Department of Real Estate
- Department of Alcoholic Beverage Control
- Department of Motor Vehicles
- Coastal Zone Commission
- Secretary of State
- Fair Employment Practice
- Uniform Commercial Code-Bulk Sale Transfer
- Board of Equalization
- Franchise Tax Board
- Industrial Relations Department
- Employment Development Department
- Unemployment Insurance Board
- Equal Employment Opportunity Commission
- Workman's Compensation Insurance
- City/Town Hall, Fictitious name, ("doing business as"), Special Licenses, Permits, etc.
- Master Plan—Planning Department
- Building Codes
- Zoning Ordinance
- Environmental Impact and Management
- Fire Department
- Police and Sheriff Departments
- Redevelopment Department
- Highway Department
- Tax Assessor or Appraiser (Tax Collector)
- Weights and Measures
- Internal Revenue Service
- Treasury Department
- Social Security Administration
- Health, Education, and Welfare Department
- Occupational Safety and Health Administration
- Federal Trade Commission
- Commerce Department
- Securities and Exchange Commission
- Department of Consumer Affairs
- Federal Power Commission
- Air Pollution
- Environmental Protection Agency
- Food and Drug Administration
- Interstate Commerce Commission
- Human Resources Development Department
- Justice Department
- Department of Energy
- Department of Commerce
- Department of Labor
- Public Utilities Commission
- Garbage Collection Company
- Business and Transportation Agency
- National Economic Development Association
- Consumer Product Safety Commission
- Export-Import Bank
- Postal Service
- United States Customs Service

There are many agencies and services that a business owner can turn to for help. Some examples are:

- General Services Administration
- Small Business Administration
- Better Business Bureau
- Chamber of Commerce
- trade associations
- public library
- bar associations

Chapter **3** Ethics

This book, with its business-opportunity bulk-sale transfer forms is designed to promote ethical practice among all parties in the listing, buying, selling, and transfer of business opportunities. A review of common practices in the business will show that procedures and salespersons' behavior frequently violate real estate rules, regulations, and code of ethics. Sloppy standards and nonadherence to these rules and codes can result in litigation or loss of real estate licenses, or both.

The nature of the world of business opportunities and our daily environment invites, and even promotes, unethical practices. As an independent contractor, the successful business-opportunity specialist must be highly competitive and aggressive and must work under very tight "time frames." These factors tend to promote cutting corners, deception, and many other types of behavior not conducive to good business practice.

Basically, there are three phases in the completion of business-opportunity bulk-sale transfers. The first is the listing phase, which requires full disclosure. It is essential that the seller's complete terms, conditions, warranties, representations, and obligations be in writing, with data to support all material facts. In business opportunities, there are many contracts within a sale of a business. All information must be contained in the listing agreement, including, but not limited to the following:

- Allocation of selling price
- Covenant-not-to-complete agreement
- Lease assignment terms
- Seller training period
- Union contracts

9

- Encumbrance assignments
- Installment-sale information
- Pension plan obligations
- Royalties
- Trade-secret agreements
- Inventory list
- Fixtures and equipment lists
- Franchise contracts
- Medical plans

- Utilities services
- Lease equipment obligations
- Financial statements
- Tax and legal liabilities
- Licenses and permits
- Special Studies Zone Act
- National Flood Control Act
- Consumer protection

The second phase is the purchase (deposit/receipt) agreement phase, which also requires full disclosure. It is essential that the buyer's offer is complete and in writing, backed by support data for all claims made about the buyer and his or her qualifications.

The final phase is the escrow phase, again requiring full disclosure. Escrow is used to collect all predetermined information, funds, and instructions necessary to complete and record a business transfer in accordance with Uniform Commercial Code–Bulk Sale Transfer requirements.

The first two phases are the most critical and the most neglected areas in business-opportunity transactions. Incomplete listing information (as explained above), unqualified buyers, and incomplete purchase agreements complicate the business-opportunity transaction, causing "loose ends" in the escrow phase. A common cause for this neglect is the salesperson's desire to "lock" the buyer and seller into the "deal." The common practice of withholding material facts, deliberately or inadvertently, is against the Department of Real Estate rules and regulations and reduces transaction survival rate to less than 50% of the escrows opened.

In order to promote ethical practices, a professional salesperson must adhere to many "do's and don'ts" when dealing in business opportunities.

A business-opportunities salesperson must:

- Keep informed of changes in laws, codes, and rules and regulations affecting and related to business opportunities, consumer protection, consumer services, real estate, business, professional, civil, administration, revenue and taxation, building and government codes, city and county ordinances, health department, Alcoholic Beverage Control, and many others. (See Chapter 2 for list of agencies.)
- Make full disclosures of all material facts, warranties, representations, obligations, terms, and conditions in writing before offering a business opportunity for sale.

- Protect the public against fraud, misrepresentation, and unethical practices.
- Recommend the use of professionals, such as attorneys, certified public accountants, and tax specialists, in all transactions.
- Recommend arbitration when necessary.
- Develop business appraisal expertise.
- Recommend that commissions or fees, where mentioned in agreements, state in boldface type: "REAL ESTATE COMMISSIONS ARE NEGOTIABLE AND NOT FIXED BY LAW."
- Disclose to all parties, in advance, when the salesperson is acting for both buyer and seller.

A business-opportunities salesperson must not:

- Give any legal or tax advice, unless qualified and licensed to do so.
- Make statements that cannot be verified.
- Discriminate against or deny services or information to any person for reasons of race, creed, sex, or national origin.
- Allow unauthorized sharing of trade secrets or personal or confidential information to fellow salespersons, clients, competitors, and others, including, but not limited to, the following information: condition of books, financial statements, formulas and recipes, methods of operation, and offers of other parties.
- Negotiate or solicit a listing, knowing that it has not expired.
- Make false representation, such as: advertising phony or already sold business listings, advertising misleading financial terms, or representing himself or a fellow agent as a buyer in an attempt to acquire a listing.

FIRM AND FAIR POLICY

There are many more parties involved in a business-opportunity transaction than in a typical residential sale. Therefore, it is imperative that all parties be handled with the same fair and ethical treatment.

In the typical transaction, an owner who is selling a business into which he or she has put years of effort, a lot of money, and an enormous amount of creative energy is giving up an important part of his or her life. The buyer, who in many cases is stepping into a world of the unknown, is asked to exchange his or her worldly fortunes for a business of questionable value.

In short, the buyer and seller are under great stress and at opposite ends of a spectrum. The business-opportunity salesperson must be skillful in his or her role as middleman in order to satisfy successfully the needs and desires of both parties. Therefore, a "professional counselor" approach or technique is necessary to guide both parties, step-by-step, through their bulk-sale transfer. This normally can be accomplished only when the salesperson successfully educates the parties as they pass through various stages, using ethical standards of business practice and adopting the Department of Real Estate's new Code of Ethics and Professional Conduct, as follows.

REGULATIONS OF THE
REAL ESTATE COMMISSIONER

Article 11
Ethics and Professional Conduct Code

2785. Code of Ethics and Professional Conduct. In order to enhance the professionalism of the California real estate industry, and maximize protection for members of the public dealing with real estate licensees, the following standards of professional conduct and business practices are adopted:

(a) **Unlawful Conduct.** Licensees shall not engage in "fraud" or "dishonest dealing" or "conduct which would have warranted the denial of an application for a real estate license" within the meaning of Business and Profession Code Sections 10176 and 10177 including, but not limited to, the following acts and omissions:

(1) Knowingly making a substantial misrepresentation of the likely market value of real property to its owner (1) for the purpose of securing a listing or (2) for the purpose of acquiring an interest in the property for the licensee's own account.

(2) The statement or implication by a licensee to an owner of real property during listing negotiations that the licensee is precluded by law, regulation or by the rules of any organization, other than the broker firm seeking the listing, from charging less than the commission or fee quoted to the owner by the licensee.

(3) The failure by a licensee acting in the capacity of an agent in a transaction for the sale, lease or exchange of real property to disclose to a prospective purchaser or lessee facts known to the licensee materially affecting the value or desirability of the property, when the licensee has reason to believe that such facts are not known to, nor readily observable by, a prospective purchaser or lessee.

(4) When seeking a listing, representation to an owner of the real property that the soliciting licensee has obtained a bona fide written offer to purchase the property, unless at the time of the representation the licensee has possession of a bona fide written offer to purchase.

(5) The willful failure by a listing broker to present or cause to be presented to the owner of the property any offer to purchase received prior to the closing of a sale, unless expressly instructed by the owner not to present such an offer, or unless the offer is patently frivolous.

(6) Presenting competing offers to purchase real property to the owner by the listing broker in such a manner as to induce the owner to accept the offer which will provide the greatest compensation to the listing broker, without regard to the benefits, advantages, and/or disadvantages to the owner.

(7) Knowingly underestimating the probable closing costs in a transaction in a communication to the prospective buyer or seller of real property in order to induce that person to make or to accept an offer to purchase the property.

(8) Failing to explain to the parties or prospective parties to a real estate transaction the meaning and probable significance of a contingency in an offer or contract that the licensee knows or reasonably believes may affect the closing date of the transaction, or the timing of the vacating of the property by the seller or its occupancy by the buyer.

(9) Knowingly making a false or misleading representation to the seller of real property as to the form, amount and or treatment of a deposit toward purchase of the property made by an offeror.

(10) The refunding by a licensee, when acting as an agent or sub-agent for seller, of all or part of an offeror's purchase money deposit in a real estate

sales transaction after the seller has accepted the offer to purchase, unless the licensee has the express permission of the seller to make the refund.

(11) Failing to disclose to the seller of real property in a transaction in which the licensee is acting in the capacity of an agent, the nature and extent of any direct or indirect interest that the licensee expects to acquire as a result of the sale. The prospective purchase of the property by a person related to the licensee by blood or marriage, purchase by an entity in which the licensee has an ownership interest, or purchase by any other person with whom the licensee occupies a special relationship where there is a reasonable probability that the licensee could be indirectly acquiring an interest in the property, shall be disclosed.

(b) **Unethical Conduct.** In order to maintain a high level of ethics in business practice, real estate licensees should avoid engaging in any of the following activities:

(1) Representing, without a reasonable basis, the nature and/or condition of the interior or exterior features of a property when soliciting an offer.

(2) Failing to respond to reasonable inquiries of a principal as to the status or extent of efforts to market property listed exclusively with the licensee.

(3) Representing as an agent that any specific serfice is free when, in fact, it is covered by a fee to be charged as part of the transaction.

(4) Failing to disclose to a person when first discussing the purchase of real property, the existence of any direct or indirect ownership interest of the licensee in the property.

(5) Recommending by a salesperson to a party to a real estate transaction that a particular lender or escrow service be used when the salesperson believes his or her broker has a significant beneficial interest in such entity without disclosing this information at the time the recommendation is made.

(6) Claiming to be an expert in an area of specialization in real estate brokerage, e.g., appraisal, property management, industrial siting, etc., if, in fact, the licensee has had no special training, preparation or experience in such area.

(7) Using the term "appraisal" in any advertising of offering for promoting real estate brokerage business to describe a real property evaluation service to be provided by the licensee unless the evaluation process will involve a written estimate of value based upon the assembling, analyzing and reconciling of facts and value indicators for the real property in question.

(8) Failing to disclose to the appropriate regulatory agency any conduct on the part of a financial institu-

tion which reasonably could be construed as a violation of The Housing Financial Discrimination Act of 1977 (anti-redlining)—Part 6 (commencing with Section 35800) of Division 24 of the Health and Safety Code.

(9) Representing to a customer or prospective customer that because the licensee or his or her broker is a member of, or affiliated with, a franchised real estate brokerage entity, that such entity shares substantial responsibility, with the licensee, or his or her broker, for the proper handling of transactions if such is not the case.

(10) Participating in the organized disclosure to a representative, agent, or employee of a public or private school, firm, association, organization or corporation conducting a real estate preparatory course the language of any question used in a state real estate license examination, at the request of such person or entity.

(11) Demanding a commission or discount by a licensee purchasing real property for one's own account after an agreement in principle has been reached with the owner as to the terms and conditions of purchase without any reference to price reduction because of the agent's licensed status.

(c) **Beneficial Conduct.** In the best interests of all licensees and the public they serve, brokers and salespersons are encouraged to pursue the following beneficial business practices:

(1) Measuring success by the quality and benefits rendered to the buyers and sellers in real estate transactions rather than by the amount of compensation realized as a broker or salesperson.

(2) Treating all parties to a transaction honestly.

(3) Promptly reporting to the California Department of Real Estate any apparent violations of the Real Estate Law.

(4) Using care in the preparation of any advertisement to present an accurate picture or message to the reader, viewer, or listener.

(5) Submitting all written offers as a matter of top priority.

(6) Maintaining adequate and complete records of all one's real estate dealings.

(7) Keeping oneself current on factors affecting the real estate market in which the licensee operates as an agent.

(8) Making a full, open, and sincere effort to coordinate with other licensees, unless the principal has instructed the licensee to the contrary.

(9) Attempting to settle disputes with other licensees through mediation or arbitration.

(10) Complying with these standards of professional conduct, and the Code of Ethics of any organized real estate industry group of which the licensee is a member.

Nothing in this regulation is intended to limit, add to or supersede any provision of law relating to the duties and obligations of real estate licensees or the consequences of violations of law. Subdivision (a) lists specific acts and omissions which do violate existing law and are grounds for disciplinary action against a real estate licensee. The conduct guidelines set forth in subdivisions (b) and (c) are not intended as statements of duties imposed by law nor as grounds for disciplinary action by the Department of Real Estate but as guidelines for elevating the professionalism of real estate licensees.

NECESSARY SKILLS

A professional business broker should have access to qualified buyers and sellers, advertising outlets, multiple-listing services, local and statewide business-opportunity exchanges, and a referral service to other business-opportunity specialists. The broker must also have his or her client's confidence in order to avoid costly pitfalls and gain maximum benefits.

An in-depth study should be conducted of a business operation and its financial status. The broker should study all the costs involved and should make recommendations for improving specific areas (e.g., labor, materials, facilities, equipment, and marketing). And last, but not least, the broker should be able to project a return on an investment based on past performance.

Chapter 4 Responsibilities

BROKER POLICY

Specialists in business opportunities must adhere to a strict set of rules and broker policies. Your own office should set up these regulations. Below are a few examples of broker policies that can be added to or deleted from as desired.

Dress casually. When calling where food or alcohol is served, do not look like an investigator for the Health Department or Internal Revenue Service (IRS) or Alcoholic Beverage Control (ABC).

Develop a friendly relationship with the owner of the business. Always have a supply of forms handy for all stages of the transaction. On your first visit to a client, it is suggested that you leave your briefcase and other materials in your car.

Remember that approvals are required by all concerned at all stages of a business transaction. Share information regarding the business with all parties. However, confidential material must remain confidential until you have permission of the parties concerned to pass it on.

Commission splits (the percentage of the selling price shared by the persons involved in the sale) must be decided in advance. Any personal transaction made must be disclosed.

Before advertising, discuss with the seller how the business is to be listed.

Office and floor time (i.e., time spent in the office) should be decided upon by personnel in your office.

15

TIME MANAGEMENT

Time is money. By developing good work habits, maintaining records on how time is spent each day, and striving to eliminate duplication of effort, time will be saved. The time saved can be used on more productive tasks. Since most people are fresher in the morning, try to make important contacts one of your first priorities.

Try to eliminate, as much as possible, unproductive tasks such as writing letters and reports. Use the telephone whenever possible. Allow yourself plenty of time to concentrate on the important matters on any given day.

Salespersons who find themselves without energy in the afternoon should try to work earlier in the day. Some people prefer to work in the evenings. The following guidelines are suggested to improve efficiency through organization of your daily activities.

1. Develop a plan to achieve your goals. Plan your activities well in advance if possible. Plan each hour of each day if possible. Do not forget to leave time for your family and friends. Try to set deadlines for attainment of goals.
2. Set yourself a goal of one listing per week. Remember, listing is the essence of a successful real estate practice.
3. Look for "Sale by Owner" advertisements each day. Telephone three of these persons. This is an excellent way to get a listing.
4. Try to contact 10 new prospects each day either by telephone or personal canvassing.
5. Call on one or two existing listings every day. Let your sellers know that you are on top of the job. If it is possible to improve the listing price or terms, do so. It may help to sell the business more quickly.
6. Mail out 20 promotional pamphlets per day. Follow up on 10 previous mailings.
7. Try to develop and cultivate relationships with people you come in contact with by following the above guidelines.
8. Do not become discouraged if you cannot achieve these goals each day. Keep on trying and eventually it will pay off.

CLIENT RELATIONSHIPS

A professional salesperson is made, not born. Selling business opportunities is a highly specialized field requiring technical competence. It is important to realize how many "sales" there are within one transaction. The following suggestions and recommendations have proved helpful to others in this field:

Sell yourself in order to sell others.

Always prospect with every contact (friends, relatives, neighbors). Inquire about persons who might be thinking of selling or buying. If you are introduced to a prospect, set up a time with this person so that you can determine what his or her needs are in regards to a business and whether he or she wants to buy, sell, or exchange.

Contact business owners. Determine if they want to sell, buy, or exchange a business. Ask them if they know of anybody requiring the services of a business-opportunity specialist. Explain the services of such a specialist. List businesses at reasonable prices and make sure that the terms are attractive.

Sell the landlord. Avoid unreasonable demands; negotiate a lease assignment or an extension of a lease. Get the buyer of a business accepted as a new tenant.

Sell the buyer. If you get a response to your advertising, have the buyer come into your office. Ask him or her to sign a "Promise Not to Disclose" contract (i.e., confidential information that has been given to a potential buyer must not be disclosed to anybody at this time). If he or she wants to make a reasonable offer after viewing the business, this must be taken by the broker to the seller for approval or rejection. Should the seller make a counter offer this must be presented to the buyer. It may be necessary to return to the seller and prospective buyer a number of times before the transaction is consummated.

Build relationships with franchisors, note holders and leasing institutions. Avoid unreasonable demands and assure the necessary contract assignments to the new buyer. Remember you are now "selling" the buyer, not the business.

COUNSELING BUYERS AND SELLERS

The specialist in business opportunities provides service and knowledge primarily through effective communication (both verbal and written). Effective communication can only be accomplished when the listener is totally receptive. Therefore, it is necessary that positive relationships between and among all parties be established. The following suggestions may be helpful:

- Educate all parties in your services, skill, and experience.
- Build confidence by your prompt follow-up and good communication.

- Use checklists and forms. "Walk" parties through all steps and expectations.
- Determine your client's goals. Early in the process, identify in writing the client's goals, experience, resources, investment and personal objectives, and tax considerations.
- Act as a counselor and consultant in all client contacts by building the proper client relationship and confidence. By doing so, you will quickly eliminate "bargain hunters" and "lookers."
- As the sale of business opportunities is a serious business try to deal with clients who are really serious.
- Every "sales step" must include the advantages and the benefits of whatever is being sold.

OBJECTIONS

Many clients in real estate and business opportunities ask numerous questions in initial contacts to test the salesperson. This is normal. Often this client reaction or behavior allows a means of establishing rapport with the salesperson. If the salesperson satisfactorily answers these objections, he or she will be able to proceed with the remainder of the presentation. This testing can sometimes be avoided by setting the stage, i.e., by asking questions to establish rapport, listening to a client's concerns, obtaining a client's undivided attention, and satisfying his or her concerns.

Another technique to counter objections is the *question method* of handling an objection. It is a way of isolating the true objection and is illustrated as follows: The client voices an objection and the salesperson counters with, "Is that your only objection?" If the client replies "yes," the single key factor that the salesperson must satisfy may be identified. However, if the client says "no," he may simply be raising a "smoke screen" before the salesperson. An appropriate question by the salesperson at this point may be, "What else do you object to?" This question, repeated in a variety of ways, will lead to the real objection. The salesperson must get down to the real problem or objection before any progress can be made.

Above all, the sales process must be handled smoothly. It must satisfy all parties. This can be done if a satisfactory relationship is established at the beginning of negotiations and if effective communications are maintained. One measure of a good salesperson is not the amount of commission in his or her pocket but the amount of repeat or referral business generated.

Let us review some of the common objections from the authors' own experiences to illustrate how effective communications can overcome objections.

Common Objections From the Seller

Wants to Sell Business Himself

This usually means that the seller does not understand the difficulties involved in finding a qualified buyer and legally completing a transaction. The seller often is not aware of the business, governmental, and professional codes, laws, and rules and regulations required in business opportunities. Show the seller the complete procedural checklist system that is necessary to ensure a complete business-opportunity transaction.

Wants All Cash

This usually means that the seller does not realize that only about 10% of all buyers pay cash for a business. Point out the advantages of taking a low downpayment to qualify for an installment sale with its capital gains tax advantages, especially if it is near the end of the calendar year.

Not Interested in Selling

Perhaps the owner has not recently evaluated some of the potentially negative aspects of his or her business. Suggest that the owner ask himself or herself such questions as:

"How many hours do I work each work?"
"How often do I work weekends?"
"What is my actual pay per hour?"
"When did I last take a vacation?"
"What is my true net profit?"
"How much stress do I have to cope with each day?"
"Do I have a retirement fund?"
"How often do I have problems with employees, customers, vendors, and others?"

Will Not Disclose Specific Information About the Business

Usually occurs if the salesperson has not established a good relationship with the business owner or the owner is not ready to sell his or her business. The salesperson should not press a business owner for disclosure of trade-secret information, although it should be made clear that such information would be part of the sale of the business. Also, remind the seller of the "Promise Not to Disclose" form the buyer must sign (see page 117).

Common Objections From the Buyer

Price is too High

This usually means that the buyer is requesting more information. He or she needs to understand and appreciate the benefits to be derived from the business, such as potential income and tax write-offs.

Wants Better Terms   Sometimes the buyer has insufficient funds for the downpayment. Restructure the financing of the business to suit the buyer's pocketbook. This can be accomplished by:

> Having the owner carry a larger loan.
> Arranging a new equipment lease or refinancing the existing lease.
> Having the seller or vendor retain title to inventory, selling to the buyer on an "as needed" basis.
> Offering note payments to the seller starting in three to six months.
> Restructuring accounts payable for lower monthly total cash outflow or extending credit for 30, 60, or 90 days.
> Increasing accounts receivable by discounting especially delinquent accounts.

Bad Location   This often means either that the buyer does not have enough information about the business operation, location, and drawing potential from the surrounding area or that he is looking for a better deal.

Uncertain About the   If all other objections have been satisfied, this usually means that the buyer
Transaction   does not have confidence in the business-opportunities salesperson. The relationship between buyer and the salesperson needs to be built up.

INQUIRIES

Telephone   In business opportunities, most inquiries are generated by newspaper advertisements under the heading "businesses for sale." The salesperson should get the name and telephone number of the caller before attempting to determine the caller's qualifications or before giving him or her too much information about the business in question. The salesperson should never disclose over the telephone specific information about any business advertised. Telephone conversations should be used to determine the buyer's basic needs, experience, motivation, and financial resources, such as available cash or sources to raise capital.

The salesperson should advise the client that he has specific details about the business for sale in his office in addition to other businesses for sale so that the client can make comparisons. An appointment should then be made to meet with the buyer in the office.

Office   When meeting the buyer in the office and establishing a relationship, the buyer should fill out the "Business Wanted" form, which will provide the specific information needed to qualify the buyer and determine his needs.

While helping the buyer to complete this form (see page 118) the salesperson can gain a great deal of insight into the buyer's true goals, objectives, motivation, experience, and abilities. The client is purchasing not just a business, but a source of income.

SALES TECHNIQUES

Much has been written about "high" and "low-pressure" sales techniques, but the authors offer no conclusive definition for either technique. Each salesperson must determine an approach that is acceptable to the many parties in the transaction.

High-pressure is usually destined to fail for a variety of reasons. High-pressure tactics cannot be sustained over the many days or months required to close a business-opportunity transaction. The decision to buy must be the buyer's based on adequate facts. High-pressure tactics often lead to a dissatisfied customer, who may at a later date resent having been forced to buy against his or her better judgment. An unhappy client will not return for repeat business or provide referrals, which is a necessary part of the business. It must be determined if the buyer wants a business for a job, investment, legacy (foreigner for citizen requirements), tax advantages, hobby, or for his or her spouse and family.

Selecting Prospective Businesses to Show

After selecting one or two businesses for the buyer to look over, the salesperson has the buyer sign the "Location of Business" form (see page 121). Specific information about each listed business can then be disclosed to the buyer. If there are no current business-opportunity listings suitable for the buyer, have him or her complete the "Buyer's Authorization" form (see page 111).

Presenting the Business

It is common in business opportunities to send the buyer out alone to see a business. However, since you have matched buyer and business so well, it is advisable to make an appointment with the owner and take the buyer to the premises.

When taking the buyer to the location, the salesperson should brief him or her on the business and advise against talking to employees or any customers on the premises at this time. All parties must protect the business' reputation and the morale of the employees and customers while the business is in the process of being sold. Explain to the potential buyer that most sellers do not want it known that the business is for sale. Also, remind the buyer not to discuss price and terms with the owner.

21

Let the buyer quietly observe the business activities for a few minutes before introducing him or her to the owner. The salesperson can further qualify the buyer and more accurately match the buyer to the business by asking additional questions about objectives, goals, and needs.

After returning to the office with the prospect the salesperson should point out the advantages and the disadvantages of the business. The salesperson should then be prepared to answer the buyer's questions or be able to get the answers in a short time.

If the business just viewed seems to match the objectives, goals, and needs of the buyer (the salesperson should be realistic, ethical, and honest) the purchase offer can then be prepared for the buyer's signature (see page 147).

Presenting the Offer

Make an appointment with the seller informing him or her that you have an offer. (Note: If you are representing both buyer and seller, it must be disclosed in writing and acknowledged by both parties.) All standard attempts should be made to present the offer and educate the seller in a proper setting—one in which there will be no interruptions during the presentation. Compare all information on the offer with seller's needs and listing agreements, especially his or her net profit compared to the number of hours spent in the business. You will soon arrive at the seller's advantages for accepting the offer. High pressure at this point simply defeats all previous efforts, so do not get overanxious. Remember, the seller has three options; he or she can accept or reject the offer, or make a counteroffer. You must educate the seller regarding each of these options and the consequences of each.

The seller must make the final decision based upon adequate facts. Your guidance must be objective, ethical, and in the best interests of both parties, otherwise you have broken the fiduciary relationship required by a real estate license and normal business relationships. Any approach not respecting these principles may suggest that you used duress in acquiring approval. This results in unfavorable consequences.

At this point, if the seller is satisfied, obtain a signature. If he is dissatisfied, make a counteroffer to reflect seller's unmet concerns.

Client Relationships

Body Language

It is useful to understand body language, such as performance, mannerisms, gestures, and facial expressions. One's body, hands, eyes, and even eyebrows often say much more than one's mouth. Although you are probably unaware of your natural gestures, learning the meaning of specific motions made by an individual can affect the degree of success you achieve as a salesperson.

Unfortunately, most people listen only with their ears. But gestures often communicate more than words. Each action has a meaning, regardless of the words accompanying it. In other words, people have a "vocabulary" of movements.

Unlike oral communication, the language of bodily movements always tells the truth. No matter how guarded people make their conversation, they reveal their true feelings through their gestures. Any alert salesperson can analyze a customer's reactions to a presentation by carefully observing his or her movements.

As a salesperson you should be aware of your own gestures when you are talking. You should try to appear open and relaxed in order to convey the same feeling to the other parties present. The following are some basic rules for interpreting body language:

- The direction in which people wave their hands tells whether they are introverted or extroverted. Swinging the hands outward from the body indicates an open and outgoing nature. Introverts invariably make inward movements, bringing their hands toward their body.
- The direction of the palms is another form of body language. People will turn their palms open toward those who are antagonizing them. This is a defensive gesture against those who seem to be posing a verbal battle. Palms close to or even touching the body indicate that the person feels friendly toward the speaker.
- Sweeping the hands up and out says the person is optimistic and enthusiastic. Hands arcing inward toward the body and down say the person is rather shy and retiring. He or she is pessimistic, lacks confidence, and tends to be easily dejected.
- Peering at the floor to avoid eye contact reveals depression or lack of confidence.
- People who habitually cover their mouths as if stifling a yawn have an inferiority complex.
- Wiping the lips unnecessarily with a hand or handkerchief is a shielding gesture. When people do this, they are evasive.
- The shape the mouth takes in a smile indicates a person's attitude. When a person is smiling to himself or herself, as if reflecting on some secret, humorous thought, the corners of the mouth move slightly upward and outward. Smiles exposing the upper teeth are somewhat friendly, but are reserved for social rather than business affairs. The broad smile is the friendly and relaxed indicator. The mouth opens and upper and lower teeth are exposed.

- Nose-rubbing is a negative gesture. People do it when they are repulsed or upset. This movement is usually done quickly.
- A person who runs a hand across his or her head in a hair-grooming gesture is tense and agitated.
- When a woman pats her hair while talking to a man, she is interested in impressing him.
- A person who tilts his or her head to the side and looks at the speaker is imaginative and has a sense of humor. He or she is lively and alert.
- When a woman dangles one foot in a swinging rhythm, she is very uneasy and bored. She has a tremendous desire to leave wherever she is.
- Women who shed a shoe or let it dangle by the toe are friendly and relaxed. They will put it back on if they are tense.
- Men who prop their elbows or arms or both across a desk or table are quite confident. They are decisive and solid.
- Men who lean back and grip the desk are aggressive. They often exhibit the strength of their moods by the amount of pressure they apply to this gesture.
- People who shift their weight from one foot to another are uneasy. They are bored and thinking about something that they would rather be doing.
- People who fold their arms are cold and aloof and sometimes physically aggressive. They are in a very defensive mood and prefer not to be bothered.
- People who use their cigarettes (or pipes, or cigars) to avoid eye contact with others are calculating. They often know something the speaker does not. They plan the conversation with precision to their own advantage.
- The salesperson can also determine what people are thinking by watching how a wife and husband interact.

These few gestures, if properly analyzed, will offer an intense insight into your client's thought and moods. They can be an invaluable asset in understanding human behavior. If we understand what the person's anxieties, needs, desires, and moods are, we can shape and control the discussion so that it becomes relaxed, informative, and interesting to the listener. Remember, you are selling yourself, your company, and your services to those who are sincerely willing to listen and believe in you.

Chapter 5 Business Frauds

INTERPRETATION OF OWNER'S ACCOUNTING RECORDS

Records are maintained to show profits and losses from business operations. Some owners may "set up" the "books" to benefit themselves (see Chapter 7 for different profit-and-loss statements) by showing different net profits to the Internal Revenue Service, banks, and potential buyers of their business. The business-opportunities salesperson must become aware of discrepancies in the books through discussions with the owner and observation of the business.

Are the Owner(s) and/or Employees "Skimming" Cash from the Business?

There are many ways to skim cash; and the following list mentions only a few of them:

- Jukeboxes, pool tables, pinball machines, and other vending machines provide a substantial amount of so-called nontraceable cash.
- Prices at the gas pump of a service station may not match pump prices used in the books. A penny or two per gallon adds up when you consider the average station pumps 50,000 gals/month.
- Invoices that are not accounted for numerically provide opportunities for invoices and cash to disappear. A second set of dummy or extra invoices can accomplish the same thing.
- Inventory might be sold for cash and not rung up on the cash register. The same can happen when a customer leaves cash on the counter and walks off, not waiting for a receipt.

25

- An employee might accept a kickback or ring up a smaller than actual sale price for the benefit of friends and relatives.
- A bartender might water the drinks, or substitute bar inventory with his or her own bottles, brought in wrapped in his or her jacket or by an accomplice. Owner should count empty bottles.
- The owner might "total out" the cash register a few hours before closing, not reporting income for the balance of the day.
- The owner or an employee might issue credits for phony customer claims or returns, pocketing the cash.
- Fictitious accounts can be used to siphon business profits into someone's pocket.
- Employees might sell copies of door keys or the combination to the safe to their friends for mutual benefit.
- Check dates on bank deposits. Owner should insist on deposits being made daily. An employee could be keeping the money for personal use.

Has the Owner Inflated Net Profit?

Inventory substitution and other expense adjustments can reduce the "cost of goods" as shown on the books. For example:

- Turkey is a cheap substitute for chicken.
- Cheap wine, bought by the gallon, can be used to refill more expensive wine bottles for resale in restaurants.
- Unreported cash purchases of inventory boosts net profit.
- Inventory brought into Business #1 and sold, but charged to Business #2, reduces the cost of goods sold for Business #1. Business #1 can then be sold at a higher price, based on its "higher" net profit.
- Long-range pension plans might not show on the books. Here is a liability to the buyer that can have far-reaching implications on long-term profitability.
- Long-term notes on bond plan payments not on the books will also affect profits.

Are Personal or Non-Deductible Expenses Being "Buried" Into Business Expenses?

- *Insurance ripoffs:* Insurance expenses might include personal automobile, medical, life, or home insurance.
- *Utilities and telephone charges:* Personal home or vacation cabin utilities and telephone charges might be deducted as business expenses.
- *Promotions and hidden expenses:* Family outings, vacations, restaurant tabs, or alimony payments might be buried in promotional expenses.

- *Mortgage, rent, or lease costs:* Personal home, vacation home, or girlfriend's apartment costs might find their way into business-rental expenses.
- *Falsified payroll:* A payroll can be padded with family, friends, or phony employees. Terminated employees might be carried on the books beyond their termination date. Also, check owner's unemployment tax rate. If it is high, it could mean the business has a high turnover problem.
- *Equipment expenses:* Personal automobile, boat, or airplane payments might be included in this category.
- *Inventory expenses:* Personal food supplies and household items might be hidden as inventory expenses.

Actual Case Histories

- A stock clerk for a shoe company parked his car at the receiving dock. He kept his trunk closed but unlocked. At 12:30 p.m., when the shipping-receiving manager was at lunch, the stock clerk threw full cartons of shoes into his trunk and then slammed it locked. Elapsed time: 18 seconds.
- Customers stood in line for one veteran saleswoman. They refused to be served by anybody else. No wonder! She switched tickets for many "special" customers, giving them substantial markdowns. The store's losses amounted to about $300 per week, not including $25 a week in increased commissions for the crooked saleswoman.
- In yet another case many returned items were marked down to a fraction of their original cost due to damage. Clerks got authorization to buy the "as is" merchandise. They then took first-rate items out of stock and substituted the damaged goods.
- Items in a thrift shop were ticketed in pencil. Moreover, some tickets were unmarked. Since the store was inadequately staffed, many customers marked down prices, switched tickets, or wrote their own prices.

"Fraud" covers a broad spectrum, even outright stealing of merchandise, equipment, cash, stamps, pencils, or even the end roll of the toilet paper from a restroom.

It is quite possible that sellers will admit to "skimming" to cover up an inability to make a profit. Never accuse or imply that a seller is operating in an illegal manner. Without proof, it is possible for an agent to become an accessory in this illegal activity. He or she may be accused by a buyer of transmitting false information or withholding material facts.

Chapter **6** Business Appraisal

BASIC PRINCIPLES

There are four basic factors of value to consider when buying or selling a business: (1) *Utility* is based upon a property's highest and best use, or its usefulness. (This factor is a "subjective value".) (2) *Scarcity*—short supply tends to increase the value of a property. (3) *Demand*—the larger the number of people seeking the same property, the more it tends to increase its value. This factor is implemented by those people having purchasing power. (4) *Transferability* is the possibility to legally convey something, in this case, a business.

APPRAISING A BUSINESS

One of the most difficult tasks in listing, buying, and selling business opportunities is appraising the business. There are three general methods of appraisal being used today. They are: the comparison (market value) approach, the cost approach, and the income capitalization approach.

Comparison (Market Value) Approach

This approach is considered unacceptable in business opportunities. This method requires that the appraiser find three or four recent sales of businesses similar in size and location. This is at best a difficult task. There are no two businesses exactly alike, so beware. You can check the "McCords," a daily publication, or multiple-listing services from your local Real Estate Board for past sales. In an attempt to qualify the sales information gathered, there is a multiple regression analysis method that may be used to measure the relationship between three or more variables, such as selling price, location, and size. Because of the large number of variables, this approach could be time-consuming and the results questionable.

Cost Approach

This approach is regarded as a disadvantage in business opportunities. First, you determine replacement cost, including the cost of all furniture, fixtures, equipment, leasehold improvements, inventory, liquor license, and so forth, less depreciation. Where real estate is part of the business, calculate building replacement cost, less depreciation, plus land value. This method ignores subjective values such as location and good will. These factors carry significant value in business opportunities.

Income Capitalization Approach

This is a questionable approach in business opportunities. The net profit is calculated by determining gross income and subtracting operating expenses. Then, the net profit divided by the capitalization rate equals the value of the property.

Income capitalization has been the most accurate method for comparing business opportunities provided expense, net profit, and capitalization rate information has been derived from the same set of guidelines. This can only be determined by adjusting each business profit-and-loss statement before applying the capitalization rate formula. This method does not take into account such factors as good will, owner's salary, depreciation, personal expenses, and service debts.

Innovative Appraising

True Selling Price Approach

Evaluation of business opportunities may be reduced to a fairly simple process. The problem is one of gathering hard facts and reducing this information to basic comparable factors. These factors may then be evaluated using a formula to establish the "true selling price." First of all, you reconstruct the profit-and-loss-statement figures. There are two steps to this process.

Step One: Establish "True Net Profit" "True net profit" (see page 31 and Buyer's Profit-and-Loss Statement on page 45) may be defined as "true gross sales" less "true business expense," which is the net income before:

- debt service
- equipment rental
- depreciation
- amortization
- income tax
- manager's salary
- owner's salary
- personal expenses

By adjusting the owner's stated net profit (by deleting the above expenses) the appraiser has, in effect, reconstructed the profit-and-loss statement as if

ESTIMATED ANNUAL "TRUE NET PROFIT"

Name _____ Address _____ Phone _____

Time period_____To _____

Net profit (sellers books–12 months) = $ _____

Add back:

    Depreciation $ _____

    Amortization $ _____

    Debt service (loan interest) $ _____

    Income tax $ _____

    Owner's salary $ _____

    Manager's salary $ _____

    Personal expenses

        Promotion $ _____

        Insurance $ _____

        Travel and entertainment $ _____

        Auto $ _____

        Other (specify) _____ $ _____

    Expenses buyer(s) may eliminate:

        Equipment rental $ _____

        Discounts and refunds $ _____

        Bad debt $ _____

        Donations $ _____

        Extra employee(s) $ _____

        Other (specify) _____ $ _____

Gross sales not reported (juke box, games, etc. that may

be verified)

(specify)_____ $ _____

Other (specify)_____ $ _____

Plus Total Adjustment = $ _____

Total Annual "True net profit" = $ _____

Less buyer(s) debts:

    Debt service (loan interest) assumed $ _____

    Equipment rental $ _____

    "New" loan payment _____ $ _____

    Other (specify) _____ $ _____

    Less Total Adjustment (debt service) = $ _____

"Net spendable cash" to new buyer(s)* $ _____

*Note: The above information has been supplied by the seller from his books and financial records. The broker, or its agent, has reviewed these books and financial records. Broker, or its agent, does not warrant the accuracy of the information contained herein.

ESTIMATED ANNUAL "TRUE NET PROFIT" (RECONSTRUCTION)

Name __AAA Cocktail Lounge__ Address _____ Phone _____

Time period _____ To _____

Net profit (sellers books–12 months) =		$ _____ 5,000 _____
Add back:		
Depreciation	$ _____ 5,000 _____	
Amortization	$ _____	
Debt service (loan interest)	$ _____ 1,300 _____	
Income tax	$ _____ 4,000 _____	
Owner's salary	$ _____ 40,000 _____	
Manager's salary	$ _____ 14,000 _____	
Personal expenses		
Promotion	$ _____ 1,000 _____	
Insurance	$ _____ 2,000 _____	
Travel and entertainment	$ _____ 1,000 _____	
Auto	$ _____ 2,000 _____	
Other (specify) _____	$ _____	
Expenses buyer(s) may eliminate:		
Equipment rental	$ _____ 5,000 _____	
Discounts and refunds	$ _____ 500 _____	
Bad debt	$ _____ 500 _____	
Donations	$ _____ 400 _____	
Extra employee(s)	$ _____	
Other (specify) _____	$ _____	
Gross sales not reported (juke box, games, etc. that may be verified)		
(specify)_____	$ _____	
Other (specify)_____	$ _____	
Plus Total Adjustment =		$ _____ 76,700 _____
Total Annual "True net profit" =		$ _____ 81,700 _____
Less buyer(s) debts:		
Debt service (loan interest) assumed	$ _____ 1,300 _____	
Equipment rental	$ _____ 5,000 _____	
"New" loan payment _____	$ _____	
Other (specify) _____	$ _____	
Less Total Adjustment (debt service) =		$ _____ 6,300 _____
"Net spendable cash" to new buyer(s)*		$ _____ 75,400 _____

*Note: The above information has been supplied by the seller from his books and financial records. The broker, or its agent, has reviewed these books and financial records. Broker, or its agent, does not warrant the accuracy of the information contained herein.

32

the buyer had paid cash for the business and operated the business on a cash basis. This allows you or the buyer to establish a useful comparison of one business to another. To determine "net spendable cash" for the buyer, add back the buyer's debt-service payments to see if his or her cash flow is positive or negative. This method is an excellent tool for securing listings at the right price and terms from the seller.

Step Two: Establish "True Selling Price" "True selling price," on the true value of the business (see form on page 39), may be defined as asset value plus good will value. The "asset value" may be defined as the total value of equipment, fixtures, leases, franchise, and any other tangible items installed, less depreciation (i.e., market value). "Good will value" may be defined as "true net profit," less return on asset investment multiplied by a risk factor.

The investment in good will is determined in part by selecting a "risk factor," using the scale shown here. Selecting a risk factor is somewhat subjective within the guidelines indicated on the risk factor scale. Since each business is different, each factor should be evaluated separately to determine an overall risk factor applicable to the business being evaluated. These factors include (but are not limited to):

> The *skill and training* a buyer would need to take over operation of the business.
> The *type of business*, i.e., how technical it is.
> The *number of potential buyers* available to buy such a business.
> The *location* of the business and character of the neighborhood.
> The *number of years* the business has been established.
> The *number of established customers* who return to do business each year.
> The *age and condition* of the building.
> The *return of investment in good will*, i.e., how long it will take for the buyer to get his or her money back.

As an example, to determine the factor for a restaurant, start with the basic factor of 2 on the scale. If the restaurant is smaller than average, you might conclude that there are more buyers available since less cash and skill would be needed to purchase and to operate the business. These factors might move the risk from 2 to 2.3. If the building is old and in need of repair and the location is less than prime, the risk factor would move down the scale from 2 to perhaps 1.6. Weighing all the facts that apply to the restaurant permits an overall factor to be selected and used in the subse-

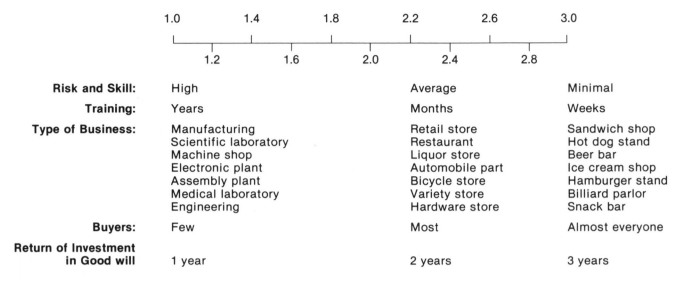

RISK FACTOR SCALE

1.0	1.4	1.8	2.2	2.6	3.0
1.2	1.6	2.0	2.4	2.8	

Risk and Skill:	High	Average	Minimal
Training:	Years	Months	Weeks
Type of Business:	Manufacturing Scientific laboratory Machine shop Electronic plant Assembly plant Medical laboratory Engineering	Retail store Restaurant Liquor store Automobile part Bicycle store Variety store Hardware store	Sandwich shop Hot dog stand Beer bar Ice cream shop Hamburger stand Billiard parlor Snack bar
Buyers:	Few	Most	Almost everyone
Return of Investment in Good will	1 year	2 years	3 years

quent calculation of good will. In this example we might wind up with an overall risk factor of, say, 1.9. This means that the buyer's investment in good will will be returned in 1.9 years.

The estimated true selling price (see form on page 39) is calculated as follows:

1. Total all business assets.
2. From the annual "true net profit" deduct 10 percent of the total asset value. (This represents a fair annual return on the asset investment.)
3. Multiply the result by the previously determined risk factor to establish the value of good will.
4. Add the total asset value to the good will value and the result is the estimated true selling price.

Theory of Value:
Lease Residual

It is not uncommon to find a business owner who has an asset in the form of a lease because of the contractual terms of the lease. (This is an asset provided the lease is assignable to a buyer with the same terms.) The problem is, how does one assign a fair market value to the lease? (Note: It is possible to have a lease with detrimental terms, creating a negative value.)

To establish the value of the lease (see next page) determine which lease terms have positive (or negative) attributes compared to the terms of a new comparable lease that the landlord would be willing to issue. The most

CASE HISTORY
LEASE RESIDUAL VALUE –

Term of original lease in years: ____

Remaining life in years: ____

Economic rent (today's market value)
    per month: $ _____

Less contract (present) rent
    per month: $ _____

Savings per month: $ _____

Savings per year: ($\times$ _____ months) $ _____

Savings over remaining life of lease

    (____ years $\times$ $____ savings per year): $ _____

Calculate future value:* $_____/month

    savings for ____years @ ____% interest
    average per annum savings account $ _____
    (Factor = _____)

Calculate present value:*

    $_____ discounted at (____% inflation rate

    plus ____% risk rate Total _____%) $ _____
    (Factor = _____)

Estimated Value of Lease: $ _____

* Note: Future value and present value tables
    may be found at your local library
    or book store.

common value found in a lease would be a savings in monthly rent, the difference being between the "economic" or today's "market" rent and the contract rent, over the remaining term of the lease.

To find the total savings from a given lease, multiply the remaining lease term (in months) times today's market rate less the actual lease rate (per month, adjusted for any rent increase over the remaining term). The result equals the total savings created by the lease terms over the remaining life of the lease.

The asset value of the lease is not equal to the total savings. A buyer will not, and cannot be expected to pay this "savings" amount for the lease because there is a time value to money that should be taken into consideration. The expected value of money saved in the future is affected by inflation and risk.

A savings of $10 in pocket today is worth $10. That $10 can be used to purchase $10 of today's goods and services. Because of inflation this savings in pocket five years from now will possibly only purchase $5 to $6 of today's goods and services. In short, future dollars must be discounted back to today's values, but, at what discount rate? We have already mentioned that the future value is affected by inflation and risk. The discount rate for inflation is based on your best estimate of expected inflation over the remaining life of the lease. The discount rate for risk is based on the terms of the lease and the longevity and profitability of the business. At best, risk discount is difficult to assess. (Note: Where the asset value of a lease is critical, contact an appraiser for a professional evaluation.)

The case history on the next page will provide some insight as to the evaluation of a lease asset.

Once the "true net profit" and "true selling price" have been established, a business may be compared to every other business without distortion or confusion.

Gross Multipliers Are Worthless (Multiplying Times Gross Income)

Let's look at two identical businesses. Assume that everything is equal (i.e., gross profit and expenses), except rent. One business in a large shopping center has a very high rent, showing a loss on the business books. The other business, in a very low-rent area, shows a good net profit on its books. Using the gross-multiplier appraising technique, both businesses would be valued at the same price. Which one would a buyer purchase?

Net Multipliers Are Next to Worthless (Multiplying Times Net Profit)

Let's again look at two businesses. A cocktail restaurant with $100,000 of "hard" assets, and an answering service with no "hard" assets. Both businesses produce the same net profit. Using the net-multiplier appraisal

CASE HISTORY
LEASE RESIDUAL VALUE –

Term of original lease in years:	20
Remaining life in years:	7.5

Economic rent (today's market value) per month:	$ 1,116.00
Less contract (present) rent per month:	$ 540.00
Savings per month:	$ 576.00
Savings per year: (× 12 months)	$ 6,912.00
Savings over remaining life of lease (7.5 years × $6,912 savings per year):	$ 51,840.00
Calculate future value:* $576/month savings for 7.5 years @ 8% interest average per annum savings account (Factor = 122.774,143)	$ 71,717.91
Calculate present value* $71,717.91 discounted at 12% inflation rate plus 6% risk rate (18%) (Factor = 0.289,981,598)	$ 20,506.89
Estimated Value of Lease:	$ 20,506.89

* Note: Future value and present value tables
  may be found at your local library
  or book store.

technique, both would be valued at the same price. What happened to the value of "hard" assets?

Buyer's "True Net Profit"

The buyer may not be able to eliminate all the seller's expenses (see "True Net Profit" form on page 31). Using the same form it is possible to estimate the buyer's "true net profit" (or, return on his investment) by recalculating each item to match the new buyer's situation. If buyer and seller agree to a full replacement value on the furniture, fixtures, and equipment, the buyer will have a good tax write-off, in the form of depreciation. The buyer may have a new loan in addition to assuming the seller's loan.

In addition, the new buyer will have an investment tax credit. The investment tax credit is a direct, dollar-for-dollar offset against tax liability. It ranges from $3\frac{1}{2}\%$ of the price of equipment to $11\frac{1}{2}\%$ for a company that makes a contribution to an employee stock-option plan. For a business that is in the 48% tax bracket, the credit is worth just about twice as much as an income-tax deduction in the equivalent amount.

Tangible personal property and certain other tangible property acquired for use in business is entitled to investment tax credit. Credit for tangible personal property includes almost anything used in business that moves and has a useful life of three or more years, including office equipment, machinery, automobiles, display racks and shelves, wall-to-wall carpeting, movable partitions, signs, individual air conditioners, and bookcases.

"Other tangible property" is the category most often overlooked. This category excludes "buildings and their components," but includes air-handling units, refrigeration units, steam boilers, temperature controls and related power outlets, electric power, air and vacuum lines, and duct work installed to provide controlled temperature and humidity in a dust-free environment in special workrooms in a factory.

Note that in taking advantage of the investment tax above, the buyer must remember that he or she has to pay a sales tax (let's use $6\frac{1}{2}\%$). Taking an average of 10% for the investment tax above, the buyer would realize a benefit of $6\frac{3}{4}\%$ as follows:

Credit		10 %
Deduction (sales tax)	$6\frac{1}{2}\%$	
Tax effect at 48%	$(3\frac{1}{4})$	$3\frac{1}{4}$
Net credit (benefit)		$6\frac{3}{4}\%$

If the business uses unskilled workers, the new owner can get a tax credit of up to 20% off for each employee if hired through the Federal Unemployment Office's W.I.N. Program, in his or her local city.

ESTIMATED "TRUE SELLING PRICE"

Name___*AAA Cocktail Lounge*___Address_____Phone_____

ALL ASSETS (Excluding good will)

Accounts receivable	$	_____
Inventory (at current wholesale cost)	$	6,000
Work in process	$	_____
Furniture, fixtures and equipment (market value installed)	$	35,000
Leasehold improvements (minus used up life)	$	_____
Franchise, trademarks and trade names	$	_____
License(s) (ABC)	$	50,000
Lease value (residual and improvements, adjusted to market value)	$	6,000
Real property _____	$	_____
Customer(s) list(s)	$	5,000
Customer(s) contract(s)	$	_____
Other assets (specify) _____	$	_____
Other assets (specify) _____	$	_____
Total asset value "A"	$	102,000

GOOD WILL:

Annual "true net profit" (see page 32) $ ___81,700___

Deduct 10% annual interest on

total asset value "A" $ ___10,200___

Subtotal $ ___71,500___

Risk factor___2___ (times subtotal) = good will $ ___143,000___

"True selling price" (asset plus good will)* $ ___245,000___

*Note: The total selling price of the business is less any outstanding liabilities, such as, liens, encumbrances (notes), etc. The above information has been supplied by the seller from his books and financial records. The broker, or its agent, has reviewed these books and financial records. Broker, or its agent, does not warrant the accuracy of the information contained herein.

ESTIMATED "TRUE SELLING PRICE"

Name_____Address_____Phone_____

ALL ASSETS (Excluding good will)

Accounts Receivable $ _____

Inventory (at current wholesale cost) $ _____

Work in process $ _____

Furniture, fixtures and equipment (market value installed) $ _____

Leasehold improvements (minus used up life) $ _____

Franchise, trademarks and trade names $ _____

License(s) (ABC) $ _____

Lease value (residual and improvements, adjusted to market value) $ _____

Real Property _____ $ _____

Customer(s) list(s) $ _____

Customer(s) contract(s) $ _____

Other assets (specify) _____ $ _____

Other assets (specify) _____ $ _____

Total asset value "A" $ _____

GOOD WILL:

Annual "true net profit" (see page 31) $ _____

Deduct 10% annual interest on

total asset value "A" $ _____

Subtotal $ _____

Risk factor_____ (times subtotal) = good will $ _____

"True selling price" (asset plus good will)* $ _____

*Note: The total selling price of the business is less any outstanding liabilities, such as, liens, encumbrances (notes), etc. The above information has been supplied by the seller from his books and financial records. The broker, or its agent, has reviewed these books and financial records. Broker, or its agent, does not warrant the accuracy of the information contained herein.

Chapter **7** Financial Statements

ANALYSIS OF SELLER'S PROFIT-AND-LOSS STATEMENT

A profit-and-loss statement in its purest form shows all the income a business has made and all the expenses it has incurred (see page 44). If every business reported income and expense by the same rules, direct comparisons and evaluations could be made from one business to another. However, they do not do this. So until a thorough investigation is made of a business for sale you cannot know what their income and expenses amount to.

Business owners have conflicting profit-and-loss statement goals, reflecting the requirements of the owner. For example, the owner may want to use the profit-and-loss statement for tax purposes (maximum expenses and least profit), or for potential sale purposes (minimum expenses and maximum profit), or to cover up something, or to acquire investors.

The question arises as to how valuable these reports are. It is very important to get at least a three-year pattern of profit or loss margins and also as much information on the business as possible in order to reconstruct the profit-and-loss statements that reflect the "real world."

In addition to a profit-and-loss statement (if not available, it can be created from scratch), ask the owner for the following:

- personal tax returns
- 1040 Schedule "C" statement
- sales tax returns
- payroll tax returns

- personal property tax returns
- real property tax returns
- business books
- utility bills

Talk to the business owner's banker, accountant, lawyer, suppliers, and, if possible, discreetly talk to his or her customers. When evaluating the information gathered, look for: understated gross sales, overstated expenses, personal expenses buried in the business, padded inventory, and illegal deductions. (See Chapters 5 and 6).

"Operating Cash Flow" Problems (see page 45)

Reconstruct the seller's profit-and-loss statement by deleting owner's personal insurance, salary, promotion, travel and entertainment, depreciation on equipment, automobile expenses, discounts and refunds, bad debt, donations, and income tax. In the example given, the "operating cash flow" equals $61,400 annually.

"True Net Profit" (see page 45)

Reconstruct the seller's profit-and-loss statement and use the "true net profit" definition (see page 32) by deleting all of the owner's personal expenses. The buyer will take over the manager's job, paying cash for the business and operating the business on a cash basis. This will result in a "true net profit" equal to $81,700 annually for the same business on which the seller declared a net profit of $5,000.

ANALYSIS OF THE BALANCE SHEET

The balance sheet represents a "snapshot" look at the condition of a business as of the date of the audit only. It is normally made up by an accounting firm. Most business-opportunities owners do not bother to have a balance sheet made up unless the business is large or has been incorporated.

If a balance sheet is available, various ratios may be checked to determine the condition of the business. Libraries, stockbrokers, and accountants will have valuable information to help establish correct ratios for the type of business being reviewed.

The current ratio (ratio of debt to equity) is the ratio of current liabilities (all items payable within a year) to current assets (cash, marketable securities, receivables, and inventory). Current ratio is a measure of a company's ability to meet its obligations over the next 12 months and still have ample funds to conduct its business effectively. A two-to-one ratio is considered a desirable minimum.

Another balance-sheet item that deserves attention is "book value," that is, total assets minus total liabilities (including preferred stock), divided by number of shares outstanding. A book value that is significantly higher than the market price of a company's stock is usually an indication that the company's assets are poorly managed.

Examine the return on the total investment, that is, net income divided by long-term liabilities and stockholders' equity.

If this is confusing, then it is suggested that you take the advice of a competent accountant. A salesperson should always recommend professional advice.

SELLERS TYPICAL PROFIT-AND-LOSS STATEMENT
AAA Cocktail Lounge

			% Sales
Gross Sales			
Bar	$160,000		40
Restaurant	240,000		60
Total Gross Sales		$400,000	100%
Cost of Sales			
Beginning Inventory	$8,000		
Ending Inventory	6,000		
Inventory Used	2,000		.50
Purchases—Bar	30,000		7.50
Purchases—Food	118,000		29.50
Total Cost of Sales		150,000	−37.50
Gross Profit		$250,000	62.50%
Operating Expenses			
Advertising	$ 1,000		.25
Cash Short (Over)	1,000		.25
Insurance—General	8,000		2.00
Laundry and Cleaning	5,500		1.38
Legal and Accounting	4,000		1.00
Licenses	3,000		.75
Office Expenses	1,000		.25
Operating Supplies	4,000		1.00
Repairs and Maintenance	10,000		2.50
Salaries—Wages	97,000		24.25
Rent	12,500		3.13
Telephone	3,500		.88
Utilities	10,200		2.55
Freight	500		.13
Bank Charges	600		.15
Credit Cards Cost	1,000		.25
Dues and Publication	500		.13
Taxes—Payroll	4,500		1.13
Personal Property Taxes	500		.13
Promotion	1,000		.25
Salaries—Manager	14,000		3.50
Insurance—Officers	2,000		.50
Salaries—Officers	40,000		10.00
Travel and Entertainment	1,000		.25
Depreciation—Equipment	5,000		1.25
Equipment Rental	5,000		1.25
Automobile Expenses	2,000		.50
Loan Payment/Interest	1,300		.33
Discounts and Refunds	500		.13
Bad-Debt Expense	500		.13
Donations	400		.10
Total Operating Expense (Before Taxes)		241,000	60.25
Taxes—Income		4,000	1.00
Total After Income Taxes		$245,000	61.25
Net Profit		5,000	1.25
Return on Investment (Based on Investment of $245,000)			2.00%

SELLERS TYPICAL PROFIT-AND-LOSS STATEMENT (RECONSTRUCTION)
AAA Cocktail Lounge

	Operating Cash Flow	% Sales	True Net Profit	% Sales
Gross Sales				
Bar				
Restaurant				
Total Gross Sales	$400,000	100%	$400,000	100%
Cost of Sales				
Beginning Inventory				
Ending Inventory				
Inventory Used				
Purchases—Bar				
Purchases—Food				
Total Cost of Sales	$150,000	37.50	$150,000	37.50
Gross Profit	$250,000	62.50%	$250,000	62.50%
Operating Expenses				
Advertising	$ 1,000	.25	$ 1,000	.25
Cash Short (Over)	1,000	.25	1,000	.25
Insurance—General	8,000	2.00	8,000	2.00
Laundry and Cleaning	5,500	1.38	5,500	1.38
Legal and Accounting	4,000	1.00	4,000	1.00
Licenses	3,000	.75	3,000	.75
Office Expenses	1,000	.25	1,000	.25
Operating Supplies	4,000	1.00	4,000	1.00
Repairs and Maintenance	10,000	2.50	10,000	2.50
Salaries—Wages	97,000	24.25	97,000	24.25
Rent	12,500	3.13	12,500	3.13
Telephone	3,500	.88	3,500	.88
Utilities	10,200	2.55	10,200	2.55
Freight	500	.13	500	.13
Bank Charges	600	.15	600	.15
Credit Cards Cost	1,000	.25	1,000	.25
Dues and Publication	500	.13	500	.13
Taxes—Payroll	4,500	1.13	4,500	1.13
Personal Property Taxes	500	.13	500	.13
Promotions				
Salaries—Manager	14,000	3.50		
Insurance—Officers				
Salaries—Officers				
Travel and Entertainment				
Depreciation—Equipment				
Equipment Rental	5,000	1.25		
Automobile Expenses				
Loan Payment/Interest	1,300	.33		
Discounts and Refunds				
Bad-Debt Expense				
Donations				
Total Operating Expense	$188,600	47.15%	$168,300	42.07%
Taxes—Income				
Total After Income Taxes				
Net Profit	$ 61,400	15.35%	$ 81,700	20.43%
Return on Investment				
($245,000)		24.56%		36.68%

Chapter 8 Identifying Business Opportunities

SOURCES OF BUSINESS-OPPORTUNITIES LEADS

To buy or sell a business, check the following sources for potential clients. There are directories at most libraries.

Referrals
Buyers
Sellers
Landlords
Attorneys
Accountants
Bankers
Management consultants
Stockholders
Owner advertisements
Better Business Bureau
Chamber of Commerce
Old listings (Multiple-listing service)
Contacts Influential Directory

Telephone books
Business directories
Newspapers
Bay Area Business Opportunity Exchange
Certified business counselors
National business-opportunities marketing meetings
Exchange meetings
Trade journals and associations
Libraries
Small Business Administration
United States Printing Office
Distributors

Identifying Types and Categories of Business Opportunities

Here are a few examples of business opportunities:

Advertising agencies
Ambulance services

Amusement centers
Answering services

Antique stores
Appliance repair stores
Art schools
Art supply stores
Auctioneers
Auto dealerships
Auto parts stores
Auto repair shops
Auto tire stores
Auto washes
Bail bonds
Bait shops
Bakeries
Barber shops
Beauty shops
Beer bars
Bicycle stores
Billiard parlors
Boat sales
Bowling alleys
Building contractors
Building materials
Bus lines
Cafes
Camera shops
Carpenters
Carpet stores
Carpet cleaners
Caterers
Clothing stores
Cocktail lounges
Coffee shops
Coin laundries
Costume shops
Dairy drive-ins
Dance studios
Delicatessens
Dentists
Dinner houses
Distributorships

Dog grooming shops
Doughnut shops
Driving ranges
Drug stores
Dry cleaners
Electricians
Employment agencies
Engineers
Exterminators
Farms
Fast foods restaurants
Fire alarm systems
Fisheries
Floor covering stores
Florists
Funeral parlors
Furniture stores
Garden supplies
Gasoline service
   stations
Gifts
Greeting cards
Grocery markets
Hamburger stands
Hardware stores
Health clubs
Heating-air condi-
   tioner shops
Hobby shops
Horse rental
Hot dog stands
Ice cream shops
Insurance agencies
Interior decorators
Janitorial services
Jewelry shops
Jobbers
Kennel clubs
Liquor stores
Machine shops

Masonry workers
Maternity shops
Medical laboratories
Motels
Moving companies
Music shops/schools
Newsstands
Nightclubs
Nurseries
Nursery schools
Nursing homes
Office supplies and
    equipment
Optometrists
Paint stores
Pest control
Pet shops
Photography studios
Picture framing stores
Pizza shops
Pool services
Print shops
Real estate agencies
Record stores
Restaurants
Riding stables
Rock shops
Roller rinks

Roofers
Sandwich shops
Scientific equipment
    stores
Secretarial services
Sheet metal fabricators
Shoe repairs
Sign and display
    suppliers
Ski shops
Small contractors
Snack bars
Surveyors
Sweeping services
Swim schools
Tailors
Taverns
Taxi services
Theaters
Title companies
Travel agencies
Trucking firms
Variety stores
Vending routes
Veterinarians
Wedding chapels
Welders
Wholesalers

Tools, Strategies, Materials, and Resources Used to Locate and List Business Opportunities

Contacts Developing contacts, customer confidence, trust and knowledge takes lots of hard work and discipline.

Identifying Businesses To Sell Primary methods in locating businesses to sell are direct market research, telephone market research, solicitation by mail, and referrals.

49

Direct Market Research   Most people fear cold canvassing of businesses. Remember, businesspersons are professionals, too. Where else can you get the feel for what is going on in the business community?

You should, for instance, select a shopping center or business strip that looks interesting. Park your car at one end and walk to the other end, stopping at every business along the way. Avoid the tendency to pass by a business because it looks too busy, too quiet, too prosperous, as if it is failing, or because it looks like a dump.

Do not evaluate a business at the door. You might decide that the business may not be for sale and not go in. Go in, be friendly. First of all, look over the merchandise and browse around the store. You may want to purchase something; at least show concern and interest. Secondly, ask to speak to the owner. If you speak to the owner, ask if you and he or she can speak together in private for just a few minutes. If the answer is "yes," take him or her off to the side and ask if the business is for sale (check before you ask this question that it has not already been listed). If it is not for sale at this time give the owner your name and company (preferably hand him or her your business card) and explain that you are a business-opportunities salesperson, and that your company specializes in selling going concerns and usually has a waiting list of clients for this kind of business. Some good questions to ask are: "Have you heard of any business like yours that might be for sale?" "Have you ever considered selling your business?"

Wait for the owner's reply (you should have read in Chapter 4 all the objections that businesspersons come up with). If the owner seems indecisive about selling and there seems a possibility that the business might be for sale at a later date, be sure that he or she understands that your company specializes in selling business opportunities.

The form for the buyer's authorization to search for a business (see Chapter 10) is an excellent tool that may be used when approaching an owner of a business. It is a form of proof that the business-opportunities salesperson actually has a buyer for the type of business the owner possesses.

You may also choose to offer a special service in order to gain greater rapport, trust, and confidence in selling youself. For instance you could offer a free market analysis. This technique is a feasibility study to determine whether or not it is wise, sensible, or practical for the owner to sell.

A last resort is to ask the seller to write down all the reasons for not selling, then all the reasons for selling. Most times the owner's reasons for selling will outweigh the reasons for not selling. He or she may have second thoughts, especially if you figure wages per hour spent operating the business. When you determine that the owner wishes to sell his or her business, go right into appraising the business (see Chapter 6). Write up the listing agreement before you leave the premises. For details of this agreement see Chapter 9.

Telephone Market Research   Proper telephone use saves a lot of time and traveling expense, and is especially well suited to looking for businesses within a specialized field and for "feeling out" potential sellers. Use a street directory or Contacts Influential Directory.

The telephone does have its limitations. Develop a pleasant telephone technique and use it to set up an appointment only, as it is best to meet your customer face-to-face, especially for your initial contact. Ascertain that the owner is alone and not too busy to see you. If a face-to-face meeting is not possible at that time, using the telephone will allow you to spread your materials in front of you making it possible to read your presentation.

Solicitation By Mail   A consistent mail-out program will help build a business-opportunities specialist's contacts. Several types of direct-mail pieces work well (see below):

- *Company brochure.*   This direct mail piece tells about your business-opportunities company and its experienced staff. This method, along with newspaper advertisements, builds long-term exposure to the business-opportunities field.
- *Publicity.*   Take advantage of free advertising. Send company information and personal activities to local newspapers for publication in their business information section.
- *Monthly newsletter.*   A well-written newsletter filled with items of interest is an excellent way to maintain contact with clients. There are many sources for information, such as a Better Business Bureau, Chamber of Commerce, police and fire departments, city and county reports, and other local businesses. A list of businesses for sale or businesses wanted is also of interest.
- *Anniversary and birthday cards.*   Clients appreciate being remembered.
- *Solicitation brochure.*   This mail piece is directed toward a specific type of business or a particular location on behalf of an interested buyer. An offer for a free business appraisal followed up with a

telephone call may produce much success in locating businesses for sale.

The following are two sample letters for making first contact with a business owner by mail. In adapting them for your purposes, be sure to use only those statements that are valid for you.

_____

_____

_____, _____

_____. 19 ____

_____

_____

_____ , _____

Dear Sir:

Are you considering selling? Buying? Merging? Expanding? Or have you possibly heard of a business like yours that might be considering these actions?

We have inquiries from many potential buyers, anxious to buy profitable businesses.

We are business brokers and have been providing such service to the business community for many years. We would like the opportunity to introduce our professional staff specialists and the services we can provide to assist you.

We would be happy to discuss your particular needs, in confidence, at your convenience. Would you prefer a meeting at your place of business or at my office?

Please contact me at the above phone.

Very truly yours,

_____

Enclosures

52

_____

_____

_____ , _____

_____ . 19 ____

_____

_____

_____ , _____

Dear Sir:

In response to your advertisement in today's newspaper, permit us to introduce our company to you.

During the past years, we have been deeply involved in initiating and transacting mergers, acquisitions, plant purchases and liquidations, both public and private. Due to this in-depth involvement, we constantly have available a select group of serious buyers.

In order to assure you, the seller, of the utmost confidentiality, we utilize a blind method of presenting your firm to the would-be buyer. Only where there is serious interest and proven financial capability will your firm's name be divulged to the buyer.

If you are interested in obtaining our services, please call to discuss your requirements in greater length, in confidence, at your convenience. Would you prefer a meeting at your place of business or at my office?

Very truly yours,

_____

Enclosures

Remember that there is no substitute for a good referral. Treat clients with respect, be honest, keep them informed, and keep in touch with them after the sale. These are things that build a good referral business.

Locating Buyers for Businesses The two primary methods in locating buyers for businesses are advertising and referrals.

Advertising Interesting advertisements make the telephone ring. The telephone should be used only to make an appointment with the buyer. Qualifying the buyer as to what he or she wants and the funds he or she has to work with should be accomplished in the office.

Newspaper advertisements by law must indicate that the business being advertised is offered by an agent or a broker. If you mention any of the following: how much down, the amount of interest, or the amount of payments, you must advertise all three. However, you may say merely "low downpayment."

Referrals You should keep old clients and buyers informed on currently available businesses for sale. They may know of somebody interested in buying a business.

Field Experience

Field experience is very important, especially to the newly licensed salesperson. He or she should go out and view many different types of businesses (even before a client comes into the picture) so that when a client desires a certain business in a specific location, the salespeson may be aware of its availability.

Comparing similar businesses in different locations is not an easy task and requires skill and practice. If, for example, a client wants a restaurant in the business section of a certain town, it will be to your advantage to sample the food in order to make a value judgment before introducing yourself to the owner of said business. You can observe the kind of clientele that is being served, the service, and how the food is prepared. By following the procedures mentioned above the salesperson will be able to judge whether the business is worth offering to a potential buyer. Of course, the salesperson should eat at several other restaurants in the area, even if they are not for sale, as a basis for comparison. Frequently an owner may be interested in selling his or her business, even if it is not listed for sale.

Field Experience Form The form on page 56 should be completed after observations have been made at certain business premises. If necessary, duplicate this form and fill in several other businesses of like nature for comparison and practice.

Field Experience
Analysis Form

This form on page 57 is an analysis form. This, again, is for practice purposes and should be completed by the salesperson to show why this business was chosen and the reason why it would be to the benefit of the seller to sell and the buyer to buy. These practice runs will prove very useful to the newly licensed salesperson when an actual sale is pending.

BUSINESS OPPORTUNITIES FIELD EXPERIENCE PRACTICE

Name of business _____Telephone no._____

Address _____City_____

Type of business _____

How contacted   ☐ phone   ☐ cold canvass   ☐ went into business (eat, buy)

REPORT: Selling price $_____.

        Approximate gross $_____ per month.   Approximate net $_____ per month.

TERMS: Downpayment $_____, with $_____ per month, _____% interest included.

REMARKS: _____

_____

_____

_____

_____

_____

_____

_____

_____

_____

_____

_____

_____

_____

_____

Listed with a real estate broker   ☐ yes   ☐ no. If yes, expires_____

Your Name _____Address _____Telephone no._____

ANALYSIS OF BUSINESS OPPORTUNITIES FIELD EXPERIENCE

Name of business _____ Telephone no._____

Address _____ City_____

Type of business _____

Report: _____

_____

_____

_____

_____

_____

_____

_____

Summary: _____

_____

_____

_____

_____

_____

_____

Would you purchase this business and why? _____

_____

_____

Chapter **9** Listing Agreement

ANALYSIS OF LISTING AGREEMENT FORM — BUSINESS OPPORTUNITY VIEWPOINT

The listing agreement is for the business owner (seller) who wishes to sell his or her business. The selling of a business is usually accomplished through a real estate agency that specializes in the sale of business opportunities. However, it can be sold by the owner.

Realistic listings are the life blood of the industry; without them there would be no sales or commissions. This chapter focuses on the technical preparation of a listing agreement (review the fundamental seller's education by the specialist, Chapter 4).

Control of a business-opportunity listing depends on the relationship between the seller and specialist. It is wise to educate the seller on every aspect of the listing agreement. This technique will benefit the seller in saving time and money and avoiding problems.

Control can be accomplished by providing a thorough explanation of the services the business opportunity specialist can provide that in most cases the owners cannot or would not do for themselves. For example, the specialist can provide:

- access to qualified buyers
- advertising outlets
- multiple-listing services
- local and statewide business-opportunity exchanges
- referral service to other business-opportunity specialists

59

- experience to negotiate a complete transaction
- accurate appraisal of the true value of the business
- advertising to qualified buyers
- tax implications
- sale negotiating
- avoidance of legal and tax pitfalls
- local, county, state, and federal rules and regulations or sources to ensure a complete bulk-sale transaction

If the seller is not familiar with all aspects of the transaction, litigation may result, taking the seller months to settle. Legal action may delay or "kill" the deal. However, an experienced salesperson has the best chance to obtain the highest price, best terms, and complete escrow in a minimum amount of time, with very few problems.

Explain to the seller that in the process of preparing a proper listing agreement, appointments must be made with the landlord, noteholders, franchiser, and any other persons connected with the transfer of the business for their approval. Seller participation is usually required (see Chapter 14).

It is essential that the seller be kept informed on a weekly basis of all responses and action on his or her property. Remind the seller not to try to sell the business himself or herself. He or she should only answer specific questions and show prospective buyers around, then refer the clients to the listing salesperson.

LISTING AGREEMENT PREPARATION — FULL DISCLOSURE

The importance of an accurate listing cannot be overstressed. Listing contracts have legal implications for all parties. Extreme care must be taken to include the seller's entire terms, conditions, warrants, covenants, representations, and so forth. *Oral agreements are unacceptable.* They are rarely enforceable or acceptable for legal action.

Business-opportunity listings are exposed to many pitfalls with less than 25% resulting in a sale. However, with careful and complete listing preparation, chances of a sale can be easily increased to 90% when the seller's complete terms and conditions are negotiated before a business is offered for sale.

The listing agreement shown on page 77 is for businesses only, i.e., the "leasehold rights." Any real property involved should have a separate agreement (contact your local Real Estate Board for necessary forms). A

Security and Exchange License is required to sell corporation stock. However, the corporation "assets" only may be sold without a Security License.

Listing Agreement Form (pages 77 through 88) *   Let us go through the listing agreement item by item:

Date—the date seller signs the agreement.

Type of business—spell out the type of business, i.e., bar, fast food, retail automobile parts, etc.

Describe Product or Service—Italian food served, pool cleaning service, etc.

Name(s)—Let us say Charles Brown, the seller, names his business "Charlie Brown, Inc.," and puts the name "Charlie's" on the marquee. Thus, he lists three different names: the name of the business is "Charlie Brown, Inc.," doing business as (dba) "Charlie's." The name of the owner is Charles Brown. Next add his home address.

The owner in this case is a corporation, and in most cases selling assets only. The salesperson must specify what the owner is selling!

We will see as we progress through the listing, that for every supporting document referred to, that document becomes a part of this agreement. In essence, the salesperson must sell a "going business" by listing a complete "package."

Exclusive Right to Sell Listing—This is an irrevocable and exclusive right to sell a business. In other words, the business owner (seller) gives the exclusive right to sell his or her business to the broker specified in the listing. Even if the owner sells the business himself or herself or through another broker, the specified broker would still earn full commission. There is a time limit (usually six months) in the agreement and the agreement continues thereafter as a nonexclusive right for a further period of one year. Once the agreement becomes nonexclusive, the party who sells the business would be entitled to the commission—or if the seller sells it, he or she would pay no commission.

However, the broker with the exclusive agreement can furnish to the owner, in writing and no later than 30 days after the exclusive agreement expires, the names of all parties with whom he or she has been negotiating or to whom he or she supplied information about the business. Then that broker would still receive the full commission if the property is sold within a specific time to one of the parties named on that written list.

---

*This form and others discussed in this chapter are grouped at the end of the chapter.

The broker is authorized to accept and hold a deposit check upon acceptance of a purchase offer by a potential buyer. The broker is also authorized to cooperate with other brokers, such as a multiple-listing service, and divide his or her commission with any broker as the brokers deem acceptable.

Other items included in the exclusive listing are as follows:

1. *Price and Terms*. What is the total price of the business and the downpayment that is to be paid at the opening of the escrow? Will there be any additional payments required to be paid 10 days before escrow closes; if so, how soon should it be paid?

   A). Are there any encumbrances (notes) that buyers may assume? If so, how much is left to be paid and at what interest rate? (Note: this listing agreement states "simple interest." It can be amortized interest or some other type of interest. It is important that the type of interest be specified in this agreement.) What are the monthly payments? "Until paid" means until the entire principal and interest is paid, or, there may be a balloon payment. That is, one extra large payment on a note at the time it is payable in full. The approximate amount of that note should be specified in the agreement. "Free and clear" means that there are no encumbrances (notes) on the business. If there are encumbrances on the business, can they be assumed by the buyer? In other words, can the new buyer take over the encumbrances? What is the amount of the encumbrances? All this information must be spelled out on the listing agreement.

   B). Will the seller take an installment note back with the business assets as security? How much? At what interest rate? How much per month? Of course, the buyer can pay all or part of the balance owed on the note, without prepayment penalties, at any time during the note period. The buyer should also be told if there is a balloon payment due at the end of the note period.

   When there are encumbrances carried by the seller, he or she may ask for additional security, that is, the seller may require a first or second note on the buyer's real property, home, car, boat, airplane, or stocks or bonds. If the buyer defaults in making payments, he or she could lose the additional security. The entire encumbrances are due and payable in full if the buyer sells or transfers the business.

   C). The seller might accept the balance of the encumbrances in a form of a deed to real property. In that case, specify the exact location and attach the legal assumption and title insurance or waive title insurance, if the seller does not require it.

D). If there is usable and saleable inventory it should be itemized on forms shown on pages (92 through 94) and only the total estimated value listed. Is this total value included in the selling price? If not, how and when will it be paid?

E). Additional terms is a catchall area to add anything else to this agreement.

2. *Assets.* The items to be included in the sale of this business must be spelled out, i.e., licenses or special permits, without which this business cannot operate legally. A complete business has to be sold in order to have a "going business."

   Does the price include the value of the Alcoholic Beverage Control license and what type is it? Also add the seller's sales tax number and ABC license number. The latter number is on the permit. The permit should be hanging on the wall near the cash register.

3. *Liabilities.* Specify what is to be excluded from this sale, for example, accounts payable, real estate encumbrances, or deposits.

4. *Installment Sales.* Does the seller want or need an installment sale? The Installment Sales Revision Act of 1980, radically revises the reporting of gain on installment sales and deferred payment sales. While some key provisions of the new law are effective only for transactions after Oct. 19, 1980, others are effective retroactively, to transactions already made. Here is a comparison of the law on installment and other deferred payment sales of real property and nondealer sales of personal property, as it existed before the changes made by the 1980 Act and as it exists after the 1980 Act amendments.

Old Law	**New Law**
No more than 30% of the selling price can be received in the taxable year of sale. *	30% rule eliminated. Amount of payment in year of sale irrelevant. 30% rule dropped retroactively for certain sales.
The contract price must be payable in two or more taxable years. *	Only requirement is that at least one payment be made in a taxable year after year of sale. Rule requiring payments in two or more years dropped retroactively for certain sales.

*These are effective January 1, 1980.

63

Old Law	**New Law**
Selling price of personal property must be more than $1,000.	No minimum sale price required.
Installment method must be elected.	Installment treatment automatic unless taxpayer elects not to have installment treatment apply.
Case law upheld installment sale treatment for installment sales to family members who later sold property outright (tax-deferred for first seller, tax-free for second).	Taxes first seller when second seller collects, with some exceptions.
Installment treatment is available for installment sales of depreciable property to family members.	Where taxpayer sells depreciable property to his or her spouse or certain 80% owned corporations or partnerships, deferred payments will be deemed to be received in the taxable year in which the sale occurs, unless absence of tax motive can be shown.
For purposes of reporting gain, like-kind property received in an installment sale qualifies for non-recognition treatment. The value of the like-kind property, however, is included in the contract price and is treated as payment received (e.g., in applying the 30% test), for purposes of reporting profit under the installment rules.	Like-kind property that can be received without recognition of gain isn't treated as payment and isn't included in the contract price for purposes of reporting profit under the installment method.
On installment sale of corporation's assets in a 12-month, Code Sec. 337 liquidation, distribution of installment obligations to shareholders doesn't qualify for installment reporting in their hands.	Distribution of installment sale obligations to shareholders in a Code Sec. 337 liquidation won't be taxed to them until the shareholders receive payment on the installment obligation.
Sales with a contingent sale price don't qualify for installment sale treatment.	Installment sale rules apply to sales with a contingent sales price.
It is unclear whether income is realized (as installment obligation disposition) by gift cancellations of the obligation or the installments as they come due.	The cancellation of an installment obligation is treated as a disposition of the obligation by the holder of the obligation.
It is unclear whether any unreported gain remaining at the death of the seller is taxed if the installment obligation is left to the obligor, because the interests of the obligor and obligee merge.	The installment obligation disposition rules can't be avoided by the bequest of an obligation to the obligor. Thus if an installment obligation is transferred by bequest to the obligor or is cancelled by the executor, the unreported gain becomes taxable to the seller's estate.

Old Law	**New Law**
A decedent's estate isn't allowed to succeed to the tax treatment which would have been available to the decedent had he or she lived to receive a reconveyance of real property in partial or full satisfaction of purchase money debt. This tax treatment, which is availalbe when the holder of the obligation is alive, provides for the limited recognition of gain.	An executor or beneficiary who receives a secured installment obligation from a decedent succeeds the decedent for purposes of qualifying for nonrecognition treatment if the real property sold by the decedent is reacquired in cancellation of the obligation.
Standby letter of credit used to secure payment held by court to be payment.	Third party guarantee (including a standby letter of credit) not taken into account in determining if buyer's evidence of indebtedness constitutes payment to seller.
Must carry an interest charge of at least 7% per annum simple interest.	Must carry an interest charge of at least 9% per annum simple interest.

Check your individual states. For example, California, as of January 1981, had not conformed to the new federal act.

Briefly, in California the seller may accept payments for the business over two or more tax years and in the year of the sale does not receive more than 30% of the gross sale price, less value of inventory, and covenant not to compete, and must carry 7% per annum simple interest charges.

An installment sale normally benefits both buyer and seller. The buyer's down payment is lower than a full cash sale, and the seller pays taxes in a lower tax bracket, while spreading taxable gain over a period of years. There are many factors affecting an installment sale. Buyer, seller, and their accountants and attorneys should all carefully review any installment sale transaction.

5. *Allocation of the Selling Price* (capital gains tax rules for business opportunities). You must allocate the purchase price or the Internal Revenue Service will do it for you, and in most cases, years later. Compliance with IRS regulations requires that the business selling price be divided (allocated) between ordinary income and long-term capital gain categories. Allocations are negotiable (within reason) and could have important tax consequences. The buyer may want maximum allocation to direct expense categories for maximum tax write off in the year of purchase. The seller wants maximum allocation to capital gain categories for minimum tax consequences on

the sale of the business. The selling price of the business would typically be divided among the following categories:

A). *Accounts receivable** (see form, page 96).

Buyer: ordinary gain or loss as accounts are paid.

Seller: ordinary gain at the time of sale.

B, C). *Inventory* (finished goods, work in progress, and raw materials)* (see form, page 92).

Buyer: ordinary gain or loss as inventory is sold.

Seller: ordinary gain or loss at time of the sale.

D). *Furniture, fixtures, and equipment* (see forms, pages 93 and 94).

Buyer: A large allocation is advantageous to the buyer because it provides a higher basis for depreciation and also for the investment tax credit. These assets are termed 1231 assets, and disposition thereof may result in either a capital gain or ordinary income. When valuing the furniture, fixtures, and equipment, remember that if the parties agree to a full replacement value, the buyer will have a good tax write off (full depreciation) and a good investment tax credit (see "True Net Profit" form on page 31 for breakdown of percent range for investment tax credits).

Seller: A low allocation reduces the seller's taxable gain and might even provide an ordinary loss, depending upon the tax basis (amount of depreciation taken) of the furniture, fixtures, and equipment.

E). *Leasehold improvements*

Buyer: A high allocation is beneficial to the buyer. The cost of the improvements is amortized over the remaining life of the lease. It is classified as a 1231 asset. Buyer pays no sales tax.

Seller: Would produce capital gains or ordinary loss to the seller.

F). *Franchises, trademarks, and trade names* (license to use a business name, equipment, or technique). Although they may appear to be costly, the benefit of using the business name, equip-

---

*Note: Accounts receivable, inventory, and work in progress can only be estimated at this point. Therefore, provisions must be made as to how these three items can be added or subtracted when inventory is actually taken the night before escrow is to close. If the seller has understated or overstated the value, what payment options will he or she give the buyer?

ment, or technique should reflect in higher gross sales than if one operated as a "lone wolf" business owner.

To establish a value, it is necessary to estimate the amount of additional net profit derived from use of the name, less the cost for use of the name. This "extra profit" may then be projected over a business' "life" and discounted back to a present value at an estimated inflation rate.

A franchise license should have a "going rate" on the open market. Talk to the franchise or licensing company and franchised business owners to determine the "going rate" in a particular area.

Tax consequences.

Seller: If seller abandons all right and interest, he or she can write this off as a tax loss.

Buyer: No effect; buyer cannot claim anything.

Seller: If seller sells all rights and interests to buyer, seller can receive capital gains tax treatment. If seller retains any right or interest, the cost will be taxed as ordinary income.

G). *ABC License.*

Buyer: A low allocation is beneficial to the buyer. The cost of the license is an investment expense with no amortization.

Seller: A high allocation is beneficial to the seller. The sale of the license results in capital gain or capital loss.

H). *Good will.* Most people consider good will to be a mysterious category where much of a business' true value lies. It is in this category that a seller assigns a value to his or her "blood, sweat, and tears" expended while building the business. It is in this category that a buyer takes most objection to the arbitrary value assigned to the business by the seller. Good will has a value. The logic in arriving at good will value must be valid and understandable to both buyer and seller before an agreement can be reached. Good will value is related to net profit and risk. Net profit represents a return in salary for the time and effort invested by the owner of the business, as well as a return on the owner's investment in the business. Excess net profit is a return from the business as a result of: length of time in business, competitive position, customers, location, business name and reputation, products, service, and various other intangible factors (for good will formula see pages 33 and 34).

Tax consequences. This is an intangible commodity and difficult to justify. A low allocation is of benefit to the buyer. "Good will" is carried on the books as a nondepreciable asset, and as such cannot be written off for tax purposes. The sale of good will results in either capital gain or loss to the seller.

I). *Covenant not to compete.* The seller covenants to the buyer, his or her successors, assignees, and representatives that he or she will not engage, directly or indirectly, in any business the same as, similar to, or in competition with the business hereby sold within a radius of (number of miles) from the principal place of business being sold for a period of (number of months, years) from date of buyer's possession, either as a principal, agent, manager, employee, owner, partner, stockholder, director or officer of a corporation, trustee, consultant or otherwise in any capacity whatsoever. This covenant is not transferable or assignable (see form, page 188).

Tax consequences.

Buyer: Able to amortize cost over term of covenant as an ordinary expense.

Seller: Reports the proceeds of the covenant as ordinary income as received. Consequently, it is to seller's advantage to allocate a lesser portion on the sales price to the covenant which should be separately identified in the contract.

J). *Lease valuation.* A lease is an exclusive right to use space or equipment at a predetermined rental rate for a specific period of time. When a lease gives a right of use for other than the economic or "going market rate" (above or below), it has a residual value (negative or positive).

The annual lease residual may be calculated by subtracting the annual lease rate from the annual "market rate." This lease residual amount is then multiplied by the remaining lease term to establish the total dollar amount of the lease residual (less lease adjustments). Because of the value of money in time, only a portion of the lease residual amount will be a valid allowance in calculating its present value to the business.

A shortcut appraisal method is to apply a one-year residual dollar amount toward the lease value, using good will calculations to account for additional savings over the remaining lease term. (Where there are large savings for long terms, the "Theory of Value: Lease Residual" technique should be used in determining the value of lease residuals. See pages 34 through 37.

Tax consequences.

Buyer: A small allocation is of benefit to the buyer. The cost of the lease is amortized over the remaining life of the lease. It is classified as a 1231 asset.

Seller: A high allocation provides the seller with a higher long-term capital gain. It is classified as a 1231 asset.

K, L). *Real property.* The sale of real property should be handled separately from the sale of the business. Tax benefits and consequences of real property will be separated from business operations on buyer's and seller's tax returns. The real property, as a rule, is subject to section 1231 tax treatment and would produce capital gains or ordinary loss for the seller. The buyer may use the allocated amount as his tax basis for depreciation.

M). *Customer list(s).* Present customers mean future income to a business. Therefore, customer lists have a value. The value of a customer list to a business depending on regular repeat sales is much higher than to a business with a low dependency on repeat sales (see form, page 97). The value of a customer list is related to the percentage amount of extra annual net income attributable to the list. This dollar amount is then multiplied by the estimated "life" of the list. This list lasts usually from three to five years, but no longer than the period of the covenant not to compete. Because of the time value, only a portion of the customer list contribution will be a valid allowance in calculating the list's present value to the business. A quick way to estimate the value of the list is to add on one year's extra net profit (attributable to the list) to account for additional value over the life of the list due to good will calculations. Where there are large extra net profits or unusual conditions in the transaction, the "Theory of Value: Lease Residual" technique should be used in determining the value of customer lists.

Tax consequences. This list must be separately identified for purposes of allocation similar to the covenant not to compete. Both the buyer and the seller must agree on a period of useful life to enable the buyer(s) to amortize its cost as an ordinary expense. A low allocation is a benefit to the seller because it is ordinary income.

N). *Customer contract(s).* Where a contract is guaranteed for a useful life and income, a buyer can amortize the cost of the contract against ordinary income.

6. *General Information.* As much information as possible should be gathered about the business.

A). Get the profit-and-loss statements for the past three years. Obtain copies of "true gross receipts" and "true net profits" for each year the seller has owned the business. (Review Chapter 6 if necessary.) What is the payroll per month? Is the seller's name on the payroll? If so, what amount does he or she draw each month? How many full-time and/or part-time workers are employed by the seller at this time? What is the average amount for utility bills per month?

B). *Lease.* How many years remain on the lease? What is the cost per month? Is there an option to renew? If so, for how many years? At what cost per month? Is the lease assumable? Any other information about the lease? Is there a security deposit required? Does the rent have to be paid in advance? (Some landlords require the first and last months rents.) How long has the business been established, and what is the length of time that the seller has owned this business? List the business hours and the number of days the business is operated per week. What is the total square footage of the business as now occupied by the present owner? Ascertain the number and type of seating. Are they in different areas? What is the parking capacity? Who are the seller's landlord, attorney, and accountant? Obtain their addresses and telephone numbers. What zoning laws and/or restrictions are placed against the business or premises? All of these questions should be fully answered so that there will be no problem with them at the completion of the transaction.

C). *Contracts.* The whole "package" must be transferred. Make lists of all the contracts, menus, recipes, etc., that will or will not go with the sale. Will the management stay? Obtain the opinion of the seller. He cannot bind the employees. The buyer might want an employment contract for these employees.

D). *Business franchise.* If a franchise is being purchased, what is the fee? Is there a transfer fee? Get the name and address of the franchiser. Is the franchise assumable?

E). *Vending machines, games, and equipment leases.* If such machines and equipment are on lease, what is the amount remaining to be paid on the notes? Are payments "until paid" or is there a balloon payment? What are the names and addresses of the vendors? Can these contracts be assumed?

F). *Furniture, fixtures, and equipment.* Make a list of items that are and are not included in the sale, and determine what is leased or owned by persons other than the seller (see forms, pages 93 through 94).

G). *Miscellaneous information*. This is another catchall to add any-thing to the contract that is not included in the categories listed above.

7. *Fee*

A). *Commission*. The seller pays the broker's commission. Note that the real estate commissions are negotiable and are not fixed by law. Brokerage commissions may be a percentage of sale price; however, some brokers charge a fixed amount irrespective of the sale price.

B,C,D). The seller agrees to pay such fee upon disposition (sale) as spelled out under "Exclusive Right to Sell Listing" agreement (see page 77).

8. *Seller's reason for selling*. Many buyers believe the seller's reasons for selling. However, it must be a legitimate reason. When specify-ing "sick," state the nature of the illness.

9. *Seller must warrant and provide proof of the following*.

A). The seller must be the legal owner and must be authorized to sign for all the sellers (assuming more than one person is involved in the sale). This authorization must be in writing.

B). The seller must state that the business is "free and clear" from any liens or notes, except as noted in the agreement.

C). The seller warrants that the business will pass all inspections (e.g., ABC, Board of Health) when the buyer takes possession.

D). The seller warrants that all property will be in good working condition when the buyer takes possession.

E). The seller is not aware that there will be any loss of customers because the business is being sold.

F). The seller must state that he or she has not received any notices that will affect the business or the right to operate said business.

G). The Special Studies Zone—the seller must inform the buyer if the business is in an earthquake area.

H). The National Flood Control Act—the buyer must be told by the seller if the business is in a flood area.

I). Sometimes the business is small so that there are no employees and there is no sales tax number. The seller in the aforementioned cases does not have to obtain "clearance receipts" (see "L" below).

J). The seller must provide a good and valid "bill of sale" to the buyer as evidence of ownership.

K). The seller agrees to sell and transfer all his or her licenses and permits necessary to legally operate the whole business.

L). If the seller has a sales tax number and employees, he or she must provide clearance receipts to show that money due to the State Board of Equalization and/or Department of Benefit Payments has been paid in full.

M). If there are any motor vehicles involved in the transaction, they must be properly described. The "pink slip(s)" must be turned over to the escrow holder at the opening of the escrow. The buyer is responsible for the sales taxes due.

N). The seller must continue to conduct business in the same and usual manner. For example, the seller cannot close the business during the course of the sale.

O). The seller must state that the business is marketable; that it can be sold as specified. If the seller misrepresents any of the facts and as a result the sale is cancelled, the seller agrees to pay the broker his or her full commission.

P). Seller must determine how he or she wishes to take title if there are any encumbrances to be carried back by the seller.

Q). The seller agrees to train the buyer or the buyer's employees for a specified period of time. The starting and finishing dates for the training period should be spelled out in writing.

R). The seller authorizes those concerned to contact the seller's associates for any information required about the business (see "Release Form" on page 91).

S). Frequently a seller knowingly or unknowingly, will list his or her business and ask for a downpayment equal to or less than total creditor claims and not include the broker's commission. If this occurs, the buyer agrees to pay said commission to the broker, reducing the selling price and downpayment amount to seller accordingly.

T). The seller agrees to prorate through escrow certain expenses.

U). The seller agrees to pay his or her share of escrow fees; usually the seller and buyer split this fee 50/50.

V). All inventory that is to be included in the sale should be listed. All inventory that is not to be included in the sale and is either owned or leased by others should be clearly described (see forms and instructions on pages 92 through 94).

W). The seller agrees to transfer ABC license at opening of escrow.

X,Y). The seller agrees as to who will be the broker and escrow holder.

Z). Occasionally a seller may delay providing the necessary information to complete the transfer of a business. He or she may be hoping the deal will fall through. This may be due to a seller's remorse, or perhaps the seller has found a better deal, or may be trying to force new terms on an overanxious buyer. This paragraph will extend the termination date of the agreement, thus eliminating the effect of the seller's delay.

AA). The seller agrees not to hold up the proceedings.

BB). The seller demands to see a financial statement with an offer. Very few statements are audited.

CC). The seller demands that someone maintain insurance to cover the period of his encumbrances. The buyer usually pays for this insurance.

DD). The seller demands that the buyer pay all sales tax as required by law. The seller is responsible and must collect and pay sales tax to the state on the furniture, fixtures, and equipment on the final sales tax return. However, the actual cost is borne by the buyer and paid through escrow, generally when escrow is opened.

10. *Corporation.* The seller must be authorized to list, sell, finance, etc., if business is owned by a corporation. A copy of the minutes stating that the corporation is for sale should be attached to the listing agreement.

11. *Covenant Not to Compete.* Seller will normally agree not to engage in the same type of business within a reasonable area and time. In a dense area, three years is considered to be a reasonable time and three miles radius a reasonable distance, depending on the type of business (see form, page 190).

12. *Default.*

A). If a seller refuses to complete the sale as required, he or she agrees to pay the broker's commission.

B). If a buyer refuses to complete the sale as required, the seller agrees that any deposit money received in excess of the amount of the commission due to the broker will be his or her liquidated damages.

C). Where a seller carries back a note on the sale of a business, this paragraph may be used if the buyer is unable to provide the seller with additional security, such as, real property, automobile, stocks, or bonds. Without this provision, the buyer could sell the inventory and assets, running the business into the ground, leaving the seller "high and dry." Often a buyer does not have sufficient assets, or is reluctant to put up his or her home as security toward a seller's note. This provision provides a compromise between buyer and seller. Where the buyer defaults by allowing either the gross sales or the inventory to fall below 75% in any three consecutive months, the seller has an option to repossess the business. However, if the seller does not want it back, a good suggestion is that he or she can go in and help the buyer increase his or her sales/inventory. This cannot include the Alcoholic Beverage Control license, as it must be free and clear at all times. A seller demands a monthly profit-and-loss statement. Except in an installment sale, a buyer has the option to pay off the note at any time. The reason for this is that the seller would lose capital gains tax advantage and would have to pay the entire capital gains tax due for the year of sale.

13. *Arbitration.* Settlement of a dispute by parties chosen to hear both sides and arrive at a decision.

14. *Hold Harmless Agreement.* To earn his or her commission, the broker, or his or her agent, needs only to find a ready, willing, and able buyer. A seller agrees to hold the broker's, or his or her agent harmless from any liability arising out of the sale.

15. *Conditions and Terms.* This agreement must contain all instructions in writing. Nothing should be agreed upon orally. This is a legal document. It should be read carefully. The broker and escrow holder are not authorized to give legal advice. This is the function of an attorney. All parties must understand everything in this agreement before signing it. Then all parties must have a copy for their files.

16. *Procuring a Buyer.* The broker agrees to find a buyer when signing this agreement. It must be dated when it is signed. The seller's name should be printed and his or her title mentioned on the agreement form. Enter the seller's Social Security number in the space provided. This can be used for further identification, if necessary, or it may be required if a loan is required at a later date. The seller should also enter his or her federal and state employer's numbers, if any, and address and telephone number. A broker or broker's agent must date and sign this form.

Change in Listing Form (see page 89). A seller changes the terms of his or her listing; the price, for example, or the downpayment, or terms. When changes are needed, this form should be completed.
Counteroffer Form (see page 90). If the seller refuses a buyer's offer, then the seller may make a counteroffer. In this case, use this form.
Release Form (see page 91). Usually a seller does not have his or her records readily available. This form should be used to acquire whatever information is necessary from third parties. Make sure that the seller signs it.

Work-In-Progress Form (see page 92). This form is usually used when dealing with manufacturing plants. Set a value to partially completed or finished goods or nontaxable inventory to establish the total value of inventory.

Inventory Forms (see pages 93 and 94). These forms are used to itemize everything that is to be sold with the business. Often the seller will say "everything goes in the sale," but the seller doesn't always own everything. By using the correct forms it is a simple matter to separate personal items, such as pictures, plants, etc., from items that may be "leased and/or owned by others." Many times equipment and signs may be leased or may belong to the landlord. The inventory forms cited are self-explanatory.

Accounts Payable Form (see page 95). Itemize all accounts. That is, are they less than 30 days old? Or are they 30 to 90 days, or over 90 days old? What is due right now? If they are considered over due, the buyer should inquire why the seller has not paid his or her bills on time. Does the seller have enough money to pay the outstanding accounts at escrow time? Total the accounts that are "currently due" and ascertain what percentage is left to pay. The buyer might want to make a "cash offer," that is, discount them and reduce the purchase price of the business accordingly. It is usual for the seller to pay these bills at escrow time.

Accounts Receivable Form (see page 96). These should be treated in the same manner as accounts payable. It is usual, and to the advantage of the buyer to assume these and, when possible, discount them. This allows for more "cash flow" in the business. It is advantageous to the buyer to handle these accounts, as the seller sometimes gets overanxious and applies too much pressure in the collection process. At this point, the seller has nothing to lose, but the new owner could lose a good account.

List of Customers Form (see page 97). Make a list of all the customers and note how long they have been doing business with the seller. Determine the useful life of these customers. This information is necessary to establish a value for tax purposes (see page 69 for tax consequences).

Special Studies Zone Act Form (see page 98). Use this form when a business is located in a geologic hazard area, for example, an earthquake zone.

National Flood Control Act Form (see page 98). Use this form when a business is located in a flood and/or mudslide zone.

Corporate Resolution Form (see page 99). If a corporation sells its assets, there must be authorization from the corporation's board of directors. Use this form for authorization to list, sell, or finance the business, or to complete any other necessary agreements.

Notice of Disclosure Form (see page 100). No later than 30 days after the listing agreement expires (as stated in the listing agreement under "Exclusive Right to Sell") the broker or the broker's agent must tell the seller just what potential buyers he or she has been negotiating with and supplying with information. This is to protect the broker's right to collect his or her commission if the seller sells either directly or indirectly to a buyer procured by the broker.

Salesperson's Checklist Form (see pages 101 through 104). This is a double-check of items in the listing agreement. The real-estate salesperson—or the seller, if he or she is selling without a real estate agent—checks off in the first column each item that is included in the transaction. If not included, just leave the item blank, and use the second column when a transaction is completed (signed) and ready for escrow.

SOLE, IRREVOCABLE AND EXCLUSIVE
RIGHT TO SELL
LISTING AGREEMENT

For Brokers Use Only	
Mgr.'s Initial	Date

Date_____, 19_____

Type of Business: _____

Describe Product or Service: _____

_____

Name of Business: _____ Phone _____

Fictitious Name of Business (DBA): _____

Address: _____

Name of Owner(s): _____ Phone _____

_____
| Address | City | State | Zip |

Owner(s) are ☐ individual/sole proprietorship ☐ husband and wife/sole proprietorship ☐ partnership
☐ limited partnership ☐ joint venture ☐ corporation ☐ corporation selling tangible assets only

☐ other (specify) _____

_____

Contract is ☐ attached ☐ will be furnished by _____, 19_____ and by reference made a part
hereof.

<u>EXCLUSIVE RIGHT:</u>

With respect to the above described business, more fully described hereafter, Owner grants to Broker the
sole, irrevocable and exclusive right to solicit, advertise, offer, sell all or a substantial part of, trade, exchange, merge, option, lease, assign or employ and give possession of, for any reason connected in any
way with anyone with whom Broker has negotiated or to whom it has supplied information about this
business, provided Broker has notified Owner in writing of such action no later than 30 days after this
agreement expires, at the price and terms specified herein, or at such other price and terms as the owner
may accept for a period of _____ months from the date hereof (exclusive listing period). Owner
authorizes Broker to use the information contained herein to procure buyers for this business. Listing term
commencing on _____, 19_____, and expiring at _____, 19_____ midnight and
continues thereafter as a non-exclusive right to dispose of said property for one year, unless revoked in
writing and delivered to Broker. Broker is hereby authorized to accept and hold on Owner's behalf a deposit

77

upon acceptance of purchase offer. Owner further authorizes Broker to cooperate with Sub-Brokers and divide such compensation acceptable to them.

1. <u>PRICE AND TERMS OF PAYMENT THROUGH ESCROW:</u>

   Total purchase price $ _____ .

   Downpayment (including deposit) of $ _____ shall be paid at the opening of Escrow ☐
   $ _____ shall be paid 10 days before close of Escrow or on _____ ,
   19_____, and the balance of the purchase price shall be made as follows:

   A. ☐ Encumbrances(s) which Buyer(s) will assume and agree(s) to pay $_____
      with principal and _____% _____ interest per annum on the unpaid balance included at
      $ _____ or more per month. ☐ until paid, ☐ balloon payment due approximately
      _____, 19_____, in the approximate amount of $_____.
      ☐ Free and clear of debt.

      Assumable ☐ yes   ☐ no.

      Holder_____Address_____Phone_____

      Holder_____Address_____Phone_____

      ☐ Note attached   ☐ Will furnish note by _____, 19_____ and by reference made a
      part hereof.

   B. ☐ Balance to Seller(s) as evidenced by an installment note and secured by the business
      assets as described herein, of $_____ with principal and _____% simple in-
      terest per annum on the unpaid balance, included at $_____ or more per
      month. ☐ until paid. ☐ balloon payment due approximately _____, 19_____, in
      the approximate amount of $_____. Additional security required? ☐ yes ☐
      no. Interest to begin at the close of escrow, first payment due _____ days thereafter. This
      note is secured by furniture, fixtures and equipment and by the business assets described
      herein and as attached and by reference made a part hereof. This note is due and payable in
      full upon the sale or transfer of this business by the Buyer(s).

   C. ☐ Balance to Seller(s) of purchase price in the sum of $_____ to be
      evidenced by a deed of trust to real property commonly known as

      _____

      Address_____City_____State_____Zip _____
      and by reference made a part hereof.

      ☐ Legal assumption attached and by reference made a part hereof.

      ☐ Title insurance attached and by reference made a part hereof.

      ☐ Title insurance waived.

D. Inventory (usable and saleable) value approximately $_____(at current whole-sale cost) included in purchase price ☐ yes ☐ no. If no, how to be purchased?

_____

_____

_____

E. Additional terms (specify): _____

_____

_____

_____

2. ASSETS:

Except as otherwise stated below, price includes all assets of the business, including, but not limited to: business records, furniture, trade fixtures and equipment, work in progress, tools, supplies, leasehold improvements, telephone numbers, customer list(s), all trade name(s), transferable permits, special license(s), sign(s), accounts receivable, good will, and all personal property used in the business (all leasehold rights) including those of all real or personal property listed herein or attached hereto, or as otherwise specified in this agreement; and (specify) _____

_____

_____

Price also includes ABC License No. _____, ☐ on license ☐ on-off license ☐ beer ☐ beer and wine ☐ cocktail. Sales tax no. _____.

3. LIABILITIES:

Price excludes liabilities, including but not limited to: cash, bank accounts, accounts payable, deposits, real estate encumbrance(s) as specified in this agreement, and (specify) _____

_____

_____

_____

4. INSTALLMENT SALE:

☐ yes ☐ no. If yes, must have at least one payment in subsequent years after the year of sale. (Value of covenant not to compete and inventory does not qualify as an installment sale.) Note must carry an interest charge of at least 9% annum simple interest on the unpaid balance. (This is the new 1981 Federal law—check your state laws.)

(Page 3 of 12)

5. ALLOCATION:

For purposes of this agreement, the purchase price shall be allocated as follows:

A.	Accounts receivable	Estimated*	$ _____
B.	Inventory (at current wholesale cost)	Estimated*	$ _____
C.	Work in progress	Estimated*	$ _____
D.	Furniture, fixtures and equipment (market value installed)		$ _____
E.	Leasehold improvements (minus used-up life)		$ _____
F.	Franchises, trademarks, and trade names		$ _____
G.	License(s): (ABC)		$ _____
H.	Goodwill		$ _____
I.	Covenant not to compete		$ _____
J.	Lease valuation		_____
K.	Real Property (improvements, buildings, etc.)		$ _____
L.	Real Property (land)		$ _____
M.	Customer(s) list(s)		$ _____
N.	Customer(s) contract(s)		$ _____
O.	Other assets (specify)_____		$ _____
P.	Other assets (specify)_____		$ _____

Total Purchase Price $ _____

*The net amount of these three items shall be added or subtracted, as the case may be, from the amount due on the purchase price at the time of escrow closing. The actual value of these three items shall be determined by Buyer(s) and Seller(s) at the time of closing escrow and adjustments, if any, shall be made at the close of escrow. Any variation in between estimated and actual values of either of these three items shall give Buyer(s) the option of paying ☐ cash ☐ increase Seller(s) note ☐ new note to the Seller(s) ☐ as follows: _____.

6. GENERAL INFORMATION:

A. Profit and Loss and Balance Sheets:
☐ Attached ☐ Will be furnished by _____, 19_____ and by reference made part hereof.

Estimate "True Gross Receipts" (not including sales tax) per year $_____.

Estimate "True Net Profit" (definition of "True Net Profit" = Net Income before Debt Service, depreciation, income tax, owner's salary, manager's salary, personal expenses, etc.) per year $_____.

(Page 4 of 12)

Payroll $_____ per month, owner on payroll ☐ no ☐ yes, at $_____ per month.
Additional employees: full time _____ part time _____.
Utilities $_____ per month.

B. Lease:

Approx. _____ years <u>left</u> at $_____ per month. Option to renew ☐ yes ☐ no. If
yes, for _____ years at $_____ per month. Security deposit $_____. Rent
due in advance $_____. Lease ☐ attached ☐ will be furnished by _____,
19_____ and by reference made a part hereof.

Established _____ year(s). Present Owner _____ year(s). Hours open _____.
Days closed _____. Est. square feet _____. Type of seating ☐ Table and chairs
☐ Booths ☐ Other _____.
Seating capacity: at bar _____ Lounge _____ Restaurant _____.
Parking capacity _____.
Assumable ☐ yes ☐ no. Miscellaneous lease information_____

_____

_____

_____

Landlord _____ Address_____ Phone _____

Attorney _____ Address_____ Phone _____

Accountant_____ Address_____ Phone _____

Zoning Law_____ Restrictions _____

C. Contracts:
☐ medical plan ☐ dental plan ☐ 2-for-one dinner plan ☐ brochures ☐ menu
☐ union ☐ employee ☐ copyrights ☐ patents ☐ trademarks ☐ royalty
☐ pension plan ☐ profit sharing plan ☐ list of customers ☐ list of suppliers
☐ price list ☐ supply ☐ services ☐ formulas ☐ recipes ☐ advertisements
☐ others

specify_____

_____

Contracts ☐ attached ☐ will be furnished by _____, 19_____ and by reference
made a part hereof. Assumable ☐ yes ☐ no.
Management will stay ☐ yes ☐ no. Remarks _____

_____

D. Business Franchise:
☐ yes ☐ no. Franchise agreements ☐ attached ☐ will be furnished by _____,

19_____ and by reference made part hereof. Franchise fee $_____.
Franchise Transfer fee $_____.

Franchise name_____ Address_____

City_____State_____ Phone _____
Assumable ☐ yes ☐ no.

   E. Vending Machine Games, Equipment Leases, Etc.:

(specify equipment)_____

_____

_____

_____

Estimate total amount remaining to be paid on all equipment $_____, with principal
and _____% _____ interest included at $_____ total per month.
☐ until paid ☐ balloon payment due _____, 19_____ of approximately
$_____.
Written contracts ☐ yes ☐ no. If yes, date expires _____, 19_____.

Vendor's name_____ Address_____ Phone _____

Vendor's name_____ Address_____ Phone _____

Contracts ☐ attached ☐ will furnish by _____, 19_____ and by reference made
a part hereof. Assumable ☐ yes ☐ no.

   F. Furniture, Fixtures and Equipment:
     ☐ included in sale ☐ not included in sale ☐ on lease or owned by others. List(s) ☐ at-
     tached ☐ will be furnished by _____, 19_____ and reference made part hereof.

   G. Miscellaneous Information:

_____

_____

_____

7. <u>FEE</u>:

   A. Seller hereby agrees to pay a commission (REAL ESTATE COMMISSIONS ARE
     NEGOTIABLE AND NOT FIXED BY LAW) to said Broker _____
     (_____%) percent of the actual total gross purchase or exchange price, including con-
     sideration other than money received; or a fee of $_____, whichever is greater.

   B. Seller hereby agrees to pay said fee to agent upon disposition of the property during the ex-
     clusive listing period, or any extensions thereof, whether brought about by Broker, or its

   (Page 6 of 12)

agent, Seller or any third party. Such fee shall also be payable after the expiration date of the exclusive listing period if Broker, or its agent is directly or indirectly responsible for the disposition of the property, provided Broker has notified owner in writing of such action no later than 30 days after this agreement expires.

C. Seller agrees to pay Broker said fee within 12 months after the exclusive listing has expired on any disposition of the property to any person, provided Broker has notified Owner in writing of such action, no later than 30 days after this agreement expires with whom negotiations commenced during the exclusive listing period.

D. Seller further agrees that the fee described above shall be due and payable to Broker immediately if the Seller, or any person acting on behalf of the Seller (other than the Broker) shall enter into a contract of sale, or accept a deposit, or open an escrow, or record a notice of intention to sell, or obtain a lease, as specified within this agreement, during the exclusive listing period and the cancellation or rescission of any of the foregoing acts shall not release Seller from his obligation to pay said fee.

8. <u>SELLER'S REASON FOR SELLING</u>:

_____

_____

_____

9. <u>SELLER(S) HEREBY WARRANT(S), REPRESENT(S), AND SHALL PROVIDE PROOF OF THE FOLLOWING</u>:

A. That he is the legal owner of the above described business and property and has full authority to execute this agreement, and warrants that he or she has written authority to do so for all Seller(s);

B. That title to the assets of such business and property is free and clear from any liens and encumbrances, except as specified herein or as attached hereto;

C. Seller(s) warrant(s) that the business premises, improvements, real property, equipment and machinery will pass all inspections necessary to conduct such business at the time of physical possession at the close of escrow;

D. Seller(s) warrant(s) that all property that is necessary in the operation of its business shall be delivered at close of escrow in good working condition and repair, ordinary wear and tear excepted;

E. Seller is not aware of any facts indicating that any customer(s) intend to cease doing business with the Seller or to materially alter the amount of the business currently being done with Seller;

(Page 7 of 12)

F. Seller has not received notice of any claim(s), litigation, investigation(s) or federal, state or local statute, law or ordinance or regulation, including building, redevelopment, zoning or other law, ordinance or regulation affecting its property or the operation of its business or any of the assets being sold, whether real or personal property;

G. There ☐ is ☐ is not appended to and made a part of this agreement an addendum which discloses information which may be pertinent to the potential use of this business or property under terms of the Special Studies Zone Act;

H. There ☐ is ☐ is not appended to and made a part of this agreement an addendum which discloses information which may be pertinent to potential use of this property under terms of the National Flood Control Act.

I. Seller warrants that he has ☐ no sales tax number ☐ no employees;

J. Seller will provide a good and valid bill of sale covering this business, free and clear of any liens and encumbrances whatsoever except those specified herein at opening of escrow;

K. Seller will provide or will transfer all the necessary licenses and permits necessary to legally conduct and operate the business described herein at opening of escrow;

L. Seller will supply clearance receipts from ☐ State Board of Equalization ☐ from Department of Benefit Payments before close of escrow;

M. Seller shall deliver at the opening of escrow the "pink slip(s)" to Motor Vehicle(s) described as follows _____

_____
Escrow holder is hereby instructed to deliver "pink slip(s)" to Buyer(s) at close of escrow. Buyer(s) agree to pay sales tax on said motor vehicles as required by the Department of Motor Vehicles before close of escrow;

N. Seller(s) will conduct the business generally in the same manner as it is now conducted and as was represented to the Buyer until close of escrow;

O. Seller(s) represent(s) and warrant(s) that said property is marketable and that all information set forth in the escrow instructions and this agreement and any attachments hereto are true and correct as of the close of escrow and are effective as of that date. Seller(s) agree(s) that if said property is made unmarketable by any voluntary act and all such representations and warranties are not true and correct and if this sale is cancelled for that reason, Seller(s) agree(s) to pay the full commission on the sales price as specified herein, as if the sale had been consummated;

P. Seller(s) shall receive Buyer(s) note(s) as ☐ an individual ☐ community property ☐ joint tenant(s) ☐ tenant(s) in common;

(Page 8 of 12)

Q. Seller(s) to train Buyer(s) or their employee(s)? ☐ yes ☐ no.
   If yes, _____ hours per day, _____ days per week for _____weeks.
   Other (specify)_____at no charge
   Buyer(s) starting _____, 19_____ and continuing through _____, 19_____;

R. Seller(s) hereby authorize(s) the Buyer(s), Buyer's Broker, agent, attorney(s) and escrow holder to contact the Seller(s) accountant, landlord, encumbrance holders, franchisors, vendors, attorneys, or anyone else connected with the above described business and all such parties are hereby authorized to give the Buyer(s), Buyer's Broker, agent, attorneys and escrow holder any information requested about the business and property, whether real or personal being sold hereunder.

S. Seller(s) hereby agree(s) that if it appears to the Broker and escrow holder that there will not be enough funds to pay in full brokers commission listed in this agreement, such obligations shall be paid by the Buyer(s) instead of the Seller(s) at close of escrow and the purchasing price and down payment to be paid by the Buyer(s) shall thereby be reduced accordingly.

T. Seller(s) hereby agree(s) that in addition to the purchase price, there shall be prorated through escrow as of the close of escrow personal property taxes, rents, interest charges, insurance and similar expenses.

U. Seller(s) hereby agree to pay all escrow fees, charges and costs as follows: ☐ one half
   ☐ Buyer(s) pay all ☐ Other_____

   For its ordinary services hereunder and upon acceptance of this escrow, the escrow agent shall be entitled to a fee of $_____, payable concurrently with its acceptance hereof. Said fee is in addition to the total consideration being paid for the business and property. Additional escrow fee(s) shall be as follows: $_____ for each creditor(s) claim in excess of three (3) paid through escrow, payable by Seller(s). $_____ for each disputed creditor(s) claim, payable by Seller(s).

V. List of work in progress, inventory, furniture, fixtures and equipment ☐ being conveyed ☐ not being conveyed ☐ on lease or owned by others shall be approved in writing by both parties at close of escrow.

W. Seller(s) agree at opening of escrow to make application for the transfer of the ABC license at the office of Department of Alcoholic Beverage Control, _____, _____. Buyer(s) shall pay such transfer fees and warrants that he is fully cognizant of the provisions of the State of _____ Alcoholic Beverage Control Act, with particular reference to his qualifications and eligibility and knows of no reason a license should be denied him. This agreement is conditioned upon such transfer.

X. Seller(s) agree that _____
   Address _____ Phone _____ is the Broker.

(Page 9 of 12)

Y. Seller(s) agree that _____, address _____
phone _____ is the Escrow Holder.

Z. Seller(s) hereby agree that if he delays the sale unreasonably during negotiations, and/or delays the delivery of any document beyond the date promised, the period of delay shall be automatically added to the purchase and sale (deposit/receipt) agreement. The Seller(s) also agree to the above and shall be automatically added to the listing term.

AA. Seller(s) hereby agree to use diligence to transfer the assets of the business.

BB. Seller(s) demand that Buyer(s) shall furnish a financial statement ⊔ audited ⊔ unaudited with his offer.

CC. Seller(s) demand that Buyer(s) shall maintain insurance to cover obligations under this agreement setting forth the ⊔ Seller(s) ⊔ Buyer(s) or their assigns as first loss payee as follows: ⊔ fire ⊔ theft ⊔ comprehensive liability.

DD. Seller(s) demand that Buyer(s) agree(s) in addition to the purchase price to pay at opening of escrow sales tax on the furniture, fixtures and equipment.

10. <u>CORPORATION</u>:

If the property to be sold hereunder is owned by a corporation, the person(s) signing this listing agreement as Owner(s) represent that he or they are duly authorized and empowered by the corporation's directors to sell and that the business and property are owned by the corporation. A copy of corporate minutes approving the sales agreement is ⊔ attached ⊔ will be furnished by _____, 19_____ and by reference made a part hereof.

11. <u>COVENANT NOT TO COMPETE</u>:

Seller(s) covenants to the Buyer(s), his successors, assigns and representatives that he will not engage, directly or indirectly, in any business the same as, similar to, or in competition with the business hereby sold within a radius of _____ miles from the principal place of business being sold for a period of _____ years from date of Buyer(s) possession, either as principal, agent, manager, employee, owner, partner, stockholder, director or officer of a corporation, trustee, consultant, or otherwise in any capacity whatsoever.

12. <u>DEFAULT</u>:

A. If Seller(s) through his own fault, fails or refuses to complete this transaction as required, the Seller(s) shall thereupon pay the Broker the Broker's full commission, as specified in the listing or commission agreement.

B. If Buyer(s) fails or refuses to complete this transaction as required, the Deposit received, or part thereof up to the full amount of the commission, shall be paid to the Broker. The balance, if any, of the deposit shall be paid to Seller(s) as liquidated damages.

(Page 10 of 12)

C. ☐ Default by Buyer(s), where Seller(s) hold Buyer(s) outstanding note on said business or property, including leasehold rights, whether real or personal, shall also occur whenever the gross sales or inventory of said business fall below 75% in any three consecutive months in comparison with the three consecutive same months in the previous year, allowing the net amount to be added or subtracted from the actual cost of living index, as determined by the federal government for the nation as a whole. Buyer(s) also agree(s) to furnish the Seller(s) a monthly Profit and Loss Statement within 10 days after the end of each month during the period of said note. Upon such default, Seller(s) shall have the option to repossess by due process in accordance with the Uniform Commercial Code the said business and property, including leasehold rights, whether real or personal, excluding the Alcoholic Beverage Control license, by giving 10 days notice in writing to Buyer(s). Buyer(s) shall have the option to pay said note in full by giving 10 days notice in writing to seller(s), excluding, if an installment sale.

13. ARBITRATION:

All parties agree to any controversy or claim arising out of or relating to this contract, or the breach thereof, shall be settled by arbitration in accordance with the rules of the American Arbitration Association, and judgement upon the award rendered by Arbitrator(s) may be entered in any court having jurisdiction thereof.

14. HOLD HARMLESS AGREEMENT:

Seller(s) agree that Broker, or its agent, in bringing Buyer(s) and Seller(s) together has fulfilled its primary brokerage function and agree to hold Broker, its agent, attorneys and Escrow Holder harmless from any liability arising out of the sale of said business.

15. CONDITIONS AND TERMS:

It is expressly understood that this listing agreement contain all instructions of Seller(s) and conditions upon which the undersigned agree(s) to the transfer ownership of said business and property.

This is a Legally Binding document. Read it Carefully. If you don't understand it, consult with your attorney and/or accountant. Broker and Escrow Holder are not authorized to give legal or tax advice.

Each of the undersigned has read the foregoing instructions, and by his signature hereto acknowledges that he understands and agrees with them.

Receipt of this listing agreement is hereby acknowledged.

16. In consideration of the execution of this contract, the undersigned Broker agrees to use diligence in procuring a purchaser.

X_____   Date_____, 19_____
Seller

Print name and title

Address _____

X_____
Seller

Print name and title

Federal I.D. No.

Address _____

X_____
Broker/Agent

Social Security No.

Phone _____

Date_____, 19_____

Social Security No.

State Employer No.

Phone _____

Date_____, 19_____

Copyrighted, American Business Consultants, Inc. 1979 and 1980   *(Page 12 of 12)*

For these forms address American Business Consultants, Inc., 1540 Nuthatch Lane, Sunnyvale, CA 94087. Tel (408) 732-8931.

CHANGE IN LISTING

Name of Business_____ Address _____ Phone _____

The undersigned Broker and Seller(s) agree to change the Sole and Exclusive Authorization to Sell (Listing) Agreement dated _____ 19_____ as follows:

Purchase Price to $_____.

Down Payment to $_____.

Balance to Seller to $_____, at $_____ per month including _____% simple interest on the unpaid balance.

Other changes (specify) _____

_____

_____

_____

_____

_____

All other terms and conditions remain the same. The person signing this change in listing, who may or may not be the sole owner of the above described business, personally warrants that he or she has written authority to do so for all owners.

Receipt of a copy of this Change in Listing is hereby acknowledged.

Executed at _____, _____ on Date _____, 19_____.

X _____   Dated _____, 19_____.
   Owner

_____
Print name and title

X _____   Dated _____, 19_____.
   Owner

_____
Print name and title

X _____   Dated _____, 19_____.
   Broker/Agent

89

COUNTER OFFER

Name _____ Address _____ Phone_____

    The undersigned accepts all the terms and conditions of the   ☐ Listing Agreement   ☐ Purchase (Deposit/Receipt) Agreement executed by _____dated _____ 19_____, except the following:

_____

_____

_____

_____

_____

_____

_____

    This counter offer shall expire unless accepted by _____ 19 _____. Receipt of a copy of this Counter Offer is hereby acknowledged.

X _____   Dated_____, 19_____.

_____
Print name and title

X _____   Dated_____, 19_____.

_____
Print name and title

I have read and accept the above Counter Offer and hereby acknowledge receipt of a copy of this Counter Offer and acceptance thereof.

X _____   Dated_____, 19_____.

_____
Print name and title

X _____   Dated_____, 19_____.

_____
Print name and title

X _____   Dated_____, 19_____.
   Broker/Agent

RELEASE

FROM: _____   Escrow Number_____

_____

_____

TO: _____   Date_____, 19_____

_____

_____

To whom it may concern:

This will serve as my instruction to you to release and furnish copies of the following to the above named broker/agent. If there are any questions regarding this instruction, please do not hesitate to contact me at

_____.

Telephone

☐ Profit and Loss Statement and Balance Sheets, etc. from_____ to_____.

☐ State Sales Tax Returns from _____ to _____. ☐ Proof of payment.

☐ Schedule C from Federal/State Income Tax records for the taxable years _____ to _____.
☐ Proof of payment.

☐ Copy of lease (including options, addendums, etc.)

☐ Copy of Contracts (specify) _____

☐ Copy of note(s) (specify) _____

☐ Copy of _____ (specify) _____

☐ Other (specify _____

☐ Other (specify) _____

Thank you for your courtesy and cooperation in this matter.

_____
Owner

_____
Print name and title

91

WORK IN PROGRESS FORM

Escrow Number_____

Name of Business _____Address _____As of Date _____ 19_____

LIST OF "PROCESS MATERIALS," "WORK IN PROGRESS," AND "FINISHED GOODS" INVENTORY . . . . .
(Non-Taxable Inventory with Resale License)

Year	Quantity	Name and Manufacturer	Percent Complete	Description	Cost

Escrow Number_____

Name of Business _____Address _____As of Date _____ 19_____

INVENTORY OF FURNITURE, FIXTURES AND EQUIPMENT—INCLUDED IN SALE

Year	Quantity	Name and Manufacturer	Description	Cost

(Page 1 of 2)

INVENTORY OF FURNITURE, FIXTURES, AND EQUIPMENT—NOT INCLUDED IN SALE

Year	Quantity	Name and Manufacturer	Description	Cost

INVENTORY OF FURNITURE, FIXTURES AND EQUIPMENT—ON LEASE OR OWNED BY OTHERS

Year	Quantity	Name and Manufacturer	Description	Lease or Owner	Cost

To be deposited with Escrow Holder _____.

Buyer and Seller hereby agree that the above list is complete and approved.

X_____Date_____19_____.   X_____Date_____19_____.
  Seller   Buyer

X_____Date_____19_____.   X_____Date_____19_____.
  Seller   Buyer

(Page 2 of 2)

94

LIST OF ACCOUNTS PAYABLE

Escrow Number_____

Name of Business_____ As of Date_____ 19_____

Address _____

Payable To Customer(s)	Amount Less 30 days	Past Due 30 to 90 days	Past Due over 90 days	Cost New	Cost current
Total					
Percent				100%	

To be deposited with Escrow Holder _____

Buyers and Sellers hereby agree that the list is complete and approved.

X _____ Dated_____19_____   X _____ Dated_____19_____
  Seller   Buyer

X _____ Dated_____19_____   X _____ Dated_____19_____
  Seller   Buyer

LIST OF ACCOUNTS RECEIVABLE

Escrow Number_____

Name of Business _____Address _____As of Date _____ 19_____

Address _____

Customer(s)	Amount Less 30 days	Amount 30 to 90 days	Amount over 90 days	Cost new	Cost current
Total					
Percent				100%	

To be deposited with Escrow Holder _____.

Buyers and Sellers hereby agree that the list is complete and approved.

X _____ Dated_____19_____.   X _____ Dated_____19_____.
  Seller   Buyer

X _____ Dated_____19_____.   X _____ Dated_____19_____.
  Seller   Buyer

LIST OF CUSTOMERS

Escrow Number_____

Name of Business _____As of Date _____ 19_____

Address _____

Name	Address	Approximate Age	Useful Life

To be deposited with Escrow Holder _____

Buyers and Sellers hereby agree that the list is complete and approved.

X _____ Dated_____19_____.   X _____ Dated_____19_____.
  Seller   Buyer

X _____ Dated_____19_____.   X _____ Dated_____19_____.
  Seller   Buyer

SPECIAL STUDIES ZONE AND FLOOD HAZARD DISCLOSURE

CALIFORNIA ASSOCIATION OF REALTORS® STANDARD FORM

This Addendum is attached as Page _____ of _____ Pages to the Real Estate Purchase Contract and Receipt for Deposit
dated _____ 19_____ in which _____

_____

is referred to as Buyer and _____

_____ is referred to as Seller.

SPECIAL STUDIES ZONE DISCLOSURE

The property which is the subject of the contract is situated in a Special Study Zone as designated under Sections 2621-2625, inclusive, of the California Public Resources Code; and, as such, the construction or development on this property of any structure for human occupancy may be subject to the findings of a geologic report prepared by a geologist registered in the State of California, unless such report is waived by the city or county under the terms of that act. No representations on the subject are made by Seller or Agent, and the Buyer should make his/her own inquiry or investigation.

Note: California Public Resources Code #2621.5 excludes structures in existence prior to May 4, 1975;

California Public Resources Code #2621.6 excludes wood frame dwellings not exceeding two (2) stories in height and mobilhomes over eight (8) feet in width;

California Public Resources Code #2621.7 excludes conversion of existing apartment houses into condominiums;

California Public Resources Code #2621.8 excludes alterations and additions under 50% of value of structure from the Special Studies Zone Act.

Buyer is allowed _____ days from date of Seller's acceptance to make further inquiries at appropriate governmental agencies concerning the use of the subject property under the terms of the Special Study Zone Act and local building, zoning, fire, health and safety codes. When such inquiries disclose conditions or information unsatisfactory to the Buyer, Buyer may cancel this agreement. If notice in writing has not been delivered within such time, this condition shall be deemed waived.

Receipt of a copy is hereby acknowledged.

DATED: _____ , 19_____   BUYER: _____

Receipt of a copy is hereby acknowledged   _____

DATED: _____ , 19_____   SELLER: _____

_____

FLOOD HAZARD ZONE DISCLOSURE

The property which is the subject of the contract is situated in a "Flood Zone" as set forth on H.U.D. "Special Flood Zone Area Map". The law requires that as a condition of obtaining financing on most properties located in a "Flood Zone", Banks, Savings and Loan Associations, and some insurance lenders will require that H.U.D. flood insurance be carried where the property or its attachments are security for the loan.

This requirement is mandated by the H.U.D. National Insurance Program, which requirement became effective March 1, 1976. The purpose of the program is to provide flood insurance to property at a reasonable cost.

The extent of coverage available in your area and the cost of this coverage may vary, and for further information you should consult your lender or insurance carrier. No representation or recommendation is made by the Seller and the Brokers in this transaction or their agents or employees, as to the legal effect, interpretation, or economic consequences of the National Flood Insurance Program and related legislation.

Receipt of a copy is hereby acknowledged.

DATED: _____ , 19_____   BUYER: _____

Receipt of a copy is hereby acknowledged   _____

DATED: _____ , 19_____   SELLER: _____

_____

NO REPRESENTATION IS MADE AS TO THE LEGAL VALIDITY OF ANY PROVISION OR THE ADEQUACY OF ANY PROVISION IN ANY SPECIFIC TRANSACTION. A REAL ESTATE BROKER IS THE PERSON QUALIFIED TO ADVISE ON REAL ESTATE. IF YOU DESIRE LEGAL ADVICE CONSULT YOUR ATTORNEY.

For these forms, address—California Association of Realtors ͯ
505 Shatto Place, Los Angeles, California 90020   SSD-FHD-11
Copyright © 1977 California Association of Realtors ͯ (Revised 1978)

Reprinted by permission, California Association of Realtors—endorsement not implied.

CORPORATE RESOLUTION

At a regular meeting of the Board of Directors of _____,
a corporation, held on _____, 19_____, pursuant to due call and notice, with a quorum present, the
following resolution was duly moved, seconded, and unanimously passed:

RESOLVED, that _____,
who is _____for this corporation, is hereby authorized
to do the following on behalf of the corporation:

    1. To execute □ sole, irrevocable and exclusive right to sell listing agreement, □ Exclusive agency listing
agreement, □ Open listing agreement, □ Purchase (deposit/receipt) agreement, □ Escrow instructions. □
Copy attached □ Will furnish by _____, 19_____ and by reference made part hereof, and the same are
hereby ratified.

    2. Without further authorization from this Board, to execute any other agreements, documents, writings, list,
sell, finance, expedite, aid the sale of, change the price, terms, conditions, orally or in writing, in whatever way or
particulars seems proper in said party's sole discretion all personal property used in the business (all leasehold
rights), including those of all real or personal property.

                                                                       Date   , 19
_____
Chairman of Board of Directors

_____
Print Name

I, the undersigned, secretary of the above-named corporation, hereby certify that the above is true and correct copy
of the Minutes of the due and proper meeting of the Board of Directors of the above-named corporation on the date
stated therein.

                                                                        Date   , 19
_____
                                 Secretary

CORPORATE
SEAL

_____
                              Print Name

99

NOTICE OF DISCLOSURE

TO:

Fictitious Business Name (D.B.A.) _____

Name of Business _____

Address _____City_____State_____Zip_____

Phone_____

As of this date _____, 19_____, your business and/or property was shown to or discussed with the following parties:

Name	Address	Date Exposed

This notice is for our mutual protection. Should you hear from these parties, please notify the undersigned.

Very truly yours,

_____ Phone_____
Broker (Agent)

_____
Address

100

SALESPERSON CHECK LIST

(Once a listing is signed)

Escrow Number_____

Business Name_____Address_____Phone_____

In	Complete	
_____	_____	Listing agreement with manager's initials.
_____	_____	Form "True Net Profit".
_____	_____	Form "True Selling Price".
_____	_____	List of ☐ Inventory ☐ work in progress ☐ raw material.
_____	_____	Release form signed.
_____	_____	List of ☐ furniture, fixtures and equipment ☐ Inventory-non-taxable included in sale.
_____	_____	List of ☐ inventory ☐ furniture, fixtures and equipment not included in sale ☐ leased or owned by others.
_____	_____	List of Leasehold Improvements.
_____	_____	Copy of existing ☐ lease ☐ assignment of lease ☐ option ☐ extension ☐ new lease.
_____	_____	Copy of equipment lease.
_____	_____	Copy of sign lease.
_____	_____	Copy of ABC license.
_____	_____	Copy of ☐ advertising agreements ☐ telephone book ☐ newspaper.
_____	_____	Copy of business ☐ licenses ☐ permits ☐ special licenses.
_____	_____	Copy of vending machine contracts.
_____	_____	Copy of notes _____
_____	_____	Copy of notes _____
_____		Copy of Contracts: ☐ medical plan ☐ dental plan ☐ 2-for-1 dinner plan ☐ brochures ☐ menu ☐ union ☐ employee ☐ copyrights ☐ patents ☐ trademarks ☐ royalty ☐ pension plan ☐ profit sharing plan ☐ list of customers ☐ list of suppliers ☐ price list ☐ supply ☐ services

101

In	Complete	
		☐ formulas ☐ recipes ☐ advertisements ☐ others (specify) __
		_____
_____	_____	Copy of franchise agreement.
_____	_____	Copy of ☐ partnership ☐ copy of by-laws.
_____	_____	Copy of ☐ corporate minutes ☐ articles of incorporation ☐ approval of listing ☐ approval of sale ☐ approval of financing.
_____	_____	Copy of insurance ☐ fire ☐ theft ☐ comprehensive liability ☐ workman's compensation ☐ others _____
_____	_____	Copy of ☐ tax records ☐ "C" schedule for 19___ to 19___. ☐ Proof of payment.
_____	_____	Copy of Profit and Loss Statement for 19___ to 19___.
_____	_____	Copy of balance sheet for 19___ to 19___.
_____	_____	Copy of sales tax return for 19___ to 19___. ☐ Proof of payment.
_____	_____	Copy of payroll tax returns for 19___ to 19___. ☐ Proof of payment.
_____	_____	Copy of personal and real estate tax bills for 19___ to 19___. ☐ Proof of payment.
_____	_____	Copy of Motor Vehicles pink slip(s) _____.
_____	_____	Copy of Special Studies Zone Act Disclosure.
_____	_____	Copy of National Flood Control Act Disclosure.
_____	_____	Copy of bank account statements.
_____	_____	Copy of unfilled orders (past and present).
_____	_____	Copy of daily production reports.
_____	_____	Accounts Receivable—aging.
_____	_____	Accounts Payable—aging.
_____	_____	Copy of employees, rates, turnover rate, absentee rate, fringe benefits, etc.
_____	_____	Zoning law (specify) _____
_____	_____	Real Estate included ☐ plat map ☐ title policy ☐ grant deed ☐ local maps ☐ state maps ☐ photographs ☐ topography

In | **Complete**

map ☐ road map ☐ purchase agreement ☐ counter offer ☐ other_____

Chamber of Commerce package on area where the business is located.

Photographs of ☐ equipment ☐ inventory ☐ business.

Landlord reasonable consent clause ☐ in lease ☐ in letter.

Lease equipment reasonable consent clause ☐ in contract ☐ in letter.

Franchisor reasonable consent clause ☐ in contract ☐ in letter.

Note holder(s) reasonable consent ☐ in contract ☐ in letter.

Appraisal of ☐ furniture, fixtures and equipment ☐ inventory.

Change in listing form.

Counter offer(s).

Credit reports.

Commission ☐ Broker ☐ Co-broker ☐ Finder's fees $ _____.

Salesperson's work sheet.

Newspaper ads (one long and one short).

Letter(s) of recommendation _____.

Other: (specify) _____.

Other: (specify) _____.

Other: (specify) _____.

Automatic extension letter(s).

Buyers Contract ("business wanted" or "buyers authorization").

Buyers "Location of business" agreement.

Buyers financial statement.

Buyers resume.

Buyers "True Net Profit" form.

Buyers Letter of Intent.

In   **Comp**

_____|_____   Salesperson comments_____

_____

_____

_____

Completed by _____   Manager OK _____

The information is provided solely as a guide and estimate of some of the more common requirements involved in transferring a business. The information above has not been verified by the Broker, its agents, attorneys, CPA or Escrow Holder, and they are not responsible for their accuracy or completeness.

Copyrighted, American Business Consultants, Inc. 1979

Chapter **10** Buyer's Agreements

BUYER'S AUTHORIZATION FORM

This form (see pages 111 through 117) is used when a buyer retains a broker as his or her exclusive agent for the purpose of locating a business property as outlined below. It also helps to qualify the buyer. (This is equivalent to a listing agreement for a seller.)

Let us go through the Buyer's Authorization form item by item.

1. *Agreement.* The buyer agrees to retain said broker as his or her sole and exclusive agent for the purpose of locating a business. This agreement generally runs for six months and after this time it continues to run for one year as a nonexclusive right, unless the buyer revokes it in writing.
2. *Business Wanted.* The kind of business required should be accurately specified, i.e., bar, fast food, electronic manufacturing plant, etc.
3. *Terms and Conditions.* Many buyers like to purchase food businesses. If a buyer wants a food and beverage concern specify percentage of food and percentage of beverage he or she wants to operate. Due to certain religions or beliefs some buyers may not want to sell alcoholic beverages. Other buyers may want to sell beer, wine, and/or cocktails. Specify the areas in which the buyer is interested. There are buyers who are not interested in buying a franchised business. With these business details settled, the buyer should be well qualified. Ask the buyer the following questions, phrased in your own way: What gross sales or net profit are you looking for? What downpayment can

you pay? How much can you pay per month? What is the maximum annual interest rate that you are willing to pay? Do you need to raise more capital? If so, how much? How much rent and what length of lease do you require? Do you want a free-standing building and real property? Do you know what size premises and lot you want? How many parking spaces? If seating is required, what capacity is required? Will your family be working in the business? How many dependents do you have to support? Will you need any instructions as to how to run the business? If so, for how long? How do you want to take title? Will you pay half the escrow fee?

4. *Financial Statement.* The seller will want a financial statement from the buyer. How soon can that be supplied?

5. *Financial Information.* This is similar to No. 4 and is self-explanatory.

6. *Employment History.* The landlord will want this information.

7. *Experience and present earnings.* What kind of experience does the buyer have? How long has the buyer been employed at his or her present and past jobs? At what salary? The buyer must be qualified very thoroughly. For example, do not expect the buyer to purchase a $100,000 business if he or she can only raise $5,000. Conversely, do not show a $5,000 business if the prospect has $100,000 to invest.

8. *Places seen.* This is a good way to find out if the buyer is sincere. Ask the buyer what businesses he or she has already seen and thinks would be a reasonable offer for them. For example, let us say the buyer saw "Charlie's Restaurant" and the salesperson knows that this property is worth $100,000. The prospect says he or she would not pay over $35,000 for it. This buyer may be just a "looker" with no money or intentions to purchase anything, and may be wasting the salesperson's time. On the other hand, the salesperson may pick up a "lead" to another business for sale that he or she was not aware of.

9. *Fee.*

   A, B). Same definition as in listing agreement (see page 71, item 7A). The buyer agrees that if he or she purchases a business of which the broker was the procuring agent, buyer will pay the broker's commission and further agrees to furnish a statement, under penalty of perjury, as to how and when the buyer and seller were brought together. It is not uncommon for a buyer and a seller to get together before the expiration date of a listing agreement and agree to eliminate the broker's commission and lower the selling price of the business. Actual paperwork of their transaction is started after the listing agreement expires.

C). The broker agrees that he or she is representing the buyer and will not accept two commissions—one from the buyer and another from the seller—unless he or she makes a full disclosure of this commission arrangement to all parties.

D). Buyer agrees when to pay the commission. This is usually at the close of escrow.

10. A). The buyer agrees to furnish a financial statement and the date it will be forthcoming.

B). One party agrees who will carry the insurance to cover the obligations. Generally, a seller will cover it until close of escrow, and a buyer thereafter, or at least until a seller's note is paid off.

C). A buyer will pay sales tax on furniture, fixtures, and equipment.

D). A buyer must agree on how to take title.

E). A buyer has to warrant that he or she has full authority to execute purchase and sales agreement of a business if there are other buyers involved (e.g., spouse, partner, etc.).

F). The buyer usually agrees to pay half of the escrow fee.

G). The buyer agrees that a list of work in progress, inventory, equipment, etc. must be in writing and approved by both parties at the close of escrow.

H). The buyer agrees to make application for transfer of an Alcoholic Beverage Control license at the opening of escrow. The buyer agrees to pay such transfer fees and states that he or she has no reason to believe himself or herself unqualified to hold such a license.

I). The buyer agrees who is to be the broker and the escrow holder.

J). A Buyer's Delay is similar to listing agreement, but from the buyer's point of view (see page 73, item AA).

K). A Buyer's Agreement is one in which the buyer acknowledges that this agreement is the entire agreement and there are no oral agreements. He or she also agrees that the escrow instructions supersede all prior agreements.

L). The buyer will not delay the transfer of the assets. Similar to the seller's agreement (see page 73, item Z).

M). Insufficient funds is the same as in the listing agreement, except from the buyer's point of view (see page 72, item S).

N). The buyer agrees that in addition to the purchase price there shall be prorated through escrow certain items such as personal property taxes, insurance, and similar charges (see page 72, item T). O). True and correct information is the same as in the listing agreement, except from the buyer's point of view (see page 72, item O).

11. *Corporation.* Same as listing agreement (see page 73, item 10).

12. *Covenant not to compete.* Same as listing agreement, except from the buyer's point of view (see page 73, item 11).

13. *Default.* Same as listing agreement, except from a buyer's point of view (see page 73, item 12).

14. *Arbitration.* Same as listing agreement, except from a buyer's point of view (see page 74, item 13).

15. *Hold harmless.* Same as listing agreement, except from a buyer's point of view (see page 74, item 14).

16. *Conditions and terms.* Same as listing agreement, except from a buyer's point of view (see page 74, item 15).

17. *Promise not to disclose.* It is common for a buyer to contact a broker just to get names and addresses of businesses for sale, planning to purchase directly from a seller at a reduced price. This paragraph makes a buyer responsible and accountable to a seller for disclosing information to third parties, especially competitors seeking information about the seller's business. The agreement obligates a buyer to pay the commission if he or she discloses information or passes on records about the business to a third party, member of the third party's family, or a friend who later purchases the business without using the broker.

18. The broker agrees to do his or her best to locate a suitable business for the buyer, and may sometimes supply information without a formal sales authorization (listing agreement). However, a buyer purchasing such a business will be liable for the broker's commission. This is a legal document (see page 117). The signatures are the same as in the listing, except that they are on the "buyer's page" (see pages 87 and 88).

BUSINESS WANTED FORM

This form is similar to the information about and qualification of a buyer required in the "Buyer's Authorization Form" (see pages 118 through 120), except that no fee is required. In most real-estate offices that handle business opportunities all buyers' identities are kept secret. This is done by circulating the "Business Wanted" form without divulging the buyer's identity. The buyer's identity is written below a perforated line that is torn off before the form is circulated. The form is numbered so that fellow salespersons can ask for assistance by using the given number when they wish to bring together a seller and buyer.

PERSONAL AND CONFIDENTIAL AGREEMENT FORM

This agreement (see pages 121 through 123) is commonly known as a "Send Out Slip." After the potential buyer has been qualified, he or she is then given personal and confidential information about a certain business or businesses.

The buyer agrees that on making a purchase through the specified broker's office, he or she does not become liable for any commission and acts as a principal, not as a broker. In consideration for furnishing the buyer with a list of businesses for sale or lease, the buyer agrees that on buying, leasing, or coming into possession of any business at the locations provided by the broker, he or she will deal with the broker's office only, so that the broker can collect his or her commission from the seller. If, however, the buyer passes on to another party any information provided by the broker within one year of the termination of the agreement, then the buyer agrees to pay the broker his or her 10% of the purchase price for services in bringing the business for sale to the buyer's attention.

After execution of the agreement, the buyer may call and ask for a list of other businesses for sale. Make sure that he or she has not already seen the business. The reasoning being that the buyer may say at a later date that he or she knew about a particular business that was for sale, in order to avoid paying the broker's commission. Mention to the buyer that it is important that he or she not discuss anything with the seller, employees, or any customers who may be on the premises of the business at the time of the visit.

The remainder of this contract (from the buyer's point of view) is the same as the listing agreement and buyer's authorization form.

ACCUMULATE DATA AND CROSS-REFERENCE

By accumulating the above agreements, you can make a systematic search in matching buyers with available listings.

109

RESUME AND FINANCIAL STATEMENT FORMS

The salesperson must get a resume from every buyer, as everything possible must be known before a buyer and business can be matched. A typical resume and financial statement are shown on pages 124 through 125.

BUYER'S AUTHORIZATION
SOLE AND EXCLUSIVE AGREEMENT

For Brokers Use Only	
Mgrs. Initial	Date

Date_____19_____

1. AGREEMENT:

The undersigned _____
(Buyer), hereby retains _____(Broker), as
his sole and exclusive agent for the purpose of locating a business property of a nature outlined below and of negotiating terms and conditions for the purchase of all or substantial part
thereof, or to trade, exchange, merge, obtain an option or lease for a period of _____ months
from the date hereof (exclusive listing period). Exclusive listing period shall be _____ 19__
to _____, 19__ midnight, and shall continue thereafter as a non-exclusive right for one year,
unless revoked in writing.

2. TYPE OF BUSINESS WANTED:

_____

_____

_____

3. TERMS AND CONDITIONS:

Food: ☐ Yes   ☐ No. If yes, _____% of sales.

ABC License: ☐ Beer   ☐ Beer and Wine   ☐ Cocktails   ☐ None

General Location: From _____ to _____.

Franchise: ☐ Yes   ☐ No

Sales: Gross $ _____ per month

Net $ _____ (minimum needed to live on)

Price: $ _____ (maximum)

Downpayment: $ _____ (maximum cash available)

Payments: $ _____ (maximum per month)

Interest on Business Loan: _____% (maximum)

111

Additional Sources of Capital: $ _____

_____

_____

☐ Equity Loan   ☐ Personal Loan   ☐ Equity   ☐ Sell _____

_____

Rent: Approximate maximum per month $_____

Lease Term _____ (minimum number of years)

Locate in shopping center: ☐ Yes ☐ No

Free standing building: ☐ Yes ☐ No

Purchase Real Property: ☐ Yes ☐ No   maximum $_____

Lot size _____   Parking Requirements _____ (number of spaces)

Approximate Square Feet: _____

Approximate Seating Capacity: at _____ Bar, _____ Lounge, _____ Restaurant Area.

Type of Seating: ☐ Table and chairs ☐ Booths ☐ Other _____

_____

Workers: How many in family will be working there _____ ☐ plus yourself.

Are you ready to buy ☐ now   ☐ 30 days   ☐ 3 months   ☐ other

_____

Union Shop: ☐ yes   ☐ no   ☐ don't care

Business Experience: ☐ currently   ☐ 0-1 year   ☐ 1-5 years   ☐ 5-10 years, or more

Instruction: How long? ☐ 2 weeks   ☐ 1 month   ☐ 2 months

☐ other_____

Title: ☐ individual   ☐ joint tenant(s)   ☐ community property
☐ tenant(s) in common   ☐ partnership   ☐ corporation

Escrow Fees: ☐ pay half   ☐ other _____

4. FINANCIAL STATEMENT:
    ☐ attached   ☐ will furnish by _____19____

5. FINANCIAL INFORMATION:

	Address	Approx. Value
Savings Account		
Checking Account		
Securities		
Real property		
Other (specify)		
Other (specify)		

6. EMPLOYMENT HISTORY:

Employer_____Address_____

How long? _____ (years)   Salary $_____ (annually)

Employer_____Address_____

How long? _____ (years)   Salary $_____ (annually)

7. ADDITIONAL INFORMATION:

8. PLEASE NAME PLACES SEEN AND COMMENTS:

9. FEE:

A. Buyer hereby agrees to pay a commission (**REAL ESTATE COMMISSIONS ARE NEGOTIABLE AND NOT FIXED BY LAW**) to said Broker_____ (____%) percent of the actual purchase or exchange price or other consideration received, or a fee of $_____ whichever is greater.

B. Should the Buyer, or any person acting directly or indirectly for Buyer or on Buyer's behalf, purchase, possess, lease, become connected with or obtain an option for, in any other interest in any business property of the nature described herein, during the term hereof, through the services of Broker or otherwise; or should Buyer or any person acting on Buyer's behalf purchase, possess, lease, or obtain an option for or any other interest in such a property or furnish information about any such property to someone else within one (1) year of the ter-

113

mination of this agreement, and if Broker presented or submitted to Buyer such property during the term hereof, Buyer hereby agrees to pay Broker ten (10) percent of the sale price of the property. Any dispute as to the agreement shall be arbitrated by the American Arbitration Association or as otherwise set forth within this agreement. Unless Buyer shall furnish a signed declaration under penalty of perjury stating how and when Buyer and Seller were brought together within 10 days of sale of such property, Buyer hereby agrees to pay Broker said commission in full as stated within.

C. Broker agrees that he will represent Buyer only and will not accept a fee from the Seller unless full disclosure thereof is made to Buyer prior to the execution of an offer to purchase, possess, lease, option or any disposition of the property.

D. Buyer agrees to pay the above commission or fee due Broker upon close of escrow or delivery of possession to Buyer, whichever occurs first.

10. BUYER(S) HEREBY AGREE AS FOLLOWS:

A. Buyer(s) agree(s) to ☐ attach   ☐ will furnish by _____, 19____ a financial statement ☐ audited   ☐ unaudited and by reference made a part hereof;

B. ☐ Buyer(s) agree to maintain insurance to cover obligations under this agreement setting forth the ☐ Seller(s)   ☐ Buyer(s) or their assigns as first loss payee as follows: ☐ fire ☐ theft   ☐ comprehensive liability;

C. Buyer(s) agree(s) in addition to the purchase price to pay at opening of escrow sales tax on the furniture, fixtures and equipment;

D. Buyer(s) shall take title to the business and property as ☐ an individual   ☐ community property   ☐ a joint tenant   ☐ tenant(s) in common   ☐ partnership   ☐ corporation;

E. Buyer(s) warrant(s) that he or she has full authority to execute the purchase and sale agreement, and that he or she has written authority to do so for all buyers;

F. Buyer(s) hereby agree to pay all escrow fees, charges and costs as follows: ☐ one half ☐ seller(s) pays all   ☐ buyer(s) pay all   ☐ other _____.
For its ordinary services hereunder and upon acceptance of this escrow, the escrow agent shall be entitled to a fee of $_____, payable concurrently with its acceptance hereof. Said fee is in addition to the total consideration being paid for the business and property. Additional escrow fee(s) shall be as follows: $_____ for each creditor(s) claim in excess of three (3) paid through escrow, payable by seller(s). $_____ for each disputed creditor(s) claim, payable by seller(s).

G. List of work in progress, inventory, furniture, fixtures and equipment ☐ being conveyed ☐ not being conveyed   ☐ on lease or owned by others shall be approved in writing by both parties at close of escrow.

114

H. ☐ Buyer(s) shall at opening of escrow, make application for the transfer of the ABC license at the office of Department of Alcoholic Beverage Control, _____.
Buyer(s) agree(s) to pay such transfer fees and warrants that he is fully cognizant of the provisions of the State of California Alcoholic Beverage Control Act, with particular reference to his qualifications and eligibility and knows of no reason a license should be denied him. This agreement is conditioned upon such transfer.

I. Buyer(s) agree that _____

Address _____Phone_____ is the Broker

and that _____Address _____

Phone_____ is the Escrow Holder.

J. Buyer(s) hereby agree that if he delays the sale unreasonably during negotiations, and/or delays the delivery of any documents beyond the date promised, the period of delay shall be automatically added to the purchase and sale (deposit/receipt) agreement and this Buyer's Authorization agreement.

K. Buyer(s) hereby agree to use diligence to transfer the assets of the business.

L. Buyer(s) agree that if it appears to the Broker and escrow holder that there will not be enough funds to pay the Broker's commission in full, as specified in the listing agreement, such obligations shall be paid by the Buyer(s) instead of the Seller(s) at close of escrow and the purchasing price and down payment to be paid by the Buyer(s) shall thereby be reduced accordingly.

M. Buyer(s) hereby agree that in addition to the purchase price, there shall be prorated through escrow as of the close of escrow personal property taxes, rents, interest charges, insurance and similar expenses.

N. Buyer(s) represent(s) and warrant(s) that all information set forth in the escrow instructions and this agreement and any attachments thereto are true and correct as of the close of escrow and are effective as of that date. Buyer(s) agree(s) that if said property is made unmarketable by any voluntary act and all such representations and warranties are NOT true and correct and if this sale is cancelled for this reason, Buyer(s) agree(s) to pay the full commission on the sale price as specified herein, as if the sale had been consummated.

11. CORPORATION:

If the property to be purchased is owned by a corporation, the person(s) signing these instructions attest(s) that he or they are duly authorized and empowered by the corporation's directors to purchase that business and property. A copy of corporate minutes approving the purchase agreement is ☐ attached ☐ will be furnished by_____, 19____ and by reference made a part hereof.

115

12. COVENANT NOT TO COMPETE:

Seller(s) covenants to the Buyer(s), his successors, assigns and representatives that he will not engage, directly or indirectly, in any business the same as, similar to, or in competition with the business hereby sold within a radius of _____ miles from the principal place of business being sold for a period of _____ years from date of Buyer(s) possession, either as a principal, agent, manager, employee, owner, partner, stockholder, director or officer of a corporation, trustee, consultant, or otherwise in any capacity whatsover.

13. DEFAULT:

A. If Buyer(s) fails or refuses to complete this transaction as required, the Deposit received, or part thereof up to the full amount of the commission, shall be paid to the Broker. The balance, if any, of the deposit shall be paid to Seller(s) as liquidated damages.

B. ☐ Default by Buyer(s), where Seller(s) hold Buyer(s) outstanding note on said business or property, including leasehold rights, whether real or personal, shall also occur whenever the gross sales or inventory of said business fall below 75% in any three consecutive months in comparison with the three consecutive same months in the previous year, allowing the net amount to be added or subtracted from the actual cost of living index, as determined by the federal government, for the nation as a whole. Buyer(s) also agree(s) to furnish the Seller(s) a monthly Profit and Loss Statement within 10 days of each month during the period of said note. Upon such default Seller(s) shall have the option to repossess by due process in accordance of the Uniform Commercial Code, the said business and property, including leasehold rights, whether real or personal, excluding the Alcohol Beverage Control license, by giving 10 days notice in writing to Buyer(s). Buyer(s) shall have the option to pay said note in full by giving 10 days notice in writing to Seller(s), excluding if this is an installment sale.

14. ARBITRATION:

All parties agree to any controversy or claim arising out of or relating to this contract, or the breach thereof, shall be settled by arbitration in accordance with the rules of the American Arbitration Association, and judgement upon the award rendered by Arbitrator(s) may be entered in any court having jurisdiction thereof.

15. HOLD HARMLESS AGREEMENT:

Buyer(s) agree that the Broker, or its Agent, in bringing Buyer(s) and Seller(s) together has fulfilled its primary brokerage function and that Buyer(s) agree to hold Broker, its Agent, attorneys and Escrow Holder harmless from any liability arising out of the sale of said business.

16. CONDITIONS AND TERMS:

It is expressly understood that these Buyer(s) Authorization instructions contain all instructions of Buyer(s) and conditions upon which the undersigned agree(s) to purchase said business and property.

17. PROMISE NOT TO DISCLOSE:

    I promise not to disclose to any third party that the business listed by Broker, or its Agents, may be for sale, exchange or transfer, or otherwise disposed of. Further agree not to disclose any facts learned about the business to third party, including employees, customers, vendors, other prospective Buyers or the owner thereof. The information and/or records about this business obtained by me shall not be used for competitive use in any business, present or future. I understand that information disclosed to others could cause a loss of business, and/or create injury in employer-employee relationships. Should any legal action be taken against me as a result of this agreement, the prevailing party shall be entitled to court costs and attorneys fees as awarded by the courts.

18. BROKER AGREES:

    Broker agrees to use his best efforts to locate a business suitable for client's needs, and will, from time to time, supply information to client on businesses which may or may not be the subject matter of a formal sales authorization.

    THIS IS A LEGALLY BINDING DOCUMENT. READ IT CAREFULLY. If you don't understand it, consult with your attorney and/or accountant. Broker and Escrow Holder are not authorized to give legal or tax advice.

    Each of the undersigned has read the foregoing instructions, and by his signature hereto acknowledges that he understands and agrees with them.

    Receipt of this Buyer Authorization is hereby acknowledged.

X_____   Date _____ 19_____
  Buyer

_____   _____
  Print name and title   Social Security number

Address _____   Phone _____

X_____   Date _____ 19_____
  Buyer

_____   _____
Print name and title   Social Security number

_____   Phone _____
Address

X_____   Date _____ 19_____
  Broker/Agent

117

BUSINESS WANTED

1. TYPE OF BUSINESS WANTED:

   _____

   _____

   _____

2. TERMS AND CONDITIONS:

   Food: ☐ Yes   ☐ No. If yes, _____% of sales.

   ABC License: ☐ Beer   ☐ Beer and Wine   ☐ Cocktails   ☐ None

   General Location: From _____ to _____.

   Franchise: ☐ Yes   ☐ No

   Sales: Gross $ _____   per month

         Net $ _____   (minimum needed to live on)

   Price: $ _____   (maximum)

   Downpayment: $ _____   (maximum cash available)

   Payments: $ _____   (maximum per month)

   Interest on Business Loan: _____% (maximum)

   Additional Sources of Capital: $ _____

   _____

   _____

   ☐ Equity Loan   ☐ Personal Loan   ☐ Equity   ☐ Sell _____

   _____

   Rent: Approximate maximum per month $_____

   Lease Term _____ (minimum number of years)

   Locate in shopping center: ☐ Yes   ☐ No

   Free standing building: ☐ Yes   ☐ No

   Purchase Real Property: ☐ Yes   ☐ No   maximum $_____

   Lot size _____ Parking Requirements _____ (number of spaces)

   Approximate Square Feet: _____

118

Approximate Seating Capacity: at _____ Bar, _____ Lounge, _____ Restaurant Area.

Type of Seating: ☐ Table and chairs ☐ Booths ☐ Other _____

_____

Workers: How many in family will be working there _____ ☐ plus yourself.

Are you ready to buy ☐ now ☐ 30 days ☐ 3 months ☐ other

_____

Union Shop: ☐ yes ☐ no ☐ don't care

Business Experience: ☐ currently ☐ 0-1 year ☐ 1-5 years ☐ 5-10 years, or more

Instruction: How long? ☐ 2 weeks ☐ 1 month ☐ 2 months

☐ other_____

Title: ☐ individual ☐ joint tenant(s) ☐ community property
☐ tenant(s) in common ☐ partnership ☐ corporation

Escrow Fees: ☐ pay half ☐ other _____

3. FINANCIAL STATEMENT:
   ☐ attached ☐ will furnish by _____ 19____

4. FINANCIAL INFORMATION:

	Address	Approx. Value
Savings Account		
Checking Account		
Securities		
Real property		
Other (specify)		
Other (specify)		

5. EMPLOYMENT HISTORY:

_____

Employer_____Address_____

How long? _____ (years) Salary $_____ (annually)

Employer_____Address_____

How long? _____ (years) Salary $_____ (annually)

6. ADDITIONAL INFORMATION:

_____

_____

_____

7. PLEASE NAME PLACES SEEN AND COMMENTS:

_____

_____

_____

8. PROMISE NOT TO DISCLOSE:

I promise not to discuss or disclose to any third party that the business listed by Broker, or its Agents, may be for sale, exchange or transfer, or otherwise disposed of. I further agree not to disclose any facts learned about the business to third parties, including employees, customers, vendors, other prospective Buyers or the owner thereof. The information and/or records about this business obtained by me shall not be used for competitive use in any business, present or future. I understand that information disclosed to others could cause a loss of business, and/or create injury in employer-employee relationships. Should any legal action be taken against me as a result of this agreement, the prevailing party shall be entitled to court costs and attorneys fees as awarded by the courts.

The above information has not been verified by the Broker, or its agents. They are not responsible for accuracy or omissions of information contained herein.

_____ Date_____ 19_____

Above this line to be circulated to all offices and agents.

Office No. _____

--tear off (copy only) ---

Below this line is confidential for procuring salesperson only.

Office No. _____
Buyer's Name _____Phone_____
Address _____Business Phone_____
Comments:_____

_____

_____

_____

120

PERSONAL AND CONFIDENTIAL AGREEMENT
LOCATION OF BUSINESS

For Brokers Use Only	
Mgrs. Initials	Date

1. Gentlemen:

It is agreed that if I make the purchase *through your office* I am *not* liable for any commission and am acting as a principal, not as a Broker.

In consideration of information furnished and concerning business listed below, including their availability for sale or lease, I agree that should I or any person acting directly or indirectly for Buyer or on Buyer's behalf, purchase, possess, lease, become connected with or obtain an option for, in any other interest in any business property of the nature of described herein, during the term hereof, through the services of Broker or otherwise; or should Buyer or any person acting on Buyer's behalf purchase, possess, lease, or obtain an option for or any other interest in such a property or furnish information about any such property to someone else within one (1) year of the termination of this agreement, and if Broker presented or submitted to Buyer such property during the term hereof, Buyer hereby agrees to pay Broker ten (10) percent of the sale price of the property. Any dispute as to the agreement shall be arbitrated by the American Arbitration Association or as otherwise set forth within this agreement. Unless Buyer shall furnish a signed declaration under penalty of perjury stating how and when Buyer and Seller were brought together within 10 days of sale of such property, Buyer hereby agrees to pay Broker said commission in full as stated within.

Also please tell me later about any other listed business you think will interest me. Your log book will be a sufficient record of phone calls to me about other businesses.

Name	Address	City	Rent	Price	Terms

Buyer(s) also agree that the undersigned Broker is the first to disclose the above information.

121

Please check daily for new listings _____

(Broker's Name and Phone Number)

PLEASE DO NOT TALK TO OWNERS OR EMPLOYEES OF ANY BUSINESS YOU ARE INTERESTED IN.

2. ARBITRATION:

All parties agree to any controversy or claim arising out of or relating to this contract, or the breach thereof, shall be settled by arbitration in accordance with the rules of the American Arbitration Association, and judgment upon the award rendered by Arbitrator(s) may be entered in any court having jurisdiction thereof.

3. HOLD HARMLESS AGREEMENT:

Buyer(s) agree that Broker, or its Agent, in bringing Buyer(s) and Seller(s) together has fulfilled its primary brokerage function and that Buyer(s) agree to hold Broker, its Agent, attorneys and Escrow Holder harmless from any liability arising out of the sale of said business.

4. PROMISE NOT TO DISCLOSE:

I promise not to discuss or disclose to any third party that the business listed by Broker, or its Agents, may be for sale, exchange or transfer, or otherwise disposed of. I further agree not to disclose any facts learned about the business to third party, including employees, customers, vendors, other prospective buyers or the owner thereof. The information and/or records about this business obtained by me shall not be used for competitive use in any business, present or future. I understand that information disclosed to others could cause a loss of business and/or create injury in employer-employee relationships. Should any legal action be taken against me as a result of this agreement, the prevailing party shall be entitled to court costs and attorneys fees as awarded by the courts.

5. BROKER AGREES:

Broker agrees to use his best efforts to locate a business suitable for client's needs, and will, from time to time, supply information to client on businesses which may or may not be the subject matter of a formal sales authorization.

This is a legally binding document. Read it carefully. If you don't understand it, consult with your attorney and/or accountant. Broker and Escrow Holder are not authorized to give legal or tax advice.

Each of the undersigned has read the foregoing instructions, and by his signature hereto acknowledges that he understands and agrees with them.

Receipt of this Location of Business Agreement is hereby acknowledged.

X_____   Date _____19_____
   Buyer

_____   _____
Print name and title   Social Security Number

_____   Phone _____
Address

X_____   Date _____19_____
   Buyer

_____   _____
Print name and title   Social Security Number

_____   Phone _____
Address

X_____   Date _____19_____
   Broker/Agent

123

TYPICAL RESUME

NAME: Joe Q. Buyer
111 Jones Street, San Jose, Ca. 94087
Telephone (415) 600-1979

SUMMARY: 17 years experience – profit and loss responsibilities for high volume paper converting, tableware, displays, point of purchase and disposable. One year – secondary fiber pulp. One year – coolers, floor furnaces, unit, wall and water heaters. Reliable, mature, effective, enthusiastic, well qualified in all phases of production, sales, and administration "from the ground up." Shirt sleeve executive.

EXPERIENCE:
July 1970
to
May 1978

Mill Manager, ABO Corporation, Boston, Massachusetts (150 employees). Full profit and loss responsibilities for the complete production of secondary fiber from poly coated board, including engineering, maintenance, training, also customer, civic, federal, state, county, and union relations. Production up 30%, 125 ton/day.

July 1968
to
July 1970

Plant Manager Engineer, AAAA Corporation, Newark, California (180 employees). Full profit and loss responsibilities for the complete paper converting operation. Responsible and supervised all engineering and maintenance, also developing new ideas and techniques with customer, salesmen, and art department for advertising and decorative displays. Represent management on union negotiations and grievance procedures. Production up 10%.

December 1958
to
July 1968

President, Plant Manager/Engineer and Founder, Smith Corporation, Bedford, Massachusetts (128 employees). Sole responsible for profit and loss for all management, office, production, and sales. Sold 90% of production. Principal products: hot and cold paper drinking cups. All equipment with my own alterations and designs was operating with top efficiency.

ADDENDA: *Manager, Mechanical Engineer/Draftsman*, (Job and consulting work). Various domestic and foreign machinery related to paper drinking cups, food containers and corrugated cartons. Paid 100% of college expenses. Formerly the Chairman, School Board Advisory Committee of San Jose, Calif. Active in civic organizations: Lions Club, PTA, church, and Boy Scouts of America. Member A.M.A.

124

PERSONAL: Married – 3 children; excellent health; pilot license; veteran.

EDUCATION: O.S.H.A. Seminar – University of Georgia, Atlanta, Ga. – 1974.
                Industrial Psychology – Jones College, San Jose, Ca. – 1969.
                Automation – University of Pennsylvania – 1968. Machine
                Design, School of Design – 1948.

SALARY: Open – Available to relocate within 10 days. Willing to travel.

FINANCIAL STATEMENT
INDIVIDUAL, PARTNERSHIP, OR CORPORATION

FINANCIAL STATEMENT OF _____ RECEIVED AT _____ BRANCH

NAME _____ BUSINESS _____

ADDRESS _____ AT CLOSE OF BUSINESS _____ 19___

To

The undersigned, for the purpose of procuring and establishing credit from time to time with you and to induce you to permit the undersigned to become indebted to you on notes, endorsements, guarantees, overdrafts or otherwise, furnishes the following (or in lieu thereof the attached, which is the most recent statement prepared by or for the undersigned) as being a full, true and correct statement of the financial condition of the undersigned on the date indicated, and agrees to notify you immediately of the extent and character of any material change in said financial condition, and also agrees that if the undersigned, or any endorser or guarantor of any of the obligations of the undersigned, at any time fails in business or becomes insolvent, or commits an act of bankruptcy, or if any deposit account of the undersigned with you, or any other property of the undersigned held by you, be attempted to be obtained or held by writ of execution, garnishment, attachment or other legal process, or if any of the representations made below prove to be untrue, or if the undersigned fails to notify you of any material change as above agreed, or if the business, or any interest therein, of the undersigned is sold, then and in such case, at your option, all of the obligations of the undersigned to you, or held by you, shall immediately become due and payable, without demand or notice. This statement shall be construed by you to be a continuing statement of the condition of the undersigned, and a new and original statement of all assets and liabilities upon each and every transaction in and by which the undersigned hereafter becomes indebted to you, until the undersigned advises in writing to the contrary.

ASSETS	DOLLARS	CENTS	LIABILITIES	DOLLARS	CENTS
Cash In _____ (NAME OF BANK)			Notes Payable to Banks _____		
Cash on Hand _____			Notes Payable and Trade Acceptances for Merchandise _____		
Notes Receivable and Trade Acceptance (Includes $_____ Past Due)			Notes Payable to Others _____		
Accounts Receivable—$_____ Less Reserves $_____			Accounts Payable (Includes $_____ Past Due) _____		
Customer's . . . (Includes $_____ Past Due)			Due to Partners, Employes, Relatives, Officers, Stockholders or Allied Companies _____		
Merchandise—Finished—How Valued _____			Chattel Mortgages and Contracts Payable (Describe Monthly Payments) . . . . . $_____		
Merchandise—Unfinished—How Valued _____			Federal and State Income Tax _____		
Merchandise—Raw Material—How Valued _____			Accrued Liabilities (Interest, Wages, Taxes, Etc.) _____		
Supplies on Hand _____			Portion of Long Term Debt Due Within One Year _____		
Stocks and Bonds—Listed (See Schedule B) _____					
TOTAL CURRENT ASSETS			**TOTAL CURRENT LIABILITIES**		
Real Estate—Less Depreciation of: $_____ Net (See Schedule A)			Liens on Real Estate (See Schedule A) $_____		
Machinery and Fixtures— Less Depreciation of: $_____ Net			Less Current Portion Included Above $_____ Net		
Automobiles and Trucks— Less Depreciation of: $_____ Net					
Stocks and Bonds—Unlisted (See Schedule B) _____			Capital Stock—Preferred _____		
Due from Partners, Employes, Relatives, Officers, Stockholders or Allied Companies _____			Capital Stock—Common _____		
			Surplus—Paid In _____		
Cash Value Life Insurance _____			Surplus—Earned and Undivided Profits _____		
Other Assets (Describe) _____			Net Worth (If Not Incorporated) _____		
TOTAL			TOTAL		

PROFIT AND LOSS STATEMENT FOR THE PERIOD FROM _____ TO _____			CONTINGENT LIABILITIES (NOT INCLUDED ABOVE)		
Net Sales (After Returned Sales and Allowances) _____			As Guarantor or Endorser _____		
Cost of Sales:			Accounts, Notes, or Trade Acceptances Discounted or Pledged _____		
Beginning Inventory			Surety On Bonds or Other Continent Liability _____		
Purchases (or cost of goods mfd.)			Letters of Credit _____		
TOTAL			Judgments Unsatisfied or Suits Pending _____		
Less: Closing Inventory			Merchandise Commitments and Unfinished Contracts _____		
Gross Profit on Sales			Merchandise Held On Consignment From Others _____		
			Unsatisfied Tax Liens or Notices From the Federal or State Governments of Intention to Assess Such Liens _____		
Operating Expenses:			**RECONCILEMENT OF NET WORTH OR EARNED SURPLUS**		
Salaries—Officers or Partners					
Salaries and Wages—Other			Net Worth or Earned Surplus at Beginning of Period _____		
Rent			Add Net Profit or Deduct Net Loss _____		
Depreciation			Total _____		
Bad Debts			Other Additions (Describe) _____		
Advertising			Total		
Interest			Less: Withdrawals or Dividends _____		
Taxes—Other Than Income			Other Deductions (Explain) _____		
Insurance			Total Deductions _____		
Other Expenses			Net Worth or Capital Funds on This Financial Statement _____		
Net Profit from Operations			**DETAIL OF INVENTORY**		
Other Income					
Less Other Expense			Is Inventory Figure Actual or Estimated? _____		
Net Profit Before Income Tax			By Whom Taken or Estimated _____ When? _____		
Federal and State Income Tax			Buy Principally From _____		
Net Profit or Loss			Average Terms of Purchase _____ Sale _____		
(To Net Worth or Earned Surplus)			Time of Year Inventory Maximum _____ Minimum _____		

126

SCHEDULE A   LIST OF REAL ESTATE AND IMPROVEMENTS WITH ENCUMBRANCES THEREON

DESCRIPTION, STREET NUMBER, LOCATION	TITLE IN NAMES OF	BOOK VALUE		MORTGAGES OR LIENS		TERMS OF PAYMENT	HOLDER OF LIEN
		LAND	IMPROVEMENTS	MATURITY	AMOUNT		
		$	$		$	$	
TOTALS		$	$		$	$	

SCHEDULE B   STOCKS & BONDS: Describe Fully. Use Supplemental Sheet if Necessary. Indicate if Stocks Are Common or Preferred. Give Interest Rate and Maturity of Bonds.

NO. OF SHARES AMT. OF BONDS	NAME AND ISSUE (DESCRIBE FULLY)	BOOK VALUE		MARKET VALUE	
		LISTED	UNLISTED	PRICE	VALUE
		$	$	$	
	TOTALS	$	$		$

SCHEDULE C   Complete if Statement is for an Individual or Sole Proprietorship

Age _____ Number of Years in Present Business _____ Date of Filing Fictitious Trade Style _____

What Property Listed in This Statement is in Joint Tenancy? _____ Name of Other Party _____

What Property Listed in This Statement is Community Property? _____ Name of Other Party _____

With What Other Business Are You Connected? _____ Have You Filed Homestead? _____

Do You Deal With or Carry Accounts With Stockbrokers? _____ Amount $ _____ Name of Firm _____

SCHEDULE D   Complete if Statement is of a Partnership

NAME OF PARTNERS (INDICATE SPECIAL PARTNERS)	AGE	AMOUNT CONTRIBUTED	OUTSIDE NET WORTH	OTHER BUSINESS CONNECTIONS
		$	$	

Date of Organization _____ Limited or General? _____ Terminates _____

If Operating Under Fictitious Trade Style, Give Date of Filing _____

SCHEDULE E   Complete if Statement is of a Corporation

	AUTHORIZED	PAR VALUE	OUTSTANDING		ISSUED FOR	
			SHARES	AMOUNT	CASH	OTHER (DESCRIBE)
Common Stock	$	$		$	$	
Preferred Stock	$	$		$	$	

Bonds—Total Issue $ _____ Outstanding $ _____ Due _____ Interest Rate _____

Date Incorporated _____ Under Laws of State of _____

OFFICERS	AGE	SHARES OWNED		DIRECTORS AND PRINCIPAL STOCKHOLDERS	SHARES OWNED	
		COMMON	PREFERRED		COMMON	PREFERRED
President				Director		
Vice President				Director		
Secretary				Director		
Treasurer						

SCHEDULE F   Complete in ALL Cases   INSURANCE

Are Your Books Audited by Outside Accountants? _____ Name _____

Date of Last Audit _____ To What Date Has the U.S. Internal Revenue Department Examined Your Books? _____

Are You Borrowing From Any Other Branch of This Bank? _____ Which? _____

Are You Applying for Credit At Any Other Source? _____ Where? _____

Have You Ever Failed in Business? _____ If So, Attach a Complete Explanation and State Basis of Settlement With Creditors _____

Lease Has _____ Years to Run, With Monthly Rental of $ _____

Merchandise $ _____

Machinery & Fixtures $ _____

Buildings $ _____

Earthquake $ _____ Is Extended Coverage Endorsement Included? _____

Do You Carry Workmen's Compensation Insurance? _____

Automobiles and Trucks:

Public Liability $ _____ M/$ _____ M

Collision $ _____

Property Damage $ _____

Life Insurance $ _____ Name of Beneficiary _____

STATEMENT OF BANK OFFICER:

Insofar as our records reveal, this Financial Statement is accurate and true. The foregoing statement is (a copy of) the original signed by the maker, in the credit files of this Bank.

The undersigned solemnly declares and certifies that the above statement (or in lieu thereof, the attached statement, as the case may be) and supporting schedules, both printed and written, give a full, true, and correct statement of the financial condition of the undersigned as of the date indicated.

Signature _____

_____ ASSISTANT CASHIER-MANAGER

By _____

(TITLE, IF CORPORATION)

127

Chapter **11** Financing

HOW TO FINANCE A BUSINESS WITH LITTLE OR NO MONEY DOWN

There are various ways to purchase a business. If a thorough study has been made of a prospective business, as outlined in this book, there can be a cash flow from the first day of operation. This immediate cash flow should cover loan obligations. The "instant business success" that one hears about, that is, taking over a going business with little or no cash down, appears to be the best that one can do. What often is not mentioned is the fact that a person must be wealthy and must put up suitable collateral (assets) at least equal in value to the loan balance owed against the business. If the buyer has a large amount of equity, there is a better chance that a seller will consider taking a lower downpayment and carry back a note for the balance. The stronger a buyer appears to be financially the better the chance that other creditors, noteholders and/or equipment lease holders will allow him or her to assume their notes or extend credit.

Let us look at several major sources of financing a new business.

1. *Personal Loans.* The buyer may rely on his or her immediate family, relatives, or others for a personal loan. Another source of personal loans would be a financial institution, for example, a bank, savings and loan association, insurance company, or finance company; the higher the risk, the higher the interest rate will be. A loan offering a lower interest is one secured by personal assets, such as real property (second mortgage), land, automobile, mobile home, boat, airplane,

stocks, bonds, or loans against insurance policies. Other collateral that most people fail to recognize is a passbook, savings account, securities, or the cash value of a life insurance policy. There are also simple commercial unsecured loans for 30 to 90 days.

2. *Inventory Loans.* There are different ways that merchandise can be obtained:

A). Merchandise can be delivered, if requested, on consignment. That is, suppliers retain ownership of inventory, receiving payment when inventory is sold.

B). Suppliers can be asked to ship inventory now and bill in 10 to 90 days.

C). A few suppliers will, on request, extend credit terms up to 120 days.

D). Cash on delivery is often required on new accounts from suppliers, or the merchant may wish to pay before delivery.

E). Suppliers will often send "seasonal" goods well before a particular season. Payment does not start or is not due until the season is under way. Monthly billing can be established if requested by the merchant.

Any combination of these billing arrangements can be set up between a supplier and a merchant.

3. *"Flooring" Financing.* This type of financing is done through a finance company. They will finance up to 100% of the merchandise. The finance company stocks the showroom, store, or other business and the merchant pays off the finance company as he or she sells off the goods. This is called a "revolving account." Title remains with the lender until the merchandise is sold. This form of financing is usually used for large items such as automobiles, home appliances, or boats.

4. *Unsecured or Secured Loans.* Unsecured or secured loans, or both, are used when a merchant will pledge all or part of his or her inventory as security to the supplier. This will ensure a dependable source of supplies and bind a merchant and the supplier closer together.

5. *Secured Notes.* A seller often carries notes against a business where a seller agrees to accept payments of part of the purchase price over an extended period of time (usually three to five years) and secure the note by assets of the business. However, one can use other assets too.

Sometimes a seller will want additional security, such as a note against a buyer's real property or against personal assets. If a buyer defaults he or she will not only lose the business but his or her additional assets as well.

It is difficult to get a bank to carry notes just against a business. In most cases, a bank will ask for additional security. Their contention is that in reality there are little or no "hard" assets with marketable value in most small-to-medium-sized businesses.

6. *Free Equipment.* It is quite common to get vending machines, such as pool tables, video games, and pinball equipment free and also receive 50% out of sales receipts.

   Suppliers and distributors often supply free equipment if one purchases their supplies. This is a good way to get things such as coffeemakers, coolers, freezers, and dispensers. Sometimes a landlord will purchase equipment for a tenant and add a little more money to the monthly rent to cover the equipment cost.

7. *Equipment and Machinery Loans.* Loans on time payments can be secured against the equipment up to 80% of its value. The loans come usually from the manufacturer, distributor, supplier, or a bank.

8. *Equipment and Machinery Leases.* Suppliers and distributors sometimes arrange leases for their own equipment by carrying the lease themselves or by using a leasing company.

9. *Leased-Back Equipment.* Ask a supplier, insurance company, or a bank to purchase the equipment that you need. Then you can lease it back at a monthly cost.

10. *Accounts Receivable — "Factoring" vs. Loans.* The major difference is that a factor organization buys all well-rated accounts receivable, some purchase orders, invoices, contracts, and secured loans and notes for immediate cash. If any of these items prove uncollectable, the factor absorbs the loss; the borrower does not incur any obligation. A commercial finance company makes loans to a borrower who *assigns* his or her accounts receivable as collateral for a *loan* and who remains responsible for any uncollected debt. This is called "with recourse," and is the usual method employed.

11. *Equity Loans.* Some suppliers will loan money for an investment in a business, based on the equity of the business, ownership of a home or other assets, or if it is a state business or industrial development corporation.

12. *Credit Line.* Usually a bank or supplier will extend credit on a combination of personal and "hard" assets for short-term funds for a maximum amount agreed upon at any one time.

13. *Trade Credit.* This represents a major source of funds, usually 2% discount on balance, when payments are made within ten days,

compared to taking 30 days to pay without a discount. Sometimes suppliers will offer up to 90 days of interest-free credit. Also, there are suppliers who will offer loans up to 200% of your equity investment, at a very low interest rate, to purchase a business or for expansion of a business. Even a credit card is a form of loan from your suppliers.

14. *Customer's Advances.* Customers sometimes make advance payments against orders for future production and delivery. This is done mostly with high-priced items with long delivery times (one third is paid when ordering, one third when the merchandise is shipped, and one third when it is installed or delivered).

15. *Federal Government Loans.* Small Business Administration (SBA) and Small Business Investment Companies (especially for minorities) loans have a very detailed requirement. It is wise to have a professional person prepare these forms. Reconstruction Finance Corporation loans are for depressed or poor economic conditions. Special aid is available to military suppliers, such as, construction and equipping of plants.

There are also special aids to victims of flood, tornadoes, drought, or other disasters. These loans are intended as rehabilitation measures.

Veteran's home loans can also be obtained for a business venture.

Intermediate loan capital is for small businesses and farmers, and credit on export sales is available.

The hottest loans are the new energy loans, for example, solar heat, insulation, and energy-saving devices. All loans must be of sound value or reasonably secured to ensure repayment.

Most sellers will not wait for SBA approval, which usually takes three to six months. SBA is an excellent source for financial counseling and reference materials.

16. *Go Public.* Sell stock in your own company. See an investment house about this method of raising money.

17. *Cash.* A business can always be purchased for cash; however, most sellers and buyers, after they have studied the tax consequences and their financial resources, will not accept or offer cash.

Chapter 12 Business-Insurance Considerations

The following discussion is not meant to replace the services of a qualified insurance agent. It is presented here to provide areas for further discussion and review.

RISK AND INSURANCE

The risk of loss is a problem for people in nearly every walk of life. Every day, most people assume a wide variety of risks, often without realizing it. Insurance is one of the major risk-handling methods. However, not every risk is insurable due to factors including legal, physical, and moral hazards. The cost of insurance sometimes seems to outweigh its economic value to the user, but if the business or individual cannot afford the insurance premiums, it is even more likely that the losses will not be affordable should they occur.

There are many factors and alternatives that must be considered before a final risk decision can be made. A life underwriter and a property-liability broker can be important members on the businessperson's advisory team, bringing valuable knowledge and experience to the decision-making process. Since not all insurers are alike, extreme care should be exercised in selecting companies and agents. Particular attention should be paid to the matters of insurance cost, financial strength, and the quantity and quality of services. *Shopper's Guides to Insurance* (published by state insurance departments), *A. M. Best's Insurance Reports*, and college-level textbooks can provide this information.

For discussion, the broad title of insurance can be divided into two parts. First of all, the life and health underwriting and secondly, the property and casualty underwriting. Separate state licenses are required for each category, though often one agent may hold both licenses. Because of the many regulatory and product changes in both areas, it is often recommended that a specialist in each area be selected to handle and coordinate the insurance program.

Life and Health

Life and health underwriting may be divided into the following areas: personal and business planning, business-continuation planning, employee benefits, and special benefits for key management. Establishing priorities and timetables for the acquisition of these benefits will be helpful. Two extremely important areas most often neglected are the businessperson's own personal and business planning. What are your priorities?

Personal Planning

When was the last time you and your spouse reviewed capital accumulation? Estate tax and liquidity planning? Family income protection? Disability income? Spouse's life insurance? Children's life insurance? Term insurance conversion? Will and trust-planning? Retirement planning? Charitable and family needs? Educational needs? Tax shelters? See your personal advisors for the coordination of your business and personal objectives. Can you use the corporate dollar to provide your personal security?

Business Planning

1. *Question*: What would you think of an idea whereby your firm could provide you with retirement benefits and disability income at an after-tax profit to the corporation?
   Comment: This refers to the utilization of a selective retirement and deferred compensation plan.

2. *Question:* Would you be interested in a plan that would enable your corporation to pay your spouse a tax-deductible dividend, and make a profit while doing it?
   Comment: This refers to a salary continuation plan with the insurance owned by the corporation and payable to the corporation.

3. *Question:* Would you be interested in seeing the nine ways in which you can get dollars out of your corporation completely free of income tax?
   Comment: The nine are: medical and dental reimbursement, group life insurance, split-dollar life insurance (explained below), pension plan, profit-sharing plan, individual retirement accounts (explained below), interest-free loans, Section 303 stock redemption (explained below), and disability salary continuation.

134

4. *Question:* What would you think of an idea whereby your corporation could carry your personal life insurance at up to a 25% discount?

   Comment: Transfer personal insurance to corporation under a split-dollar plan. The discount is due to the corporation being in a lower tax bracket.

5. *Question:* Would you be interested in an idea that could provide your family with additional tax-free income, and would enable you to make a profit from the plan?

   Comment: This refers to a split-dollar plan where the corporation would get back a factor for the use of its money in addition to the premiums paid.

6. *Question:* What would you think of an idea that would enable you to cut the inheritance taxes on your estate in half and then arrange for up to a 95% discount on the balance?

   Comment: This refers to the utilization of a trust arrangement in connection with insurance to pay the estate taxes.

7. *Question:* Would you like to see an arrangement that would double the benefits from your present life insurance program without increasing your annual cash outlay and with no reduction in guaranteed cash benefits at retirement?

   Comment: This refers to a piggyback arrangement where the cash value from an existing policy is used to help pay the premium on a new policy.

8. *Question:* Could you write a check today for one third of your net worth?

   Comment: This refers to the estate taxes that would ultimately be due.

9. *Question:* How much would you have to pay in estate taxes if your wife died?

   Comment: This is the estate-planning question that executives and business owners have totally disregarded.

10. *Question:* Do you enjoy paying taxes? Do you enjoy paying insurance premiums? If we could use tax dollars to pay your insurance premiums would you be interested?

    Comment: This refers to utilizing a pension or profit-sharing plan to acquire insurance with before-tax dollars.

11. *Question:* What steps have you taken to avoid the unnecessary double taxation of your estate?
    Comment: This involves the utilization of a trust arrangement.

12. *Question:* What are you doing to provide yourself (and your key employees) with special tax-favored benefits through your corporation?
    Comment: This refers to the utilization of selective retirement and deferred compensation plans and split-dollar, and so forth.

13. *Question:* What steps have you taken to ensure that your family gets the maximum value for your business interest?
    Comment: This refers to the utilization of insurance to fund a buy-and-sell agreement (explained below) and to provide additional benefits through salary-continuation plans, pensions, profit-sharing plans, and split-dollar life insurance.

Business-Continuation Planning

Key-Management Insurance. This is insurance owned, paid by, and the proceeds payable to the business entity. Premiums are not deductible. Indemnifies the employer for the loss of his most important asset, his key person.

Business Valuation. This is the determination of the "fair market" value of the business entity. It is a requirement for the business-continuation agreement.

Buy-and-Sell Agreement. This constitutes a plan to effect the orderly change in the ownership of a business at the death of the owner. It solves the problems of creating a market for the business interest, establishing a price at which the business agrees to buy and the owners agree to sell their interest, and providing the money to fund the plan.

Disability Buyout. This plan will effect the orderly buyout of a disabled owner.

Section 303 Stock Redemption. Within stipulated limits, a corporation can redeem part of a deceased stockholder's shares without the redemption price being treated as a dividend (taxable in full as ordinary income).

Employee Benefits

Group Insurance. Discounted insurance is available for a group of two or more employees. Most employers are convinced that such plans make employment more attractive or lead to greater productivity by their employees, or both. Plans include: major medical, dental, life, supplemental life, accidental death, and disability insurance.

136

Salary Savings. Payroll deduction programs can be made available to employees.

Individual Retirement Account. This is available to an employee under the age of $70\frac{1}{2}$ years who is not an active participant in: a qualified pension or Keogh plan (explained below), state or federal government plan, or a tax-sheltered annuity (explained below). Contributions are limited to 15% of annual earnings or $1500, whichever is less. If spouse is not employed $1750 may be contributed. Contributions are deductible from gross income, with no current tax on interest. Funding vehicles include: annuities, mutual funds, real estate, government bonds, and savings accounts.

Tax-Sheltered Annuities. This is available to employees of public schools and certain tax-exempt, nongovernmental organizations, (listed in Section 501(c) 3 of the Internal Revenue Code). Contributions to this plan, together with other employer-paid retirement benefits, cannot exceed 20% of "included income." Contributions are deductible from gross income. Funding vehicles include: annuities, life insurance, and mutual funds.

Keogh Plan (HR-10). This is available to anyone with income earned from self-employment. (Even if you are under a pension plan, you can qualify if you have "outside" income.) Contributions are limited to up to 15% of income earned by self-employment, not to exceed $7500 per year. Contributions are deductible from gross income. Funding vehicles include: annuities, life insurance, savings accounts, and trust or custodial accounts.

Corporate Pension Plans. These are available to employees of an incorporated business. Contributions are limited up to 25% of income from the incorporated business, not to exceed $32,000 or an annual amount that would provide a retirement lifetime income of not greater than 100% of pay. This annual amount may exceed 25% in some cases.

Corporate Profit-Sharing Plans. A profit-sharing plan is a corporate retirement plan in which annual contributions can be varied according to annual corporate profits. This is often combined with a corporate pension plan.

Other Retirement Plans. Other retirement plans include: stock bonus plan, savings or thrift plans, and employee stock ownership plans. Consult your professional advisor as to which plans best fit your personal needs.

Special Benefits for Key Management

Split-Dollar Life Insurance. This is a life-insurance plan for the executive, which provides personal insurance at a lower cost through the sharing of premiums. It enables the employer to retain key executives with a fringe benefit that has a minimal effect on current cash flow and surplus account. The employer pays the amount equal to the increase in cash value. The executives pay the balance. At death, the employer receives the cash value equal to his premium contribution and the executive's beneficiary receives the remainder of the face amount of the life insurance. Premiums are not deductible.

Bonus Plan. This is a corporate executive's personal life-insurance plan. The corporation gives the annual premium to the executive as a bonus. The executive or a third party applies for the policy. The executive pays the premium, or he makes a gift of the premium to a third party. The bonus to the executive is deductible to the corporation as reasonable compensation. The bonus is taxable ordinary income to the executive. Death proceeds are free of estate tax provided executive has no incidents of ownership.

Supplemental Group Term (Section 79). In this plan, the corporation pays deductible group term premiums on an employee's life. No income tax is attributable to the insured on the first $50,000 of term coverage. If the employee holds no incidents of ownership in the policy, the proceeds are received free of estate tax. This terminates at retirement.

Retired Lives Reserve. This plan provides term insurance during employment and sets up a fund to pay for continued coverage after retirement. The premiums are deductible to the corporation.

Deferred Compensation. Payment for current rendered services are postponed until a future date. This has the effect of postponing the taxation until the payment is received. A corporation may pay for its obligation by setting aside a fund composed of life insurance contracts, annuities, mutual funds, and securities, among other things, without adverse tax consequences to the employee, so long as the fund remains the unrestricted asset of the corporation and the employee has no interest in the fund. Corporate contributions are not deductible until received by the employee.

Low or No-Interest Loans. These have possible income and gift-tax consequences. Consult your personal advisors.

Property and Casualty Property and casualty underwriters have developed package policies that combine multiple-peril property coverage with comprehensive general liability coverage. While it is impossible to list all risks that should be considered, we have attempted to review the more common types. Three general divisions of concern are: loss of property (business and personal), loss of income, and loss due to legal liability.

138

Loss of Real Property   Loss can occur to business or personal property on or off the premises, in transit, or in the mail. These physical assets include: buildings, equipment, inventory, tenants' improvements, property of others, accounts receivable, and valuable papers. Damage to these assets can be caused by fire, windstorm, hail, explosion, riot, civil commotion, aircraft, motor vehicles, smoke, vandalism, theft, malicious mischief, earthquake, sprinkler leakage, flood, and many other perils.

Fire Insurance. With minor variations in some states, the 1943 Standard Fire Policy is used throughout the country. This covers direct loss caused by fire and lightning. Additional forms and endorsement may be added, such as:

1. *The Building and Contents Form* covers declared structures, all permanent fixtures, and machinery used in building service, i.e., air conditioning, boilers, and elevators. Several different locations may be covered.

2. *Extended Coverage Endorsement* extends a fire insurance policy to include all direct loss or damage caused by windstorm, hail, explosion, riot and civil commotion, aircraft, motor vehicles, and smoke.

3. *Vandalism and Malicious Mischief* is an endorsement to Extended Coverage which expands coverage to loss or damage caused by vandalism or mischief.

4. *Replacement Cost Endorsement* provides for full reimbursement for the actual cost of repair or replacement of property, without deduction for depreciation. This endorsement amends the "actual cash value" basis found in the standard fire insurance policy. In the basic fire insurance contract, the measure of actual cash value (loss) is the current replacement cost of destroyed property less an allowance for estimated depreciation.

"Named-Peril" and All-Risk Insurance. There are two general approaches used in drafting insurance agreements. The traditional one is the "named peril" approach. Only the perils specified in the policy are covered. Those not named, of course, are not covered. The other type of insurance policy is "all-risk." This covers all risks of loss to the described property except those perils specifically excluded.

Glass Insurance. This insurance covers replacement of plate glass windows and structural glass that is accidentally or maliciously broken.

Water Damage Insurance. This type of policy indemnifies all direct loss or damage caused by accidental discharge, leakage, or precipitation of water or steam. Sprinkler leakage and flood damage are not covered.

139

Sprinkler Leakage Insurance. Direct loss to building or contents caused by sprinkler installation leakage, freezing, or breaking is covered by this policy.

Earthquake Insurance. Insurance can be obtained to cover earthquake damage.

Improvements and Betterments Insurance. Improvements and betterments made by the insured to a nonowned building can also be insured.

Motor Vehicle Insurance. Motor vehicle insurance can be comprehensive or can cover only collisions.

Loss of Income

Income can be lost because of a reduction in earnings or rental income. Also, a loss can be due to increased expenses caused by damage to physical assets (see Loss of Real Property). Some common contracts are:

Business Interruption. The insured can be reimbursed for lost income due to interrupted business operations caused by specific hazards.

Contingent Business Interruption. When damage is sustained by a supplier, the insured can collect for losses due to his own interrupted business operations.

Extra Expense. You may sometimes need to conduct business in temporary quarters due to damage to buildings or contracts by fire or other insured hazards. This policy insures against additional expenses incurred under these circumstances.

Loss Due to Legal Liability

Loss due to legal liability can occur on premises, from operations, contracts, products, completed operations, automobiles, aircraft, and watercraft. The perils that can cause these losses include: bodily injury, property damage, personal injury, medical payments, professional liability, bailee's liability, employee injury, and inability to perform. Some of the more common contracts are:

Personal Injury. The insured is protected against injury due to false arrest, malicious prosecution, willful detention, libel, slander, or defamation of character.

Specified Liabilities. An individual or business can be insured for comprehensive general liability; owners', landlords', and tenants' liability; and contractual liability.

Umbrella Liability Insurance. General liability, automobile, and homeowners' liability policies may be extended to a greater specified limit.

Product Liability. This policy protects from loss due to claims arising from bodily injury caused by consumption or use of a product processed or sold by the insured.

Motor Vehicle Insurance. Endorsements are available to cover automobile liability, employer's nonownership liability, hired cars, medical payments, collision, comprehensive, and fleet plans.

Professional Liability Insurance. This policy protects professional people from third-party claims alleging bodily injury or property damage arising from the rendering of or failure to render professional service.

Bailee's Customers Floater Policies. Customers' property is covered while in the custody of the insured.

Worker's Compensation. Worker's compensation is social insurance designed to provide employers with common-law liability and workers with disability benefits. It covers employees who suffer on-the-job injuries or occupational diseases.

Surety Bonds. Surety bonds guarantee the performance of an obligation.

Crime Insurance. This policy covers theft and employee dishonesty.

Fidelity Bonds. These bond employees who handle merchandise or money.

License and Permit Bonds. These are usually required by law prior to acquiring a liquor, beer, and wine license.

TAX CONSEQUENCES

The following are tax-deductible corporation benefits:

1. Group insurance, including
   a) medical,
   b) life,
   c) disability,
   d) dental, and
   e) prescription insurance.

2. Medical reimbursement plans.

3. Qualified retirement plans, including
   a) pension plans,
   b) profit-sharing plans, and
   c) employee stock ownership plans.

4. Business overhead expense insurance.

5. Tax preferred personal life insurance.

6. $5,000 widow's death benefit.

Non-deductible corporation plans include

1. Key-man life insurance,
   a) stock redemption (including Section 303),
   b) split-dollar insurance,
   c) salary continuation, and
   d) deferred compensation (nonqualified).

Nondeductible individual plans are

1. Cross-purchase life insurance,

2. Cross-purchase disability insurance,

3. Split-dollar life insurance,

4. Personal estate-planning insurance, and

5. Salary savings.

Chapter 13 Purchase (Deposit/Receipt) Agreement Form

The professional business-opportunities salesperson must be familiar with all aspects of the contract form he or she is using. The offer represents all of the intentions of the buyer, and, once accepted, the seller's too. Before an attempt is made to write an offer, the salesperson should be familiar with all terms and conditions in the listing agreement as well as the information in the buyer's authorization form. This information is the basis for writing a reasonable offer for the buyer.

A complete transaction must have every variable defined clearly and legally. Complete every blank on the contract form. Fill in appropriate boxes. Define open-ended problems. Plan a solution and a completion schedule. All contingencies require a time limit. Protect the buyer and the seller.

To present an offer to a seller (review Chapter 4), a complete presentation package will be required. You are now selling the buyer, not the business.

The salesperson should have the following information available:

1. A purchase (deposit/receipt) agreement (see pages 147 through 157), signed by the buyer,
2. A listing agreement,
3. The buyer's financial statement,
4. The buyer's resume,
5. The buyer's authorization or business wanted agreement, signed by the buyer,

6. A letter of intent—to be presented to the landlord. (The seller must know the content of this last item if he or she is carrying a note on the business.)

This purchase agreement is for the business only, i.e., the "leasehold rights." Any real property involved should have *separate* agreements. Contact the local Real Estate Board for the necessary forms.

The salesperson will now begin to see some continuity of all the forms. The forms must contain the same information throughout. Otherwise there must be addendums or waivers of contingencies before proceeding to the next step. All forms must be accurate before they are taken to the escrow officer.

The purchase agreement is the same as the listing form (see Chapter 9), with the following exceptions. If the buyer agrees that the listing agreement is in order, then the agreement under discussion can just be copied, if not, add what the buyer wishes. Remember this is the buyer's offer.

DEPOSIT

The buyer must put up some type of collateral, usually a check payable to the escrow holder, as specified in the listing. However, a buyer might suggest something else to use as collateral. This would have to be negotiated. The broker may hold the money until acceptance of the offer by the seller. After the seller signs this form, he or she has agreed to sell and the buyer has agreed to buy the seller's business.

CLOSE OF ESCROW AND POSSESSION OF THE PREMISES

These two events are usually accomplished at the same time. It is not a good idea to allow a buyer to operate the business before escrow closes. The buyer usually wants to make changes. He may run up a big telephone bill or buy more merchandise. If the sale does not go through, it can cause many problems. In some states it is illegal to take possession before close of escrow.

After a buyer signs this agreement (see page 156), the offer is presented to the seller. If the offer is acceptable to the seller, then he or she signs it. If not, the seller writes "rejected" on the form and signs it. However, if the seller wishes to make changes, a counteroffer is made (refer to page 90), and the seller can check off - "The undersgned accepts all of the terms and conditions [above] except the following . . . ." Seller then signs

144

the agreement and the counteroffer agreement. This is then presented to the buyer for his or her acceptance or another counteroffer. Counteroffering can go on for several days, until the buyer and the seller agree on each and every point.

DECLARATION OF SATISFACTION AND WAIVER OF CONTINGENCIES FORM

The buyer states that he or she has made an independent investigation and is satisfied (see page 158). The buyer waives any and all contingencies that he or she has made, acknowledges having inspected this business, and states that he or she can operate it. The seller's financial statements, books and records are approved with a clear understanding that no profits are guaranteed. The buyer also agrees to (or assumes) the lease, contracts, agreements, and conditions, as specified. The total amount of money owed is spelled out. The payment rate is decided upon. The interest rate must be specified, along with the terms of the note.

A buyer usually agrees to maintain the insurance if there are any obligations to the seller, or his or her assignees, the seller being designated as first loss payee.

ESTIMATED CLOSING COSTS WORK SHEET FORM

Now that the business is about to change hands the buyer, and sometimes the seller, wants to know how much money will be needed at the close of escrow. When completing this form (see page 159), especially the part that deals with the utility companies, check the outstanding bills to see what deposit will be demanded from the new owner. (Note: If a higher than usual deposit is required, it generally means that the buyer is a questionable risk or there may have been problems in collecting from him in the past.)

BUYER'S AND SELLER'S CHECKLIST

This is a useful list (see pages 215 through 218) of names and addresses for the buyer (and the seller) of persons, companies, and government organizations that will be helpful when setting up a business where improvement and expansion is planned. (This list was prepared for Santa Clara County, California. Substitute names, addresses, and telephone numbers from your own area.)

145

SELLER'S REFUNDS

At the close of escrow the seller may have some deposits to be returned to him or her by various organizations, such as the utility companies and equipment companies (see pages 220 and 221). He or she may also want to pay off some bills that are outstanding, such as notes or loans. The seller generally comes out ahead at closing time.

PURCHASE (DEPOSIT/RECEIPT) AGREEMENT

For Brokers Use Only	
Mgrs. Initial	Date

Date_____19_____

DEPOSIT: Received from _____, called the "BUYER", the sum
of $_____, ☐ cash ☐ check or money order payable to _____
called the "ESCROW HOLDER". Broker is authorized to hold the deposit check until acceptance of that

certain business known as Fictitious Business Name (D.B.A.) _____

Name of Business _____

Address_____City_____State_____Phone_____

Owner(s) are ☐ individual/sole proprietorship ☐ husband and wife/sole proprietorship ☐ partnership
☐ limited partnership ☐ joint venture ☐ corporation ☐ corporation selling
tangible assets only ☐ other (specify) _____

Witnesseth: Whereas the Seller(s) agree(s) to sell and the Buyer(s) hereby agree(s) to purchase the above
described business from the Seller(s) on the following terms and conditions.

1. PRICE AND TERMS OF PAYMENT THROUGH ESCROW:

    Total purchase price $_____

    Downpayment (including deposit) of $_____ shall be paid at the opening of
    escrow. ☐ $_____ shall be paid 10 days before close of Escrow or on
    _____, 19_____, and the balance of the purchase price shall be paid as follows:

    A. ☐ Encumbrance(s) which Buyer(s) will assume and agree(s) to pay $_____
        with principal and _____% simple interest per annum on the unpaid balance included at
        $_____ or more per month. ☐ until paid, ☐ balloon payment due approximately
        _____, 19_____, in the approximate amount of $ _____
        ☐ free and clear of debt. Assumable ☐ yes ☐ no.

        Holder _____Address _____Phone _____

        Holder _____Address _____Phone _____

        ☐ Note Attached, ☐ will furnish note by _____, 19_____ and by refer-
        ence made a part hereof.

    B. ☐ Balance to Seller(s) as evidenced by an installment note and secured by the business
        assets as described herein, of $_____ with principal and _____% simple interest
        per annum of the unpaid balance, included at $_____ or more per month. ☐ until
        paid. ☐ balloon payment due approximately _____, 19_____, in the approximate
        amount of $_____.

147

Additional security required? ☐ no ☐ yes. If yes, interest to begin at the close of escrow, first payment due _____ days thereafter. This note is secured by furniture, fixtures and equipment and by the business assets described herein and as attached and by reference made part hereof. This note is due and payable in full upon the sale or transfer of this business by the Buyer(s).

C. ☐ Balance to Seller(s) of purchase price in the sum of $ _____ to be evidenced by a deed of trust to real property commonly known as

_____

Address _____City_____State_____Zip_____
and by reference made a part hereof.

☐ Legal assumption attached and by reference made a part hereof.

☐ Title insurance waived.

☐ Title insurance attached and by reference made a part hereof.

D. ☐ Inventory (usable and saleable) value approximately $_____ (at current wholesale cost) included in purchase price

☐ yes ☐ no. If no, how to be purchased? _____

_____

_____

E. Additional terms (specify): _____

_____

_____

_____

_____

2. ASSETS:

Except as otherwise stated below, price includes, but not limited to: all assets of the business, including business records, furniture, trade fixtures and equipment, work in progress, tools, supplies, leasehold improvements, telephone numbers, customer list(s), all trade name(s), transferrable permits, special license(s), sign(s), accounts receivable, goodwill, and all personal property used in business (all leasehold rights), including those of all real or personal property listed herein or attached hereto, or as otherwise specified in the agreement; and

(specify) _____

_____

Price also includes ABC License No. _____, ☐ on license ☐ on-off license

☐ beer ☐ beer and wine ☐ cocktail. Sales tax No. _____.

3. LIABILITIES:

Price excludes liabilities, including but not restricted to: the following listed cash, bank accounts, accounts payable, deposits, real estate encumbrance(s) as specified in this agreement, and (specify)

_____

_____

_____

4. INSTALLMENT SALE:

☐ yes ☐ no. If yes, must have at least one payment in subsequent years after the year of sale. (Value of covenant not to compete and inventory does not qualify as an installment sale.) Note must carry an interest charge of at least 9% annum simple interest on the unpaid balance. (This is a new 1981 Federal law—check your state laws.)

5. ALLOCATION:

For purposes of this agreement, the purchase price shall be allocated as follows:

A.	Accounts receivable	Estimated*	$ _____
B.	Inventory (at current wholesale cost)	Estimated*	$ _____
C.	Work in progress	Estimated*	$ _____
D.	Furniture, fixtures & equipment (market value installed)		$ _____
E.	Leasehold improvements (minus used up life)		$ _____
F.	Franchises, Trademarks and Trade names		$ _____
G.	License(s) ABC		$ _____
H.	Goodwill		$ _____
I.	Covenant not to compete		$ _____
J.	Lease value (residual and improvements, adjusted to market value)		$ _____
K.	Real property (improvements, buildings, etc.)		$ _____
L.	Real property (land)		$ _____
M.	Customer(s) list(s)		$ _____
N.	Customer(s) contract(s)		$ _____
O.	Other assets (specify) _____		$ _____
P.	Other assets (specify) _____		$ _____
	Total Purchase Price		$ _____

149

*The net amount of these three items shall be added or subtracted, as the case may be, from the amount due on the purchase price at the time of escrow closing. The actual value of these three items shall be determined by Buyer(s) and Seller(s) at time of closing escrow and adjustments, if any, shall be made at the close of escrow. Any variation in between estimated and actual values of either of these three items shall give Buyer(s) the option of paying ☐ cash ☐ increase Seller(s) note ☐ new note to the Seller(s) ☐ as follows:_____

6. SELLER(S) HEREBY WARRANT(S), REPRESENT(S), AND SHALL PROVIDE PROOF OF THE FOLLOWING:

   A. Seller is the legal owner of the above-described business and property and has full authority to execute this agreement, and warrants that he or she has written authority to do so for all Seller(s);

   B. That title to the assets of such business and property is free and clear from any liens and encumbrances, except as specified herein or as attached hereto;

   C. Seller(s) warrant(s) that the business premises, improvements, real property, equipment and machinery will pass all inspections necessary to conduct such business at the time of physical possession at the close of escrow;

   D. Seller(s) warrant(s) that all property that is necessary in the operation of its business shall be delivered at close of escrow in good working condition and repair, ordinary wear and tear excepted;

   E. Seller is not aware of any facts indicating that any customer(s) intend to cease doing business with the Seller or to materially alter the amount of the business currently being done with Seller;

   F. Seller has not received notice of any claim(s), litigation, investigation(s) or federal, state or local statute, law or ordinance or regulation, including building, redevelopment, zoning or other law, ordinance or regulation affecting its property or the operation of its business or any of the assets being sold, whether real or personal property;

   G. There ☐ is ☐ is not appended to and made a part of this agreement an addendum which discloses information which may be pertinent to the potential use of this business or property under terms of the Special Studies Zone Act;

   H. There ☐ is ☐ is not appended to and made a part of this agreement an addendum which discloses information which may be pertinent to potential use of this property under terms of the National Flood Control Act.

   I. Seller warrants that he has ☐ no sales tax number, ☐ no employees;

J. Seller will provide a good and valid bill of sale covering this business, free and clear of any liens and encumbrances whatsoever except these specified herein at opening of escrow;

K. Seller will provide or will transfer all the necessary licenses and permits necessary to legally conduct and operate this business described herein at opening of escrow.

L. Seller will supply clearance receipts from ☐ State Board of Equalization ☐ from Department of Benefit Payments before close of escrow;

M. ☐ Seller shall deliver at the opening of escrow the "pink slip(s)" to Motor Vehicle(s) described as follows:

_____

_____

Escrow holder is hereby instructed to deliver "pink slip(s)" to Buyer(s) at close of escrow. Buyer(s) agree(s) to pay sales tax on said motor vehicles as required by the Department of Motor Vehicles before close of escrow;

N. Seller(s) will conduct the business generally in the same manner as it is now conducted and as was represented to the Buyer until close of escrow;

O. Seller(s) represent(s) and warrant(s) that all information set forth in the escrow instructions and this agreement and any attachments thereto are true and correct as of the close of escrow and are effective as of that date. Seller(s) agree(s) that if all such representation and warranties are *not* true and correct and if this sale is cancelled for that reason, seller(s) agree(s) to pay the full commission on the sales price as specified herein, as if the sale had been consummated.

P. Seller(s) shall receive Buyer(s) note(s) as ☐ an individual ☐ community property ☐ joint tenant(s) ☐ tenant(s) in common.

Q. Seller(s) to train Buyer(s) or their employee(s)? ☐ yes ☐ no.
If yes, _____ hours per day, _____ days per week for _____ weeks
other (specify) _____at no charge,
Buyer(s) starting _____,19_____ and continuing through _____, 19_____.

R. Seller(s) hereby authorize(s) the Buyer(s), Buyer's Broker, agent, attorney(s) and escrow holder to contact the Seller(s) accountant, landlord, encumbrance holders, franchisors, vendors, attorneys, or anyone else connected with the above described business and all such parties are hereby authorized to give the Buyer(s), Broker, agent, attorneys and escrow holder any information requested about the business and property, whether real or personal being sold hereunder.

7. BUYER(S) HEREBY AGREE(S) TO ASSUME AND TO PAY THE FOLLOWING:

A. *Lease:* Approx. _____ *years left* at $_____ per month. Option to renew ☐ yes ☐ no.

If yes for _____ years at $_____ per month. Security deposit $_____.
Rent due in advance $_____. Lease ☐ attached ☐ will be furnished by _____, 19_____
and by reference made a part hereof.

Established _____year(s). Present Owner _____year(s)
Hours open _____. Days closed _____.
Estimated square feet _____. Type of seating ☐ table and chairs ☐ Booths ☐ Other

_____

Seating capacity: at bar _____, lounge _____, restaurant _____.
Parking capacity_____

Assumable ☐ yes ☐ no. Miscellaneous lease information:_____

_____

_____

_____

Landlord _____Address _____phone_____

Attorney _____Address _____phone_____

Accountant_____Address_____phone_____

Zoning Law _____ Restrictions _____

Buyer(s) acknowledge(s) that he has examined the said ☐ existing lease ☐ new lease
☐ option, and that he does accept the terms and conditions there of and by reference made a
part hereof.

B. CONTRACTS: ☐ medical plan ☐ dental plan ☐ 2 for 1 dinner plan
    ☐ brochures ☐ menu ☐ employee ☐ copyrights ☐ patents
    ☐ trademarks ☐ royalty ☐ Pension Plan ☐ profit sharing plan
    ☐ list of customers ☐ list of suppliers ☐ price list ☐ supply ☐ services
    ☐ formulas ☐ recipes ☐ advertisements ☐ other (specify)_____
    Contracts ☐ attached ☐ will be furnished by _____, 19_____ and by reference made
    a part hereof. Assumable ☐ yes ☐ no.
    Management will stay ☐ yes ☐ no. Remarks _____

C. *Business Franchise:* ☐ yes ☐ no. Franchise agreements ☐ attached ☐ will be fur-
    nished by _____, 19_____ and by reference made part hereof. Franchise fee $ _____.
    Franchise Transfer fee $_____. Franchise name _____
    Franchise address _____, City_____State_____Phone_____.
    Assumable ☐ yes ☐ no.

D. *Vending Machine Games, Equipment Leases, etc.:* (specify equipment)

_____

_____

152

Estimated total amount remaining to be paid on all equipment $_____,
with principal and _____% _____ interest included at $_____ total per
month. ☐ until paid ☐ balloon payment due _____, 19_____ of approximately $_____. Written contracts ☐ yes ☐ no. If yes, date expires _____
19_____.

Vendor's name _____ Addres _____ Phone_____

Vendor's name _____ Address _____ Phone_____

Contracts ☐ attached ☐ will furnish by _____, 19_____ and by reference
made part hereof. Assumable ☐ yes ☐ no;

E. *Furniture, Fixtures and Equipment:* ☐ included in sale ☐ not included in sale ☐ on
lease or owned by others. List(s) ☐ attached ☐ will be furnished by _____,
19_____, and reference made part hereof.

F. *MISCELLANEOUS INFORMATION:* _____

_____

_____

G. Buyer(s) agree(s) to ☐ attach ☐ will furnish by _____, 19_____ a financial
statement ☐ audited ☐ unaudited and by reference made part hereof;

H. ☐ Buyer(s) ☐ Seller(s) agree to maintain insurance to cover obligations under this agreement setting forth the ☐ Seller(s) ☐ Buyer(s) or their assigns as first loss payee as follows:
☐ fire ☐ theft ☐ comprehensive liability;

I. Buyer(s) agree(s) in addition to the purchase price to pay at opening of escrow sales tax on the
furniture, fixtures and equipment;

J. Buyer(s) shall take title to the business and property as ☐ an individual ☐ community
property ☐ a joint tenant ☐ tenant(s) in common ☐ partnership ☐ corporation

K. Buyer(s) warrant(s) that he or she has full authority to execute the purchase and sale agreement, and that he or she has written authority to do so for all buyers;

L. Buyer(s) has examined the Seller(s) financial statements, books and records and hereby approves same with a clear understanding that no one has promised or represented to him how
much net profit, "true net profit", gross receipts, "true gross receipts", or cash flow the
business generates and that all profits are future.

8. BUYER(S) AND SELLER(S) HEREBY AGREE AS FOLLOWS:

   A. Buyer(s) and Seller(s) hereby agree to pay all escrow fees, charges and costs as follows:
   ☐ one-half each ☐ seller(s) pays all ☐ Buyer(s) pays all ☐ other _____

153

For its ordinary services hereunder and upon acceptance of this escrow, the escrow agent shall be entitled to a fee of $ _____ payable concurrently with its acceptance hereof. Said fee is in addition to the total consideration being paid for the business and property. Additional escrow fee(s) shall be paid as follows: $ _____ for each creditor(s) claim in excess of three (3) paid through escrow, payable by seller(s). $_____ for each disputed creditor(s) claim, payable by seller(s).

B. List of work in progress, inventory, furniture, fixtures and equipment ☐ being conveyed ☐ not being conveyed ☐ on lease or owned by others shall be approved in writing by both parties at close of escrow.

C. ☐ Buyer(s) and Seller(s) shall immediately make application for the transfer of the ABC license at the office of Department of Alcoholic Beverage Control, _____. Buyer(s) agree(s) to pay such transfer fees and warrants that he is fully cognizant of the provisions of the State of _____ Alcoholic Beverage Control Act, with particular reference to his qualifications and eligibility and knows of no reason a license should be denied him. This agreement is conditioned upon such transfer.

D. Buyer(s) and Seller(s) agree that _____

_____Address _____

Phone _____are the Broker(s) and that _____

_____Address _____

Phone _____is the Escrow Holder.

E. Buyer(s) and Seller(s) hereby agree that if either delays the sale unreasonably during negotiations, and/or delays the delivery of any documents beyond the date promised, the period of delay shall be automatically added to the purchase and sale (deposit/receipt) agreement. The Seller(s) also agrees to the above and shall be automatically added to the listing term.

F. Buyer(s) and Seller(s) hereby agree to use diligence to transfer the assets of the business.

G. The closing of escrow and possession of the premises, business and property shall take place ☐ at the office of_____

_____at _____ on or after _____, 19_____ ☐ upon the transfer of the Alcoholic Beverage Control license, ☐ at such other time and place as the parties may have agreed to in writing and provided only that all contracts and escrow requirements have been met.

H. Buyer(s) and Seller(s) each agree that if it appears to the Broker and escrow holder that there will not be enough funds to pay in full any obligation of Seller(s) and listed in this agreement, such obligations shall be paid by the Buyer(s) instead of the Seller(s) at close of escrow and the purchasing price and down-payment to be paid by the Buyer(s) shall thereby be reduced accordingly.

I. Buyer(s) and Seller(s) each hereby agree that in addition to the purchasing price, there shall be prorated through escrow as of the close of escrow, personal property taxes, rents, interest charges, insurance and similar expenses.

9. CORPORATION:

If the property to be purchased hereunder is being purchased by a corporation, the person(s) signing these Purchase Agreements as Buyer(s) represent that he or they are duly authorized and empowered by the corporation's directors to purchase the business and real and personal property. A copy of corporate minutes approving the sales agreement is ☐ attached ☐ will be furnished by _____, 19_____ and by reference be made a part hereof.

10. COVENANT NOT TO COMPETE:

Seller(s) covenants to the Buyer(s), his successors, assigns and representatives that he will not engage, directly or indirectly, in any business the same as, similar to, or in competition with the business hereby sold within a radius of _____ miles from the principal place of business being sold for a period of _____ years from date of Buyer(s) possession, either as a principal, agent, manager, employee, owner, partner, stockholder, director or officer of a corporation, trustee, consultant, or otherwise in any capacity whatsover.

11. DEFAULT:

A. If Seller(s) through his own fault fails or refuses to complete this transaction as required, the Seller(s) shall thereupon pay the Broker the full Broker's commission, as specified in the listing or commission agreement.

B. If Buyer(s) fails or refuses to complete this transaction as required, the Deposit received, or part thereof up to the full amount of the commission, shall be paid to the Broker. The balance, if any, of the deposit shall be paid to Seller(s) as liquidated damages.

C. ☐ Default by Buyer(s), where Seller(s) hold Buyer(s) outstanding note on said business or property, including leasehold rights, whether real or personal, shall also occur whenever the gross sales or inventory of said business fall below 75% in any three consecutive months in comparison with the three consecutive same months in the previous year, allowing the net amount to be added or subtracted from the actual cost of living index, as determined by the federal government for the nation as a whole. Buyer(s) also agree(s) to furnish the Seller(s) a monthly Profit and Loss Statement within 10 days of end of each month during the period of said note. Upon such default Seller(s) shall have the option to repossess by due process in accordance with the Uniform Commercial Code the said business and property, including leasehold rights whether real or personal, excluding the Alcoholic Beverage Control license, by giving 10 days notice in writing to Buyer(s). Buyer(s) shall have the option to pay said note in full by giving 10 days notice in writing to Seller(s), excluding if an installment sale.

D. This offer shall expire unless accepted by _____, 19_____.

155

12. ARBITRATION:

All parties agree to any controversy or claim arising out of or relating to this contract, or the breach thereof, shall be settled by arbitration in accordance with the rules of the American Arbitration Association, and judgement upon the award rendered by Arbitrator(s) may be entered in any court having jurisdiction thereof.

13. HOLD HARMLESS AGREEMENT:

Buyer(s) and Seller(s) each agree that Broker, or its Agent, in bringing Buyer(s) and Seller(s) together has fulfilled its primary brokerage function and that Buyer(s) has examined the business and property, real or personal, Business Financial Statements and found the business and property suitable for use and has satisfied himself of his ability to conduct said business. Both parties agree to hold Broker, its Agent, attorneys and Escrow Holder harmless from any liability arising out of the sale of said business.

14. CONDITIONS AND TERMS:

It is expressly understood that these instructions contain all instructions of Buyer(s) and Seller(s) and conditions upon which the undersigned agree(s) to the transfer ownership of said business and property.

THIS IS A LEGALLY BINDING DOCUMENT. READ IT CAREFULLY. If you don't understand it, consult with your attorney and/or accountant. Broker and Escrow Holder are not authorized to give legal or tax advice.

Each of the undersigned has read the foregoing instructions, and by his signature hereto acknowledges that he understands and agrees with them.

Receipt of this Purchase (Deposit/Receipt) Agreement is hereby acknowledged.

X_____   Date _____, 19_____
  Buyer

_____   _____
Print name and title   Social Security No.

Address _____   Phone _____

X_____   Date _____, 19_____
  Buyer

_____   _____
Print name and title   Social Security No.

Address _____   Phone _____

X_____   Date _____, 19_____
  Broker/Agent

_____
Print title and name

156

Address _____   Phone _____

The above offer is hereby ☐ accepted.   ☐ We accept all terms and conditions above except as listed in counter offer. Dated _____, 19_____
Attached and by reference made a part hereof.
Broker's commission as agreed $_____.

X_____   Date _____, 19_____
   Seller

_____   _____
Print name and title   Social Security No.

Address _____   Phone _____

X_____   Date _____, 19_____
   Seller

_____   _____
Print name and title   Social Security No.

_____   _____
Federal I.D. No.   State Employer No.

Address _____   Phone _____

DECLARATION OF SATISFACTION AND WAIVER OF CONTINGENCIES

BUSINESS _____ADDRESS _____PHONE_____

In connection with the purchase (deposit/receipt) agreement with respect to the above described business, and as part of the escrow instructions, the undersigned buyer declares that he or she has made an independent investigation and hereby acknowledges his complete satisfaction and waives any and all contingencies.

Buyer has personally inspected this business and is satisfied that he or she has the ability to conduct same. Also, buyer has checked the seller's financial statements, books and records, and hereby approves same with a clear understanding that the profits are not guaranteed.

Buyer does agree to: ☐ lease agreement ☐ sub-lease ☐ new lease ☐ lease-option and by said agreement is by reference made a part hereof. ☐ Buyer does assume the following: ☐ contracts ☐ agreements ☐ conditions ☐ contingencies

(specify) _____

_____

_____

Balance owed of $_____ to be paid $_____ per month at _____% _____interest included and said agreement is by reference made a part hereof.

☐ Buyer agrees to maintain fire and theft insurance to cover the term of these obligation(s). One policy(s) or binder(s) shall set forth the seller, or his assigns, as first loss payee. ☐ Additional contingencies (specify) _____

_____

_____

_____

Executed on _____, 19____ at _____, _____

X _____   Dated _____, 19_____
   Buyer

_____
Print name and title

X _____   Dated _____, 19_____
   Buyer

_____
Print name and title

158

ESTIMATED CLOSING COSTS WORK SHEET

(Prorate Costs Where Applicable)

Dated_____19_____

Name of Business _____Address_____

_____

Customer's Name _____Phone_____

	Estimated Cost	
	Buyer	Seller
☐ Electric Co. – Service	$	$
☐ Electric Co. – Deposit		
☐ Gas and Oil Co. – Service		
☐ Gas and Oil Co. – Deposit		
☐ Sewer and Water Co. – Service		
☐ Sewer and Water Co. – Deposit		
☐ Telephone Co. – Service		
☐ Telephone Co. – Deposit		
☐ Service Co. (janitorial, rubbish, etc.)		
☐ Advertising – phone book		
☐ Advertising – other(s)		
☐ Accounting		
☐ Legal Fees		
☐ Rent – Security Deposit		
☐ Rent – First & Last Months in advance		
☐ Insurance – Business		
☐ Insurance – Fire and Theft		
☐ Insurance – Worker's Compensation		
☐ Intent to Sell – Notice Fee		
☐ License – Business		
☐ License – Health Department		
☐ License Permits (city)		
☐ License Permits (county)		
☐ License – ABC Liquor or Transfer		
☐ License – Other		
☐ Taxes – Unsecured Personal Property		
☐ Taxes – Real Property		
☐ Taxes – Department of Benefit Payments		
☐ Escrow Fees		

(Page 1 of 2)

☐	Taxes – State Board of Equalization	
☐	Downpayment	
☐	Other (specify)	
	TOTAL	

Prepared by _____ Phone _____
                          Agent/Broker

The above information is provided solely as a guide to some of the more common expenses involved when beginning a business. This information has not been verified by a Broker, his agent or an Escrow Holder, and they are not responsible for its accuracy.

Copyrighted, American Business Consultants, Inc. 1979 and 1980   *(Page 2 of 2)*

Chapter **14** Negotiations

When dealing with sellers, landlords, noteholders, lessors, creditors, and franchisers, negotiations require a lot of preparation and presentation. When the right answers to potential questions are presented in a straightforward manner, the battle is half won. The remainder is a matter of adjusting terms (needs) in a reasonable way that is fair to all parties involved.

First, review all terms and all conditions of leases, notes, and contracts. Check to see that the phrase "will not unreasonably withhold consent to assignment," is contained in the contract. If this phrase is not in the contract, the broker must get this commitment from the lessors and assignors.

Second, contact each lessor/assignor whose consent will be required for an assignment of lease, note, or contract. Establish a relationship of effective communication, confidence, and trust with lessors/assignors. Obtain from each party a commitment to assign, extend, or rewrite the lease, note, or contract. Determine revisions to existing conditions, terms, new applications required, or other demands.

ESTOPPEL-COMMITMENT METHOD

Estoppel means that a person is forbidden to contradict or deny his own previous statement, act, or position. It is not uncommon for a lessor/assignor to verbally agree to an assignment or revision of a lease, note, or contract with favorable terms to a buyer of a business, only to change his or her mind at crucial moments after the offer and just before the close of escrow. The estoppel-commitment method is designed to avoid problems of this nature.

161

First of all obtain a verbal commitment to assign, revise, or rewrite a lease, note, or contract, including all terms and conditions. Secondly, reduce the above to a written letter, stating all terms and conditions per your conversation, mentioning that the promises were very much appreciated. Thirdly, send the letter to the lessor/assignor (not his agent), purchasing a "Certificate of Mailing" from the Post Office. Finally, keep a copy of the letter with the "Certificate of Mailing." You have now applied the principle of estoppel along with the proof that the letter of commitment was mailed. This action will prevent a lessor/assignor from denying at a later date commitments made.

PREPARATION

Landlords and creditors are looking for buyers with a good credit rating, experience in the business, business plans, and ability to repay obligations. The following package should be prepared in advance of negotiations. It should contain most of the information required when negotiating with any of the parties in the transaction. The salesperson should make sure that there are enough copies of each of these documents for each party involved before negotiation proceedings commence:

1. Purchase (deposit/receipt) Agreement.
2. Buyer's Financial Statement.
3. Buyer's Resume.
4. Buyer's Authorization Agreement.
5. Letter of Intent.
6. Completed Lessor/Assignor Application.
7. Assignment forms.

Seller

A seller's attitude toward a buyer will be based (in most cases) on how strong the buyer is financially. Another point is that the seller wants a buyer who is able to run the business satisfactorily. A well-prepared resume and financial statements will create a good impression with the seller. The buyer wants the seller to accept his purchase offer and his financing terms. When a positive impression can be created in the mind of the seller, there is less reason for concern about the buyer's business abilities and the risk involved in carrying back financing. If the buyer signs the Promise Not To Disclose Information form (see page 117), it will put the seller more at ease. He or she will then be willing to show his or her books, records, and operating information to the potential buyer.

Landlords, Note-holders, Lessors, Creditors, and Franchisers

Each of these people has goals and motives. Try to analyze the position of each before making an appointment for a presentation. Generally their goal is to better their financial situations. There may be motivation for increase in security, potential long-term gain, property improvement, improved payment schedule, or an increase in business.

The approach to each of these parties is similar to the approach used for the financial statement (explained above) and is very important. In addition, try to get the following applications filled out: Assignment Forms, Purchase (deposit/receipt) Agreement, and a Prospectus of Business Intent (see page 164). These forms should include:

1. Redecoration plans.
2. Items to be repaired, replaced, etc.
3. New equipment purchase plans.
4. Changes to be made in product and/or service.
5. Time schedule and budget information to accomplish intended plans.
6. Advertising plans.
7. Growth projections of gross sales.
8. Management and organization plans.

A well-thought-out business plan will show each party the buyer's strength and positive direction. The potential buyer is asking the landlord, noteholder, lessors, creditors, and franchisers to invest in his or her ability. They need good reasons to believe in the buyer, a stranger, who is taking over obligations from a seller, whom they already know. Do not give them any reason to say no, but rather reasons to say yes.

LETTER—PROSPECTUS OF
BUSINESS INTENT

_____

_____ , _____

_____ , 19_____

_____

_____

_____ , _____

Dear Sir:

As prospective owners of _____ located at
_____ , we propose to implement several
changes for the purpose of increasing the gross sales of the Business.

My wife and I will be involved in the operation and management of
this business.

Several physical improvements, repairs, replacements are antici-
pated as follows:

The interior will be redecorated in Spanish decor, adding new tile,
wall paint, carpets, pictures and light fixtures. Repairs will be made to
the kitchen sink and a new stove will be installed to improve kitchen
thru-put time. The men's room wall tile will be replaced. We have bud-
geted $30,000 to accomplish these improvements.

Within four months from takeover of the business, we will have a
"Grand Opening," supported by a substantial advertising campaign with
10,000 announcement flyers which will be distributed in conjunction
with 6 months of heavy newspaper advertisement. We believe in substantial budget allocation for a continuing advertisement program.

We project that the improvements, serving Spanish food and with
Spanish decor, supported by advertising and good management, will
increase our gross sales by 40% within the year, and will greatly enhance the attraction of your shopping center.

Very truly yours,

_____
                                    Buyer

(Caution, use only the statements that are true.)

164

ASSIGNMENT OF LEASE

The undersigned Lessee(s) in that certain ☐ lease ☐ sub-lease dated _____,
19_____, covering the premises known as _____
_____Adddress _____, _____
do(es) hereby sell, assign, and transfer all our (my) right, title, and interest in and to the said lease, to
_____
_____

including lease deposit in the amount of $_____.

X _____   _____   _____, 19____
   Lessee   Address   Date

X _____   _____   _____, 19____
   Lessee   Address   Date

ASSUMPTION OF LEASE

In consideration of the above Assignments and written consent of the Lessor(s) thereto, I (we) hereby
assume and agree to be bound by all of the terms and conditions of the said Lease, dated _____,
19_____, and to pay the rental therein provided.

X _____   _____   _____, 19____
   Buyer   Address   Date

X _____   _____   _____, 19____
   Buyer   Address   Date

CONSENT TO ASSIGNMENT

The undersigned Lessor(s) hereby consent to the above assignment of Lease, waiving none of our (my)
rights thereunder.

X _____   _____   _____, 19____
   Lessor   Address   Date

X _____   _____   _____, 19____
   Lessor   Address   Date

165

ASSIGNMENT OF LEASE AS COLLATERAL SECURITY

For value received, the undersigned, Lessee in that certain lease dated _____, 19____,
covering premises known as _____
_____Address _____
does hereby assign and transfer all right, title and interest in and to said lease to the holder of that certain
promissory note dated _____, 19____, as collateral security therefore.

It is understood that the holder of said note shall not exercise any right as Lessee unless and until the
undersigned shall be in default under the terms of said note or the above mentioned lease.

Following a default under the note and/or lease, the assignee, at his election, may treat the undersigned as his agent, or licensee with respect to the latter's occupancy of the premises, and the parties acknowledge that the assignee may bring unlawful detainer or other legal proceedings should the undersigned fail to surrender possesion upon demand.

This assignment shall become null and void upon payment in full of all obligations of the undersigned
to the holder of said note.

X _____   _____   _____, 19____
    Lessee   Address   Date

X _____   _____   _____, 19____
    Lessee   Address   Date

CONSENT TO ASSIGNMENT AS COLLATERAL SECURITY

For value received, the undersigned Lessor hereby consents to the above assignment and grants to
the holder of said promissory note the right of substitution of a third party in the event of default in the
terms and/or conditions of said promissory note or lease. This assignment shall become null and void
when all obligations of the promissory note have been paid in full to the holder thereof. In the event a
default occurs under the terms and conditions of the lease, the Lessor agrees to give the holder of said
promissory note notice thereof within ten (10) days thereafter by registered or certified mail in order that
the same may be cured.

X _____   _____   _____, 19____
    Lessor   Address   Date

X _____   _____   _____, 19____
    Lessor   Address   Date

166

ASSIGNMENT—GENERAL

The undersigned in that certain _____
dated _____ day of _____, 19_____ executed by _____
_____

does hereby sell, assign and transfer all his (our) right, title and interest in and to _____
_____

including lease deposit in the amount of $_____.

X _____   _____   _____, 19____
    Seller   Address   Date

X _____   _____   _____, 19____
    Seller   Address   Date

ASSUMPTION OF ASSIGNMENT

In consideration of the above assignment, I (we) hereby assume and agree to be bound by all of the
terms and conditions of the above-referenced document, dated _____ day of _____,
19_____ and to make payments (if any) as therein specified.

X _____   _____   _____, 19____
    Buyer   Address   Date

X _____   _____   _____, 19____
    Buyer   Address   Date

CONSENT TO ASSIGNMENT

The undersigned hereby consent(s) to the above assignment, waiving none of our (my) rights contained in the above-referenced document dated _____, 19_____.

X _____   _____   _____, 19____
                              Address   Date

X _____   _____   _____, 19____
                              Address   Date

167

Chapter **15** Escrow Instructions

ESCROW PREPARATION

Before submitting documents to escrow, all parties—the real-estate sales-person, the buyer, and the seller—must review and complete the sales-person's checklist (see pages 101 through 104). This is to double-check that all the supporting documents are completed.

Complete the Estimate of Closing Cost Work sheet (see page 159). Check over buyer's Purchase (deposit/receipt) Agreement (see pages 147 through 157). Does it match the seller's Listing Agreement (see pages 77 through 88)? If they do not agree, there must be an addendum or a Waiver of Contingencies agreement attached spelling out the discrepancies (see page 158). The buyer and seller must agree to these contingencies.

Before all the parties are brought together with the escrow holder, the real-estate salesperson must review the escrow holder's checklist (before the escrow holder prepares all the documents) (see pages 213 and 214), and the escrow holder's duty to complete this transaction under the Uniform Commercial Code-Bulk Sale Transfer Law.

Once all the documents are prepared and typed a meeting can be arranged with the escrow holder and all the parties for their signatures. It is best that all parties be present at the same time in case there are some changes. If there should be any last-minute changes, or errors, they all can initial the changes as they come to an agreement, otherwise there will have to be further negotiations to acquire all the necessary signatures and initials.

The meeting is conducted by the escrow holder, who will go through each document and thoroughly explain each section and answer all questions. When everything is satisfactory to all parties, the escrow holder will ask the buyer and the seller to sign in the proper places.

When the escrow holder has finished his or her duty, the salesperson will go through the buyer's checklist (see pages 215 through 218), and check off what the buyer has to do and when. There will be a separate copy of the same checklist for the seller, telling him or her what to do and when to do it.

When the meeting is over the buyer and the seller should go through the checklists, especially if an Alcoholic Beverage Control License and Board of Health License are required. The ABC Form 207A must be posted near the front door of the business for a minimum of 30 days beginning the day it is posted.

While all parties are reviewing all the documents, completing their checklists, and waiting for escrow to close, each must be assured that the transaction is complete. The salesperson must go through the Salesperson/ Manager's Checklist (see page 219) before all parties return for the close of escrow to sign the closing statements (see pages 220 and 221). After escrow closes, the salesperson must be sure that all parties receive their proper copies of all documents.

1. *Escrow Instructions Form* (see pages 175 through 186). The continuity of all the forms can now be seen. Everything that the buyer and the seller have agreed to on the listing agreement and purchase (deposit/receipt) agreement must be copied exactly. All contingencies and waivers of contingencies together with all supporting documents are attached and made part of this agreement. Escrow instructions are the same as the Listing and Purchase Agreements except as follows.

9. *Escrow Holder's Duties* (see page 183)

   A,B) The escrow holder's duties include completing this transaction as laid down by law. He or she is only a stakeholder; that is, the escrow holder only holds all the documents, money, etc., until the law says that he or she can close a transaction. The escrow holder cannot give advice.

   C) The sale must be published in the local judicial district and in the local newspaper in the city and/or county where the business is being sold. The advertisement must appear in the newspaper for 12 business days before the sale closes.

   D) It is customary when opening escrow to file a Uniform Commercial Code (UCC)-3 form to check if there are any liens against the business. It is suggested that a second UCC-3 be filed at the exact time that escrow is scheduled to close. It was possible, in the past, that a seller could arrange a note on the business, wait until the first UCC-3 cleared, then complete his or her loan, complete the sale of the business during the next day or so, and collect the escrow money too. Of course, this is illegal, but it can happen. The filing of a second UCC-3 form exactly when escrow closes prevents this from happening, although this will hold up disbursement of the seller's proceeds.

E,F) The escrow holder must prorate cost as agreed. He or she must also pay the broker's commission (if there is one). Both parties must be aware of the amount of the commission.

G) Sometimes there are notes that will be replaced by money coming into escrow before it closes. This paragraph instructs the escrow holder to cancel or exchange the notes for money when received but not before all creditors are paid.

H) When the entire transaction is completed by law, escrow can be closed.

I) When notes are drawn up at the opening of escrow it is not known what date, exact balance of the notes, interest accrued date, or the date when the first payment is due as in many cases the exact closing date cannot be determined. For example, when an ABC license is involved, often it is not known on what date ABC will issue the license and escrow cannot be closed until the license is issued.

J) A seller cannot receive any monies until all clearance receipts are in the hands of the escrow holder.

K) Escrow holder must submit all creditor claims to the seller for approval or disapproval. However, if the seller rejects any claim it is customary to hold in trust with the escrow holder one and one-half times the disputed amount from a seller's proceeds at closing of escrow, and go ahead with the escrow. On resolving the disputes, the seller may return to the escrow holder with the properly paid bills and releases for his or her money.

3. *Department of Business Taxes Letter* (see page 187). This is all the information that is required by the Board of Equalization. Do not send them anything else, unless they ask for it.

4. *Employment Tax Field Office Letter* (see page 188). Treat this the same as the Department of Business Taxes letter.

5. *Commission Authorization Form* (see page 189). This is the seller's authorization to pay a broker's commission as agreed upon. The escrow holder is instructed to break down the commission and pay it accordingly.

6. *Covenant Not to Compete Form* (see page 190). This is the same as in the Listing Form (see page 86). For IRS purposes, this agreement must be a separate document. There are tax consequences (see page 68).

7. *Bill of Sale Form* (see page 191). The seller agrees to sell, transfer, assign, and agrees to warrant and defend this sale as specified in this agreement. Describe the property, all the stock in trade, fixtures, equipment, good will, and noncompetitive agreement of that certain (name of the business) at (address).

8. *Security Agreement Form* (see page 192). For value received, the debtor grants to the receiving party, a security interest in the property. The debtor shall not move, sell, or transfer without written consent of the secured party. Be sure to check off either "resale approved" or "resale not approved" by the secured party.

9. *Straight Note Form* (see page 193). This is a promissory note stating how and when payment will be made.

10. *Assignment of Note Form* (see page 194). This is an an agreement to sell, assign, and transfer all rights, title, and interest in a promissory note.

11. *Uniform Commercial Code (UCC)-1 Form* (see page 195). This will give public notice of the security interest and protect the interest of the second secured party (lender).

12. *Uniform Commercial Code (UCC)-2 Form* (see page 196). Any changes in the filing can be made by merely checking the appropriate box.

13. *Uniform Commercial Code (UCC)-3 Form* (see page 197). This is used by anyone interested in information as to possible liens on personal property that may be filed with the Secretary of State.

14. *Notice to Creditors of Bulk Transfer Form* (see page 198). Notice must be given to all creditors that a bulk sale is about to take place. State where and when. If not done properly, the sale is void, insofar as the creditors are concerned. They have rights to attach the property to satisfy their claims.

15. *Alcoholic Beverage Control License Forms* (see pages 199 through 209). It is strongly advised that all parties go to the ABC office and request the proper forms as the business exists and then request any changes or additions. There are many types and purposes of licenses. These forms are only the highlights of a typical ABC transfer. Its only purpose is to familiarize the parties with the typical questions being asked by ABC. They are interested mostly in the moral

character of the applicant. They also want to know if he or she has had any problems with the law where alcoholic beverages were involved, i.e., drunk driving, fighting, and so forth. A person can only be in either the wholesale or retail business, but not both at the same time. The ABC may ask where the business is located, is it in the vicinity of a church, school, or public playground? Where is the money coming from?

A diagram is required of the business floor plan. Check with the seller for the existing diagram. Find out if any changes in the layout have been made since it was drawn up.

Should the sale fall through make sure that the parties sign a "Notice of Withdrawal of Application" (see pages 207 through 209).

16. *Fictitious Business Name Statement* (see page 210). Any name that is used for business purposes that is not the true name of the owner, that is, if the owner's name is Charles Brown and he calls his business "Charlie's," then "Charlie's" is the fictitious name. This fictitious name must be filed not later than 40 days from the beginning of the business transactions. A fee is required for this filing and must be sent to the County Clerk's office at the time of filing.

    Within 30 days after a fictitious business name statement has been filed it must be published in a newspaper of general circulation in the county where the principal place of business is located, once a week for four consecutive weeks.

17. *Abandonment of Fictitious Name* (see page 211). This must be executed by the seller, published, and filed in the same manner as a fictitious name statement.

18. *Affidavit and List of Creditors and Unpaid Taxes Form* (see page 212). Sellers must list all creditors and unpaid taxes, as well as their indebtedness.

19. *Escrow Holder's Checklist* (see pages 213 and 214). This is a double checklist to ensure that the transaction is complete. The escrow holder has all the supporting documents for this transaction. Use the first column marked "in" when material received. Use the second column marked "comp" when item is completed.

20. *Buyer's and Seller's Checklist and Salesperson/Manager Checklist.* Often a buyer and seller do not know where to find certain names and addresses needed in their business for licenses, permits, transfers, and so forth. A list is given on pages 215 through 218 for Santa Clara, Calif. only. Substitute information for your own area.

    The salesperson/manager checklist (page 219) should be used to make sure all steps have been completed before closing escrow.

21. *Closing Statement* (pages 220 and 221). The closing statement is very important. It gives the escrow holder, the buyer's and the seller's final instructions in writing. For example: What is the actual inventory? Has the buyer accepted the keys? Is all the equipment working properly? Are all the assets listed in the escrow on the premises on the day of physical possession? Have all parties signed this form and given it to the escrow holder?

This statement must account for all monies and state what documents in this transaction must be delivered to the buyer and seller.

ESCROW INSTRUCTIONS

Escrow No. _____

Date _____ ,19_____

Business Name _____

Fictitious Business Name (D.B.A.) _____

Address _____City_____State_____Phone_____

Buyer(s) _____

Address _____City_____State_____Phone_____

Seller(s) _____

Address _____City_____State_____Phone_____

Owner(s) are ☐ individual/sole proprietorship ☐ husband and wife/sole proprietorship ☐ partnership ☐ limited partnership ☐ joint venture ☐ corporation ☐ corporation selling tangible assets only ☐ other (specify) _____

Witnesseth: Whereas the Seller(s) hereby agree(s) to sell and the Buyer(s) hereby agree(s) to purchase the above described business from the Seller(s) on the following terms and conditions, Escrow Holder is hereby instructed to proceed as follows:

1. PRICE AND TERMS OF PAYMENT THROUGH ESCROW:

   Total purchase price $_____

   Downpayment (including deposit) of $_____ shall be paid at the opening of escrow. ☐ $ _____ shall be paid 10 days before close of escrow ☐ or on _____, 19_____, and the balance of the purchase price shall be paid as follows:

   A. ☐ Encumbrance(s) which Buyer(s) will assume and agree(s) to pay $ _____ with principal and _____% _____ interest per annum on the unpaid balance included at $_____ or more per month. ☐ until paid, ☐ balloon payment due approximately _____, 19_____, in the approximate amount of $ _____.
   ☐ Free and clear of debt.

   Assumable ☐ yes ☐ no.

   Holder _____Address _____Phone _____

   Holder _____Address _____Phone _____

   ☐ Note attached ☐ Will furnish note by _____, 19_____ and by reference made a part hereof.

B. ☐ Balance to Seller(s) as evidenced by an installment note and secured by the business assets as described herein, of $_____ with principal and _____% simple interest per annum on the unpaid balance, included at $_____ or more per month. ☐ until paid. ☐ balloon payment due approximately _____, 19_____, in the approximate amount of $_____.

Additional security required? ☐ no ☐ yes. If yes, interest to begin at the close of escrow, first payment due _____ days thereafter.

This note is secured by furniture, fixtures and equipment and by the business assets described herein and as attached, and by reference made part hereof. This note is due and payable in full upon the sale or transfer of this business by the Buyer(s).

C. Balance to Seller(s) of purchase price in the sum of $_____ to be evidenced by a deed of trust to real property commonly known as _____

_____

Address _____City_____State_____Zip_____
and by reference made a part hereof.

☐   Legal assumption attached and by reference made a part hereof.

☐   Title insurance attached and by reference made a part hereof.

☐   Title insurance waived.

D. ☐ Inventory (usable and saleable) value approximately $_____ (at current wholesale cost) included in purchase price ☐ yes ☐ no.

If no, how to be purchased? _____

_____

_____

E. Additional terms (specify): _____

_____

_____

_____

_____

2. ASSETS:

Except as otherwise stated below, price includes: all assets of the business, including, but not limited to: business records, furniture, trade fixtures and equipment, work in progress, tools, supplies, leasehold improvements, telephone numbers, customer list(s), all trade name(s), transferrable permits, special license(s), sign(s), accounts receivable, goodwill, and all personal property

176

used in business (all leasehold rights), including those of all real or personal property listed herein or attached hereto, or as otherwise specified in the agreement; and (specify) _____

_____

Price also includes ABC License No. _____, ☐ on license ☐ on-off license ☐ beer ☐ beer and wine ☐ cocktail. Sales tax No. _____.

3. LIABILITIES:

Price excludes including, but not limited to: listed cash, bank accounts, accounts payable, deposits, real estate encumbrance(s) as specified in this agreement and (specify):

_____

_____

_____

4. INSTALLMENT SALE:

☐ yes ☐ no. If yes, must have at least one payment in subsequent years after the year of sale. (Value of covenant not to compete and inventory does not qualify as an installment sale.) Note must carry an interest charge of at least 9% annum simple interest on the unpaid balance. (This is the new 1981 Federal law—check your state laws.)

5. ALLOCATION:

For purposes of this agreement, the purchase price shall be allocated as follows:

A.	Accounts receivable	Estimated*	$ _____
B.	Inventory (at current wholesale cost)	Estimated*	$ _____
C.	Work in progress	Estimated*	$ _____
D.	Furniture, fixtures & equipment (market value installed)		$ _____
E.	Leasehold improvements (minus used up life)		$ _____
F.	Franchises, Trademarks and Trade names		$ _____
G.	License(s) (ABC)		$ _____
H.	Goodwill		$ _____
I.	Covenant not to compete		$ _____
J.	Lease value (residual and improvements, adjusted to market value)		$ _____
K.	Real property (improvements, buildings, etc.)		$ _____
L.	Real property (land)		$ _____
M.	Customer(s) list(s)		$ _____

177

N. Customer(s) contract(s) $ _____

O. Other assets (specify) _____ $ _____

P. Other assets (specify) _____ $ _____

    Total Purchase Price $ _____

*The net amount of these three items shall be added or subtracted, as the case may be, from the amount due on the purchase price at the time of escrow closing. The actual value of these three items shall be determined by Buyer(s) and Seller(s) at time of closing escrow and adjustments, if any, shall be made at the close of escrow. Any variation in between estimated and actual values of either of these three items shall give Buyer(s) the option of paying ☐ cash   ☐ increase Seller(s) note   ☐ new note to the Seller(s)   ☐ as follows: _____

6. SELLER(S) HEREBY WARRANT(S), REPRESENT(S), AND SHALL PROVIDE PROOF OF THE FOLLOWING:

A. That he or she is the legal owner of the above described business and property and has full authority to execute this agreement, and warrants that he or she has written authority to do so for all Seller(s);

B. That title to the assets of such business and property is free and clear from any liens and en-cumbrances, except as specified herein or as attached hereto;

C. Seller(s) warrant(s) that the business premises, improvements, real property, equipment and machinery will pass all inspections necessary to conduct such business at the time of physical possession at the close of escrow;

D. Seller(s) warrant(s) that all property that is necessary in the operation of the business shall be delivered at close of escrow in good working condition and repair, ordinary wear and tear excepted;

E. Seller is not aware of any facts indicating that any customer(s) intend to cease doing business with the Seller or to materially alter the amount of the business currently being done with Seller;

F. Seller has not received notice of any claim(s), litigation, investigation(s) or federal, state or local statute, law or ordinance or regulation, including building, redevelopment, zoning or other law, ordinance or regulation affecting its property or the operation of its business or any of the assets being sold, whether real or personal property;

G. There ☐ is   ☐ is not appended to and made a part of this agreement an addendum which discloses information which may be pertinent to the potential use of this business or property under terms of the Special Studies Zone Act;

178

H. There ☐ is ☐ is not appended to and made a part of this agreement an addendum which discloses information which may be pertinent to potential use of this property under terms of the National Flood Control Act;

I. Seller warrants that he has ☐ no sales tax number, ☐ no employees;

J. Seller will provide a good and valid bill of sale covering this business, free and clear of any liens and encumbrances whatsoever except these specified herein at opening of escrow;

K. Seller will provide or will transfer all the necessary licenses and permits necessary to legally conduct and operate this business described herein at opening of escrow.

L. Seller will supply clearance receipts from ☐ State Board of Equalization ☐ from Department of Benefit Payments before close of escrow;

M. ☐ Seller shall deliver at the opening of escrow the "pink slip(s)" to Motor Vehicle(s) described as follows:

_____

_____

Escrow holder is hereby instructed to deliver "pink slip(s)" to Buyer(s) at close of escrow. Buyer(s) agree to pay sales tax on said motor vehicles as required by the Department of Motor Vehicles before close of escrow;

N. Seller(s) will conduct the business generally in the same manner as it is now conducted and as was represented to the Buyer until close of escrow;

O. Seller(s) represent(s) and warrant(s) that said property is marketable and all information set forth in the escrow instructions and this agreement and any attachments thereto are true and correct as of the close of escrow and are effective as of that date. Seller(s) agree(s) that if said property is made unmarketable by any voluntary act and all such representation and warranties are not true and correct and if this sale is cancelled for that reason, seller(s) agree(s) to pay the full commission on the sales price as specified herein, as if the sale had been consummated.

P. Seller(s) shall receive Buyer(s) note(s) as ☐ an individual ☐ community property ☐ joint tenant(s) ☐ tenant(s) in common;

Q. Seller(s) to train Buyer(s) or their employee(s)? ☐ yes ☐ no. If yes, _____ hours per day, _____ days per week for _____ weeks other (specify) _____

at no charge, Buyer(s) starting _____,19_____ and continuing through _____, 19_____.

R. Seller(s) hereby authorize(s) the Buyer(s), Buyer's Broker, agent, attorney(s) and escrow holder to contact the Seller(s) accountant, landlord, encumbrance holders, franchisors, vendors, attorneys, or anyone else connected with the above described business and all such parties are hereby authorized to give the Buyer(s), Buyer's Broker, agent, attorneys and escrow holder any information requested about the business and property, whether real or personal being sold hereunder.

7. BUYER(S) HEREBY AGREE(S) TO ASSUME AND TO PAY THE FOLLOWING:

A. Lease: Approx. _____ *years left* at $_____ per month. Option to renew ☐ yes ☐ no. If yes, for _____ years at $_____ per month. Security deposit $_____. Rent due in advance $_____. Lease ☐ attached ☐ will be furnished by _____, 19_____ and by reference made a part hereof.

Established _____year(s). Present Owner _____year(s).
Hours open _____. Days closed _____.
Estimated square feet _____. Type of seating ☐ table and chairs ☐ Booths ☐ Other

_____

Seating capacity: at bar _____, lounge _____, restaurant _____.
Parking capacity_____
Assumable ☐ yes ☐ no. Miscellaneous lease information:_____

_____

_____

Landlord _____Address_____Phone _____

Buyer's Attorney_____Address_____Phone _____

Buyer's Accountant _____Address_____Phone _____

Seller's Attorney_____Address_____Phone _____

Seller's Accountant _____Address_____Phone _____

Zoning Law _____Restrictions _____

Buyer(s) acknowledge(s) that he has examined the said ☐ existing lease ☐ new lease ☐ option, and that he does accept the terms and conditions there of and by reference made a part hereof.

B. CONTRACTS: ☐ medical plan ☐ dental plan ☐ 2-for-1 dinner plan
☐ brochures ☐ menu ☐ union ☐ employee ☐ copyrights ☐ patents
☐ trademarks ☐ royalty ☐ pension plan ☐ profit sharing plan
☐ list of customers ☐ list of suppliers ☐ price list ☐ supply ☐ services
☐ formulas ☐ recipes ☐ advertisements ☐ other (specify) _____

_____

_____

180

Contracts ☐ attached ☐ will be furnished by _____, 19_____ and by reference made a part hereof. Assumable ☐ yes ☐ no.
Management will stay ☐ yes ☐ no. Remarks _____

C. Business Franchise: ☐ yes ☐ no. Franchise agreements ☐ attached ☐ will be furnished by _____, 19_____ and by reference made part hereof. Franchise fee $ _____.
Franchise transfer fee $ _____. Franchise name _____.
Franchise address _____, City_____State_____Phone_____.
Assumable ☐ yes ☐ no.

D. Vending Machine Games, Equipment Leases, etc.: (specify equipment)

_____

_____

Estimated total amount remaining to be paid on all equipment $ _____, with principal and _____% _____ interest included at $_____ total per month.
☐ until paid ☐ balloon payment due _____, 19_____ of approximately $_____. Written contracts ☐ yes ☐ no. If yes, date expires_____ 19_____.

Vendor's name _____Address _____Phone_____

Vendor's name _____Address _____Phone_____

Contracts ☐ attached ☐ will be furnished by _____, 19_____ and by reference made part hereof. Assumable ☐ yes ☐ no;

E. Furniture, Fixtures and Equipment: ☐ included in sale ☐ not included in sale ☐ on lease or owned by others. List(s) ☐ attached ☐ will be furnished by _____, 19_____, and reference made part hereof.

F. MISCELLANEOUS INFORMATION: _____

_____

_____

G. Buyer(s) agree(s) to ☐ attach ☐ furnish by _____, 19_____ a financial statement ☐ audited ☐ unaudited and by reference made part hereof;

H. ☐ Buyer(s) ☐ Seller(s) agree to maintain insurance to cover obligations under this agreement setting forth the ☐ Seller(s) ☐ Buyer(s) or their assigns as first loss payee as follows: ☐ fire ☐ theft ☐ comprehensive liability;

I. Buyer(s) agree(s) in addition to the purchase price to pay at opening of escrow sales tax on the furniture, fixtures and equipment;

181

J. Buyer(s) shall take title to the business and property as ☐ an individual ☐ community property ☐ a joint tenant ☐ tenant(s) in common ☐ partnership ☐ corporation;

K. Buyer(s) warrant(s) that he or she has full authority to execute the purchase and sale agreement, and that he or she has written authority to do so for all buyers;

L. Buyer(s) has examined the Seller(s) financial statements, books and records and hereby approves same with a clear understanding that no one has promised or represented to him how much net profit, "true net profit", gross receipts, "true gross receipts", or cash flow the business generates and that all profits are future.

8. BUYER(S) AND SELLER(S) HEREBY AGREE AS FOLLOWS:

A. Buyer(s) and Seller(s) hereby agree to pay all escrow fees, charges and costs as follows: ☐ one-half each ☐ seller(s) pays all ☐ Buyer(s) pays all ☐ other _____ For its ordinary services hereunder and upon acceptance of this escrow, the escrow agent shall be entitled to a fee of $_____, payable concurrently with its acceptance hereof. Said fee is in addition to the total consideration being paid for the business and property. Additional escrow fee(s) shall be paid as follows: $ _____ for each creditor(s) claim in excess of three (3) paid through escrow, payable by seller(s). $_____ for each disputed creditor(s) claim, payable by seller(s).

B. List of work in progress, inventory, furniture, fixtures and equipment ☐ being conveyed ☐ not being conveyed ☐ on lease or owned by others shall be approved in writing by both parties at close of escrow.

C. ☐ Buyer(s) and Seller(s) shall immediately make application for the transfer of the ABC license at the office of Department of Alcoholic Beverage Control, _____. Buyer(s) agree(s) to pay such transfer fees and warrants that he is fully cognizant of the provisions of the State of _____ Alcoholic Beverage Control Act, with particular reference to his qualifications and eligibility and knows of no reason a license should be denied him. This agreement is conditioned upon such transfer.

D. Buyer(s) and Seller(s) agree that _____

_____Address _____

Phone _____are the Broker(s) and that _____

_____Address _____

Phone _____is the Escrow Holder.

E. Buyer(s) and Seller(s) hereby agree that if either delays the sale unreasonably during negotiations, and/or delays the delivery of any documents beyond the date promised, the period of delay shall be automatically added to the purchase and sale (deposit/receipt) agreement and the escrow instructions. The Seller(s) also agrees to the above and shall be automatically added to the listing term.

182

F. Buyer(s) and Seller(s) hereby agree to use diligence to transfer the assets of the business.

G. The closing of escrow and possession of the premises, business and property shall take place
    ☐ at the office of _____

    _____ at _____ on or after _____, 19_____
    ☐ upon the transfer of the Alcoholic Beverage Control license, ☐ at such other time and
    place as the parties may have agreed to in writing and provided only that all contracts and
    escrow requirements have been met.

H. Buyer(s) and Seller(s) each agree that if it appears to the Broker and escrow holder that there
    will not be enough funds to pay broker's commission in full as listed in this agreement, such
    obligations shall be paid by the Buyer(s) instead of the Seller(s) at close of escrow and the pur-
    chasing price and downpayment to be paid by the Buyer(s) shall thereby be reduced accord-
    ingly.

I. Buyer(s) and Seller(s) each hereby agree that in addition to the purchase price, there shall be
    prorated through escrow as of the close of escrow, personal property taxes, rents, interest
    charges, insurance and similar expenses.

9. ESCROW HOLDER'S DUTIES:

A. To complete this transaction in accordance with the Bulk Transfer Division of the Uniform
    Commercial Code and as set forth herein by the closing date of escrow as set forth herein;

B. Buyer(s) and Seller(s) agree that escrow holder liabilities herein are that of stakeholder only;

C. At the expense of the parties herein, to record and publish in a newspaper located in judicial
    district in the county of _____, at least twelve (12) business days prior to
    the date of transfer a notice to creditors of bulk sale transfer;

D. File two financing statements with the Secretary of State, one upon execution of this docu-
    ment, and one upon close of escrow; and to request UCC-3 information with respect to all
    liens against the business and property, whether real or personal. The Seller(s) shall not re-
    ceive any disbursement of funds until the second statement has been received in escrow with
    certificates to be delivered to Buyer;

E. To prorate costs as of the day of possession as specified herein;

F. To pay a brokerage commission of $_____. Commission authorization agreement
    attached hereto and made a part hereof;

G. All note(s) herein are to be exchanged or cancelled at close of escrow only after all creditor(s)
    claim(s) have been satisfied pursuant to Section _____ of the _____ Business and Pro-
    fessions Code;

183

H. To distribute the monies and documents to the respective parties when both UCC-3 statements have been received in escrow without further notice or authorization;

I. Without further notice or authorization, to insert on all note(s) security agreement(s) and other documents herein, the principal balance of the encumbrance, the interest accrued date and the date of first payment as determined at close of escrow;

J. Not to disburse funds to the Seller(s) until the clearance receipts from State Board of Equalization and Department of Benefit Payments have been received in escrow;

K. To submit all claims to Seller(s) for his approval or disposition on or before the date specified in the notice to creditors of escrow closing date.

10. CORPORATION:

If the property is to be sold or purchased by a corporation, the person(s) signing these escrow instructions as Owner(s) and/or Buyer(s) represent that he or they are duly authorized and empowered by the corporation's directors to sell or purchase the business and real or personal property. A copy of corporate minutes approving the sales agreement is ☐ attached ☐ will be furnished by _____, 19_____ and by reference be made a part hereof.

11. COVENANT NOT TO COMPETE:

Seller(s) covenants to the Buyer(s), his successors, assigns and representatives that he will not engage, directly or indirectly, in any business the same as, similar to, or in competition with the business hereby sold within a radius of _____ miles from the principal place of business being sold for a period of _____ years from date of Buyer(s) possession, either as a principal, agent, manager, employee, owner, partner, stockholder, director or officer of a corporation, trustee, consultant, or otherwise in any capacity whatsoever.

12. DEFAULT:

A. If Seller(s) fail(s) or refuse(s) to complete this transaction as required, the Seller(s) shall thereupon pay the Broker the full Broker's commission, as specified in the listing or commission agreement.

B. If Buyer(s) fails or refuses to complete this transaction as required, the Deposit received, or part thereof up to the full amount of the commission, shall be paid to the Broker. The balance, if any, of the deposit shall be paid to Seller(s) as liquidated damages.

C. ☐ Default by Buyer(s), where Seller(s) hold Buyer(s) outstanding note on said business or property, including leasehold rights, whether real or personal, shall also occur whenever the gross sales or inventory of said business fall below 75% in any three consecutive months in comparison with the three consecutive same months in the previous year, allowing the net amount to be added or subtracted from the actual cost of living index, as determined by the federal government for the nation as a whole. Buyer(s) also agree(s) to furnish the Seller(s) a monthly Profit and Loss Statement within 10 days of end of each month during the period of said note. Upon such default Seller(s) shall have the option to repossess by due process in accordance with the Uniform Commercial Code the said business and property, including leasehold rights, whether real or personal, excluding the Alcoholic Beverage Control license, by giving 10 days notice in writing to Buyer(s). Buyer(s) shall have the option to pay said note in full by giving 10 days notice in writing to Seller(s), excluding if an installment year.

13. ARBITRATION:

All parties agree to any controversy or claim arising out of or relating to this contract, or the breach thereof, shall be settled by arbitration in accordance with the rules of the American Arbitration Association, and judgement upon the award rendered by Arbitrator(s) may be entered in any court having jurisdiction thereof.

14. HOLD HARMLESS AGREEMENT:

Buyer(s) and Seller(s) each agree that Broker, or its Agent, in bringing Buyer(s) and Seller(s) together has fulfilled its primary brokerage function and that Buyer(s) has examined the business and property, real or personal, Business Financial Statements and found the business and property suitable for use and has satisfied himself of his ability to conduct said business. Both parties agree to hold Broker, its Agent, attorneys and Escrow Holder harmless from any liability arising out of the sale of said business.

15. CONDITIONS AND TERMS:

It is expressly understood that these escrow instructions contain all instructions of Buyer(s) and Seller(s) and conditions upon which the undersigned agree(s) to the transfer of ownership of said business and property.

THIS IS A LEGALLY BINDING DOCUMENT. READ IT CAREFULLY. If you don't understand it, consult with your attorney and/or accountant. Broker and Escrow Holder are not authorized to give legal or tax advice.

Each of the undersigned has read the foregoing instructions, and by his signature hereto acknowledges that he understands and agrees with them.

Receipt of these escrow instructions are hereby acknowledged.

X_____ Date _____, 19_____
   Buyer

_____ _____
Print name and title   Social Security No.

Address _____ Phone _____

X_____ Date _____, 19_____
   Buyer

185

Print name and title

Address _____

X_____
   Seller

Social Security No. _____

Phone _____

Date _____, 19_____

Print name and title

Address _____

X_____
   Seller

Social Security No. _____

Phone _____

Date _____, 19_____

Print name and title

Federal I.D. No.

Address _____

X_____
   Escrow Holder

Social Security No. _____

State Employer No.

Phone _____

Date _____, 19_____

Copyrighted, American Business Consultants, Inc. 1979 and 1980

_____

_____ , _____

Date _____ , 19_____

Escrow No. _____

Department of Business Taxes
Board of Equalization

State of _____

_____

_____ , _____

Name of Business: _____

Address: _____

Your Account No. _____

Name of Seller(s) _____

Address: _____

Name of Buyer(s) _____

Address: _____

Sales Tax No. _____

Fixture and Equipment Value $ _____

Purchase Price $ _____

Gentlemen:

We hereby request, on behalf of the Buyers, that you issue a "Clearance Certificate" after your requirements have been met with respect to above-referenced sale. Please forward said certificate to the undersigned, in accordance with your current procedures.

Very truly yours,

_____

Escrow Holder

187

_____

_____ , _____

Date _____ , 19_____

Escrow No. _____

Employment Tax Field Office
Department of Benefit Payments

State of _____

_____

_____ , _____

Name of Business:_____

Address: _____

Your Account No. _____

Name of Seller(s) _____

Address: _____

Name of Buyer(s) _____

Address: _____

Closing Date: _____

Gentlemen:

We hereby request, on behalf of the Buyers, that you issue a "Clearance Certificate" after your requirements have been met, with respect to above-referenced sale. Please forward said certificate to the undersigned, in accordance with Section 18802.8 to 18826 inclusive of the Revenue and Taxation Code and Section 1732 (a) of the Unemployment Insurance Code.

Very truly yours,

_____
Escrow Holder

188

COMMISSION AUTHORIZATION

To Escrow Holder _____Escrow Number_____

    You are hereby authorized and instructed by the undersigned principal of (Name of Business) _____
_____(Address)_____
to pay upon the close of escrow to (Broker) _____
Address _____a broker's commission in the total sum of $_____
for services rendered and completed. Please mail payments directly to the following: (on the closing statement, do not itemize them; list only the total paid as "Broker's Commission.")

Broker (above) $ _____

Associated Broker $ _____   Name _____Address _____

Listing Salesperson $_____   Name _____Address _____

Selling Salesperson $_____   Name _____Address _____

Finders Fee $ _____   Name _____Address _____

Misc. (specify) $ _____   Name _____Address _____

    This order is irrevocable on the part of the undersigned, unless the consent of the Broker is obtained
in writing.

Executed on _____, 19_____ at _____, _____.

X_____   Dated _____, 19_____
  Seller

_____
Print name and title

X_____   Dated _____, 19_____
  Seller

_____
Print name and title

                            Very truly yours,

                        _____
                        Broker/Agent

189

COVENANT NOT TO COMPETE

Escrow Number_____

Business Name_____Address_____Phone_____

    Seller does covenant to the Buyer, his successor and assigns, that he will not engage, directly or indirectly, in any business similar to or in competition with the business hereby sold within a radius of _____ miles from the premises at (address)_____ for a period of _____ years from the date of Buyer's possession thereof, either as a principal, agent, manager, employee, owner, partner, stockholder, director or officer of a corporation, trustee or consultant, or otherwise in any other capacity or be connected therewith in any other manner.

    The value placed on this covenant is the sum of $ _____.

    Executed on_____, 19_____ at _____, _____.

X_____   Dated _____, 19_____.
  Seller

_____
Print name and title

X_____   Dated _____, 19_____.
  Seller

_____
Print name and title

X_____   Dated _____, 19_____.
  Buyer

_____
Print name and title

X_____   Dated _____, 19_____.
  Buyer

_____
Print name and title

BILL OF SALE

For a valuable consideration paid and received _____

_____
(Seller)

hereby sells and conveys to _____

_____
(Buyer)

his executors, administrators and assigns the following property:

Seller for his heirs, executors and administrators, covenants and agrees to warrant and defend this sale of said property, goods and chattels, against all and every person and persons claiming the same.

Executed at _____ , _____ on Date _____ , 19_____.

X_____   Date _____ , 19_____.
   Seller(s)

_____
Print name and title

X_____   Date _____ , 19_____.
   Buyer(s)

_____
Print name and title

191

SECURITY AGREEMENT

For value received, _____

_____
(Name and address of Debtor)

hereafter called debtor, grants to_____

_____
(Name and address of Secured Party)

hereafter called secured party, a security interest in the following described property, hereafter called collateral, to secure payment of the following obligations of debtor to secured party and of performance of this agreement, hereafter called the obligations:

Said collateral is described as follows:

1. Debtor shall not sell or offer to sell, transfer, assign, mortgage, pledge, lease, rent, bail or encumber the collateral, or any part thereof or interest therein, or remove same, or any part thereof, from the state, without written consent of secured party first had and obtained; except that if this agreement is subscribed "resale approved", the debtor, so long as he is not in default hereunder, may, in the regular course of his business, sell the collateral for cash, or on terms approved in advance by secured party, for not less than the minimum sales prices set opposite said respective collateral.

2. Secured party may insure collateral against the hazards of fire and theft during the term hereof in the amount of its replacement and debtor agrees to pay the premiums and charges for such insurance to secured party on demand.

3. Secured party may inspect the collateral at any reasonable time, wherever located.

4. Debtor agrees to keep the collateral in good order and repair at all times and to keep the same free of liens and encumbrances.

5. Debtor agrees to pay when due all taxes and assessments on the collateral. Secured party must pay taxes or assessments on the collateral not satisfied by debtor on or before the due date thereof. Debtor agrees on demand to reimburse secured party for any such payment.

6. The following constitute defaults under this agreement: default in payment or performance of any obligation, agreement, term or condition of this agreement, insolvency of or insolvency proceedings by or against the debtor, as such terms are defined in the _____ Uniform Commercial Code; attachment of or levy upon the collateral, or any part thereof; damage or destruction of or loss or theft of the collateral, or any part thereof; or sale, termination or failure of the business of debtor.

In the event of any default hereunder secured party may declare immediately due and payable all obligations secured hereby and shall have all remedies accorded a secured party by the _____ Uniform Commercial Code. If action is commenced to enforce any term or provision hereof or to collect any moneys due or which may become due hereunder, debtor agrees to pay reasonable attorney's fees.

Executed in duplicate at _____, _____, on _____, 19_____

☐ Resale Approved
☐ Resale Not Approved

X_____
  Debtor

X_____
  Secured Party

_____
Print name and address

_____
Print name and title

Receipt of duplicate copy of the foregoing agreement is hereby acknowledged:

X_____
  Debtor

192

STRAIGHT NOTE

$ _____ , _____ , _____ , 19_____

_____after date, for value received,

I promise to pay_____

_____, or order, at

_____

the sum of _____DOLLARS

with _____ interest from _____, until paid at

the rate of_____per cent annum, payable_____

_____

_____

_____

_____

_____

_____

_____

_____

_____

_____

_____

_____

_____

Principal and interest payable in lawful money of the United States of America. Should interest not be so paid it shall thereafter bear like interest as the principal, but such unpaid interest so compounded shall not exceed an amount equal to simple interest on the unpaid principal at the maximum rate permitted by law. Should default be made in payment of any installment of principal or interest when due the whole sum of principal and interest shall become immediately due at the option of the holder of this note. If action is instituted on this note I promise to pay such sum as the Court may fix as Attorney's fees. This note is secured by

X_____   X_____
  Seller   Buyer

_____   _____
Print name and title   Print name and title

_____   _____
Address   Address

193

ASSIGNMENT OF NOTE

FOR VALUE RECEIVED, THE UNDERSIGNED DOES HEREBY SELL, ASSIGN AND TRANSFER ALL OF HIS/HER RIGHT, TITLE AND INTEREST IN AND TO THAT CERTAIN NOTE, DATED _____,
IN THE PRINCIPAL AMOUNT OF $_____, IN WHICH _____
IS THE MAKER AND_____
IS THE PAYEE: TO

_____, WITH/WITHOUT
RECOURSE.

Executed at _____, _____, on Date _____, 19_____.

X_____   Date _____, 19_____.

_____
Print name and title

_____
Address

X_____   Date _____, 19_____.

_____
Print name and title

_____
Address

X_____   Date _____, 19_____.

_____
Print name and title

_____
Address

UCC-1   This FINANCING STATEMENT is presented for filing pursuant to the California Uniform Commercial Code.

1. DEBTOR (LAST NAME FIRST - IF AN INDIVIDUAL)		1A. SOCIAL SECURITY OR FEDERAL TAX NO.
1B. MAILING ADDRESS	1C. CITY, STATE	1D. ZIP CODE
2. ADDITIONAL DEBTOR (IF ANY) (LAST NAME FIRST - IF AN INDIVIDUAL)		2A. SOCIAL SECURITY OR FEDERAL TAX NO.
2B. MAILING ADDRESS	2C. CITY, STATE	2D. ZIP CODE
3. DEBTOR'S TRADE NAMES OR STYLES (IF ANY)		3A. FEDERAL TAX NUMBER

4. SECURED PARTY — 4A. SOCIAL SECURITY NO., FEDERAL TAX NO. OR BANK TRANSIT AND A.B.A. NO.
NAME
MAILING ADDRESS
CITY   STATE   ZIP CODE

5. ASSIGNEE OF SECURED PARTY (IF ANY) — 5A. SOCIAL SECURITY NO., FEDERAL TAX NO. OR BANK TRANSIT AND A.B.A. NO.
NAME
MAILING ADDRESS
CITY   STATE   ZIP CODE

6. This FINANCING STATEMENT covers the following types or items of property **(include description of real property on which located and owner of record when required by instruction 4).**

7. CHECK IF APPLICABLE ☒   7A. ☐ PRODUCTS OF COLLATERAL ARE ALSO COVERED   7B. DEBTOR(S) SIGNATURE NOT REQUIRED IN ACCORDANCE WITH INSTRUCTION 5(A) ITEM: ☐(1) ☐(2) ☐(3) ☐(4)

8. CHECK IF APPLICABLE ☒   ☐ DEBTOR IS A "TRANSMITTING UTILITY" IN ACCORDANCE WITH UCC § 9105 (1) (N)

9. ▶ SIGNATURE(S) OF DEBTOR(S)   DATE:

TYPE OR PRINT NAME(S) OF DEBTOR(S)

▶ SIGNATURE(S) OF SECURED PARTY(IES)

TYPE OR PRINT NAME(S) OF SECURED PARTY(IES)

CODE: 1 2 3 4 5 6 7 8 9 0

10. THIS SPACE FOR USE OF FILING OFFICER (DATE, TIME, FILE NUMBER AND FILING OFFICER)

11. Return copy to:
NAME
ADDRESS
CITY
STATE
ZIP CODE

(1) FILING OFFICER COPY   FORM UCC.1 - FILING FEE $3.00
Approved by the Secretary of State

UCC-2   This **STATEMENT** is presented for filing pursuant to the California Uniform Commercial Code

1. FILE NO OF ORIG FINANCING STATEMENT	1A. DATE OF FILING OF ORIG FINANCING STATEMENT	1B. DATE OF ORIG FINANCING STATEMENT	1C. PLACE OF FILING ORIG FINANCING STATEMENT

2. DEBTOR (LAST NAME FIRST)	2A. SOCIAL SECURITY OR FEDERAL TAX NO

2B. MAILING ADDRESS	2C. CITY, STATE	2D. ZIP CODE

3. ADDITIONAL DEBTOR (IF ANY) (LAST NAME FIRST)	3A. SOCIAL SECURITY OR FEDERAL TAX NO

3B. MAILING ADDRESS	3C. CITY, STATE	3D. ZIP CODE

4. SECURED PARTY   4A. SOCIAL SECURITY NO FEDERAL TAX NO OR BANK TRANSIT AND A B A NO

    NAME

    MAILING ADDRESS

    CITY   STATE   ZIP CODE

5. ASSIGNEE OF SECURED PARTY (IF ANY)   5A. SOCIAL SECURITY NO FEDERAL TAX NO OR BANK TRANSIT AND A B A NO

    NAME

    MAILING ADDRESS

    CITY   STATE   ZIP CODE

6.

    A. CONTINUATION-The original Financing Statement between the foregoing Debtor and Secured Party bearing the file number and date shown above is continued. If collateral is crops or timber, check here ☐ and insert description of real property on which growing or to be grown in Item 7 below.

    B. RELEASE-From the collateral described in the Financing Statement bearing the file number shown above, the Secured Party releases the collateral described in Item 7 below.

    C. ASSIGNMENT-The Secured Party certifies that the Secured Party has assigned to the Assignee above named, all the Secured Party's rights under the Financing Statement bearing the file number shown above in the collateral described in Item 7 below.

    D. TERMINATION - The Secured Party certifies that the Secured Party no longer claims a security interest under the Financing Statement bearing the file number shown above.

    E. AMENDMENT-The Financing Statement bearing the file number shown above is amended as set forth in Item 7 below. (Signature of Debtor required on all amendments.)

    F. ☐ OTHER

7.

8.

    (Date)_____19___

    By:_____
        SIGNATURE(S) OF DEBTOR(S)   (TITLE)

    By:_____
        SIGNATURE(S) OF SECURED PARTY(IES)   (TITLE)

CODE
1
2
3
4
5
6
7
8
9

9. This Space for Use of Filing Officer (Date, Time, Filing Office)

10. **Return Copy to**

    ┌   ┐

NAME
ADDRESS
CITY, STATE
AND ZIP

    └   ┘

(1) FILING OFFICER COPY

196

UCC-3   REQUEST FOR INFORMATION OR COPIES. Present in Duplicate to Filing Officer

1. ☐   INFORMATION REQUEST. Filing officer please furnish certificate showing whether there is on file any presently effective financing statement naming the Debtor listed below and any statement of assignment thereof, and if there is, giving the date and hour of filing of each such statement and the names and addresses of each secured party named therein.

1A. DEBTOR (LAST NAME FIRST)		1B. SOC. SEC. OR FED. TAX NO.
1C. MAILING ADDRESS	1D. CITY. STATE	1E. ZIP CODE
1F.		

Date_____19____   Signature of Requesting Party_____

2. CERTIFICATE:

FILE NUMBER	DATE AND HOUR OF FILING	NAME(S) AND ADDRESS(ES) OF SECURED PARTY(IES) AND ASSIGNEE(S), IF ANY

The undersigned filing officer hereby certifies that the above listing is a record of all presently effective financing statements and statements of assignment which name the above debtor and which are on file in my office of _____19____at_____ __M.

_____19_____
(DATE)

_____
(FILING OFFICER)

By:_____

3. ☐   COPY REQUEST. Filing officer please furnish_____copy(ies) of each page of the following statements concerning the debtors listed below   ☐ Financing Statement   ☐ Amendments   ☐ Statements of Assignment   ☐ Continuation Statements   ☐ Statement of Release   ☐ Termination Statement   ☐ All Statements on file.

FILE NUMBER	DATE OF FILING	NAME(S) AND MAILING ADDRESS(ES) OF DEBTOR(S)	DEBTORS SOC. SEC. OR FED. TAX NO.

Date_____19____   Signature of Requesting Party_____

4. CERTIFICATE:

The undersigned filing officer hereby certifies that the attached copies are true and exact copies of all statements requested above.

_____19_____
(DATE)

_____
(FILING OFFICER)

By:_____

5   **Mail Information or Copies to**

NAME
MAILING
ADDRESS
CITY, STATE
AND ZIP

⌐   ¬

L   ⌐

197

Escrow No. _____

NOTICE TO CREDITORS OF BULK TRANSFER

(Secs. 6101–5107 U.C.C.)

Notice is hereby given to creditors of the within named parties that a bulk sale transfer is intended to be made on personal property hereinafter described.

The name(s) and business address of the intended transferor(s) are:

The name(s) and business address of the intended transferee(s) are:

The property pertinent hereto is described in general as: Materials, supplies, merchandise, equipment, fixtures, furniture,

and is located at: _____

_____

Last day to file claims: _____, 19_____.

That said bulk transfer is intended to be consummated at the office of _____

_____

on or after _____, 19_____.

So far as is known to said intended Transferee(s) said intended Transferor(s) used following additional business names and addresses within the three years last past:
(If "none," so state.)

Executed at _____, _____, on Date _____, 19_____.

X_____   Date _____, 19_____.
    Transferee

_____
Print name and title

_____
Address

X_____   Date _____, 19_____.
    Transferee

_____
Print name and title

_____
Address

Do not detach—Return all copies   *Do Not Write Above This Line—For Headquarters Office Only*

APPLICATION FOR ALCOHOLIC BEVERAGE LICENSE(S)	1. TYPE(S) OF LICENSE(S)	FILE NO.
To: Department of Alcoholic Beverage Control		FEE NO.
1215 O Street		
Sacramento, Calif. 95814 ———————— (DISTRICT SERVING LOCATION)		GEOGRAPHICAL CODE
The undersigned hereby applies for licenses described as follows:		Date Issued
2. NAME(S) OF APPLICANT(S)		Temp. Permit

Applied under Sec. 24044 ☐
Effective Date: Effective Date:

3. TYPE(S) OF TRANSACTION(S)	FEE	LIC. TYPE
	$	

4. Name of Business

5. Location of Business—Number and Street

City and Zip Code County	RECEIPT NO. TOTAL	$

6. If Premises Licensed, Show Type of License   7. Are Premises Inside City Limits?

8. Mailing Address (if different from 5)—Number and Street   (Temp) (Perm)

9. Have you ever been convicted of a felony?   10. Have you ever violated any of the provisions of the Alcoholic Beverage Control Act or regulations of the Department pertaining to the Act?

11. Explain a "YES" answer to items 9 or 10 on an attachment which shall be deemed part of this application.

12. Applicant agrees (a) that any manager employed in on-sale licensed premises will have all the qualifications of a licensee, and (b) that he will not violate or cause or permit to be violated any of the provisions of the Alcoholic Beverage Control Act.

13. STATE OF CALIFORNIA   County of ....   Date...............

Under penalty of perjury, each person whose signature appears below, certifies and says: (1) He is the applicant, or one of the applicants, or an executive officer of the applicant corporation, named in the foregoing application, duly authorized to make this application on its behalf; (2) that he has read the foregoing application and knows the contents thereof and that each and all of the statements therein made are true; (3) that no person other than the applicant or applicants has any direct or indirect interest in the applicant's or applicants' business to be conducted under the license(s) for which this application is made; (4) that the transfer application or proposed transfer is not made to satisfy the payment of a loan or to fulfill an agreement entered into more than ninety (90) days preceding the day on which the transfer application is filed with the Department or to gain or establish a preference to or for any creditor of transferor or to defraud or injure any creditor of transferor; (5) that the transfer application may be withdrawn by either the applicant or the licensee with no resulting liability to the Department.

14. APPLICANT SIGN HERE ....

APPLICATION BY TRANSFEROR

15. STATE OF CALIFORNIA   County of ....   Date...............

Under penalty of perjury, each person whose signature appears below, certifies and says: (1) He is the licensee, or an executive officer of the corporate licensee, named in the foregoing transfer application, duly authorized to make this transfer application on its behalf; (2) that he hereby makes application to surrender all interest in the attached license(s) described below and to transfer same to the applicant and/or location indicated on the upper portion of this application form, if such transfer is approved by the Director; (3) that the transfer application or proposed transfer is not made to satisfy the payment of a loan or to fulfill an agreement entered into more than ninety days preceding the day on which the transfer application is filed with the Department or to gain or establish a preference to or for any creditor of transferor or to defraud or injure any creditor of transferor; (4) that the transfer application may be withdrawn by either the applicant or the licensee with no resulting liability to the Department.

16. Name(s) of Licensee(s)	17. Signature(s) of Licensee(s)	18. License Number(s)

19. Location   Number and Street   City and Zip Code   County

Do Not Write Below This Line; For Department Use Only

Attached: ☐ Recorded notice,
☐ Fiduciary papers,
☐ .... (OTHER)   COPIES MAILED ....

☐ Renewal: Fee of.............Paid at.....................Office on.............Receipt No..............

ABC 211 (6-74)   SEPT T OSP

199

STATE OF CALIFORNIA
DEPARTMENT OF
ALCOHOLIC BEVERAGE CONTROL

PERSONAL AFFIDAVIT IN SUPPORT OF APPLICATION

F. P. NO.	F. P. DATE	FILE NO.

1. FULL NAME	2. PREVIOUS NAME(S) *(Maiden, Prior Married Name, etc.)*	3. SOC. SEC. NO.

4. PREMISES ADDRESS	(WHERE LICENSE TO BE ISSUED)	(ZIP)	PHONE

5. HOME ADDRESS	(STREET)	(CITY)	(ZIP)	PHONE

6. AGE:	SEX:	HT:	WT:	HAIR:	EYES:	PRESENT BUSINESS PHONE

7. I AM OR WILL BE [ ] SOLE OWNER [ ] PARTNER [ ] OFFICER [ ] DIRECTOR [ ] STOCK-HOLDER [ ] MGR. [ ] RESTAURANT LESSEE
OF PERSONS OR COMPANY

8. DRIVERS LICENSE NO.	PLACE OF BIRTH	DATE OF BIRTH

9. DO YOU NOW HAVE ANY DIRECT, OR INDIRECT, INTEREST IN ANY OTHER ALCOHOLIC BEVERAGE BUSINESS, OR HAVE YOU EVER BEEN AN ALCOHOLIC BEVERAGE LICENSEE OR AN OFFICER OR DIRECTOR OF A CORPORATE LICENSEE? [ ] NO [ ] YES *(If Yes, Explain Fully)*

10. HAVE YOU AS AN INDIVIDUAL, A PARTNER, OR WHILE AN OFFICER, DIRECTOR OR STOCKHOLDER OF A CORPORATE APPLICANT OR LICENSEE EVER HAD AN ALCOHOLIC BEVERAGE LICENSE DENIED, SUSPENDED, REVOKED, OR AN OFFER IN COMPROMISE ACCEPTED OR REJECTED? [ ] NO [ ] YES *(If Yes, Explain Fully)*

11. CURRENT AND PAST EMPLOYMENT (FOR AT LEAST PAST FIVE YEARS) *(Use additional sheets if necessary)*

FROM MO./YR.	TO MO./YR.	TYPE OF WORK	FIRM NAME	CITY

12. WILL YOUR SPOUSE WORK ON PREMISES? [ ] NO [ ] YES	SPOUSES NAME	PLACE AND DATE OF MARRIAGE

13. Have you ever, anywhere or at any time, (1) forfeited bail, (2) been convicted, (3) fined, or (4) placed on probation for any violation of the law? (If any of these events has occurred, this question must be answered "Yes" regardless of subsequent court action resulting in expungement, unless an order sealing records under Section 1203.45 of the Penal Code, relating to persons under age 18 years, has been issued. If no order has been issued, the answer must be "Yes".)
[ ] No [ ] Yes (If yes, explain each event fully.)

DATE OF ARREST	PLACE ARRESTED	OFFENSE	RESULTS

I have read all of the above and declare under penalty of perjury that each and every statement made is true, correct and complete.

PLACE	SIGNED

ATTEST– (ABC EMPLOYEE OR NOTARY PUBLIC)	DATE

ABC 208 (5-79)

DEPARTMENT OF ALCOHOLIC BEVERAGE CONTROL

INDIVIDUAL FINANCIAL AFFIDAVIT

This affidavit is made in connection with the following application for an alcoholic beverage license:

APPLICANT(S)

AFFIDAVIT OF	DBA

PREMISES ADDRESS (STREET)	(CITY)

I am or will be a ☐ Partner ☐ Stockholder ☐ Corporate Officer ☐ Director ☐ Financier
in the above-described licensed business.

PLEASE READ INSTRUCTIONS BELOW BEFORE COMPLETING THE FOLLOWING.

My total personal contribution will be $_____ . Of this amount, $_____ will be in cash and the cash will be or has been derived from the following sources (describe in detail):

_____

_____

_____

_____

INSTRUCTIONS: Explain the source of cash fully. If cash is from savings, indicate the source from which it was saved, where the money was or is kept, and the period of time necessary to save it. If the source was from the sale of property, indicate what was sold, the address if real estate, when it was sold, the name and address of the buyer, and the net proceeds from the sale. If a loan is involved, show the date, amount, terms, security, name, address and occupation of the lender. Fully describe any other sources such as inheritances or gifts. List any and all bank accounts in the following spaces by identifying the bank, type of account, number of account, and authorized signatures:

BANK ACCOUNT(S). (BANK, LOCATION, TYPE OF ACCOUNT, ACCOUNT NUMBER.)

_____

_____

_____

_____

_____

Authorized Signature	Authorized Signature

APPLICANT(S) UNDERSTAND THAT FALSIFICATION OF THE INFORMATION ON THIS FORM MAY CONSTITUTE GROUNDS FOR DENIAL OR REVOCATION OF THE LICENSE(S).

For a period of 90 days from this date, I/we hereby authorize the Department of Alcoholic Beverage Control, or any of its officers, to examine and secure copies of financial records consisting of signature cards, checking and savings accounts, notes and loan documents, deposit and withdrawal records, and escrow documents of my/our financial institution(s) or any financial records established in connection with this business. This authorization to examine records at any financial institution may be revoked at any time.

I/We also authorize the Department of Alcoholic Beverage Control, or any of its officers, to examine and secure copies of any business records or documents established in connection with this business including, but not limited to, those on file with my/our bookkeeper or with the above-named escrow holder.

I/We have also read all of the above and declare under penalty of perjury that each and every statement is true and correct.

Applicant(s) Signature(s) _____

Title(s) _____

Date _____ Place _____ Attest _____
ABC-242 A (4-78)   (ABC Employee or Notary Public)

DEPARTMENT OF ALCOHOLIC BEVERAGE CONTROL

FINANCIAL AFFIDAVIT IN SUPPORT OF APPLICATION

1. APPLICANT(S)

2. PREMISES ADDRESS (STREET)	(CITY)	TELEPHONE

3. LESSOR OR OWNER	ADDRESS (STREET)	(CITY)	(STATE)

4. LESSEE OR RENTER	ADDRESS (STREET)	(CITY)	(STATE)

5. MONTHLY RENTAL $	EXPIRATION DATE OF LEASE	6. DOES LEASE OR RENTAL AGREEMENT INCLUDE FURNITURE AND FIXTURES? □ ALL □ SOME □ NONE

PURCHASE AND INVESTMENT INFORMATION

7. Item	Purchased from	Cost
a. LICENSE		$
b. GOODWILL		$
c. REALTY OR INTEREST THEREIN		$
d. FURNITURE/FIXTURES		$
e. INVENTORY		$
f. NON-COMPETE COVENANT		$
8. FEES FOR OTHER LICENSES, PERMITS, AND DEPOSITS (APPROXIMATE)		$
9. WORKING CAPITAL (APPROXIMATE)		$
10. OTHER (SPECIFY)		$
TOTAL INVESTMENT (Items 7 through 10)		$

11. ESCROW HOLDER	ADDRESS (STREET)	(CITY)	ESCROW NUMBER

12. Indicate what part of the Total Investment will be in cash and from what source(s) it will be or has been derived. $ _____ (EXPLAIN - USE REVERSE IF NECESSARY)

13. Indicate the amount remaining and how it will be paid. $ _____ (EXPLAIN - USE REVERSE IF NECESSARY)

14. IF FRANCHISED, NAME FRANCHISOR

15. BOOKKEEPER OR ACCOUNTANT	ADDRESS (STREET)	(CITY)	TELEPHONE

16. BUSINESS BANK ACCOUNT (BANK(S) AND ACCOUNT NO(S).)

AUTHORIZED SIGNATURE(S)

17. OTHER BANK ACCOUNT(S) (BANK(S) AND ACCOUNT NO(S).)

AUTHORIZED SIGNATURE(S)

APPLICANT(S) UNDERSTAND THAT FALSIFICATION OF THE INFORMATION ON THIS FORM MAY CONSTITUTE GROUNDS FOR DENIAL OR REVOCATION OF THE LICENSE(S).

For a period of 90 days from this date, I/we hereby authorize the Department of Alcoholic Beverage Control, or any of its officers, to examine and secure copies of financial records consisting of signature cards, checking and savings accounts, notes and loan documents, deposit and withdrawal records, and escrow documents of my/our financial institution(s) or any financial records established in connection with this business. This authorization to examine records at any financial institution may be revoked at any time.

I/We also authorize the Department of Alcoholic Beverage Control, or any of its officers, to examine and secure copies of any business records or documents established in connection with this business including, but not limited to, those on file with my/our bookkeeper or with the above-named escrow holder.

I/We have also read all of the above and declare under penalty of perjury that each and every statement is true and correct.

Applicant(s) Signature(s) _____

Title(s) _____

Date _____ Place _____ Attest _____

(ABC Employee or Notary Public)

ABC-242 (4-78)

202

(DO NOT WRITE ABOVE. Govt. Code Sec. 27361.6 reserves space above for exclusive use of County Recorder.)

NOTICE OF INTENDED TRANSFER OF RETAIL ALCOHOLIC BEVERAGE LICENSE UNDER SECTIONS 24073 AND 24074, CALIFORNIA BUSINESS AND PROFESSIONS CODE

1. LICENSEE'S NAME(S)   SOCIAL SECURITY NUMBER(S)   MAILING ADDRESS (OTHER THAN LICENSED PREMISES)   ZIP CODE

2. INTENDED TRANSFEREE'S NAME(S)   SOCIAL SECURITY NUMBER(S)   ADDRESS   ZIP CODE

3. KIND OF LICENSE(S) INTENDED TO BE TRANSFERRED (NAME AND NUMBER)

4. PREMISES ADDRESS(ES) TO WHICH THE LICENSE(S) HAS (HAVE) BEEN ISSUED

5. NAME AND ADDRESS OF ESCROW HOLDER OR GUARANTOR

6. Total consideration to be paid for the business and license (to include inventory whether actual cost, estimated cost, or a not-to-exceed amount)

   Cash .... $ _____
   Checks .... _____
   Promissory Notes .... _____
   Tangible and/or intangible property .... _____
                     TOTAL AMOUNT $ _____

7. The parties agree that the consideration for the transfer of the business and the license(s) is to be paid only after the Department of Alcoholic Beverage Control has approved the proposed transfer. The parties also agree and herein direct the above-named escrow holder to make payment or distribution within a reasonable time after the completion of the transfer of the license as provided in Section 24074 of the California Business and Professions Code.

TRANSFEROR(S) SIGNATURES   TRANSFEREE(S) SIGNATURES

One copy of this notice, certified by the County Recorder, together with an additional copy must accompany the application for transfer for the license.

See Form ABC-522, Department of Alcoholic Beverage Control Instructions re Escrow and Public Notice Requirements for most Retail License Transfers.

ABC-227 (2-76)

203

STATE OF CALIFORNIA
DEPARTMENT OF ALCOHOLIC BEVERAGE CONTROL

DIAGRAM OF LICENSED PREMISES

APPLICANT(S)

PREMISES ADDRESS *(Street)*   *(City)*   TYPE OF LICENSE

The diagram below is a true and correct description of the entrances and boundaries of the premises to be licensed, and is the only area where alcoholic beverages will be sold, served, consumed, possessed or stored. (If only a portion of the floor plan is to be licensed, please outline in red the area where alcoholic beverages will be sold, served, consumed, possessed or stored.)

DIAGRAM:

It is hereby declared that the above-described boundaries and entrances will not be changed without first notifying and securing prior approval of the Department of Alcoholic Beverage Control. I declare under penalty of perjury that the foregoing is true and correct.

Date: _____   _____
                                                                     SIGNATURE

Place: _____   _____
                                                                     SIGNATURE

Special Instructions for Applicants for Public Premises Type Licenses

Your signature above acknowledges that you are aware that in premises operated as a Public Premises no persons under 21 years of age are to be allowed. A sign at least 7'' x 11'' stating ''No Person Under 21 Allowed'' must be posted near each entrance and at a prominent place in the interior of the premises.

DEPARTMENT use only.

Inspected on: _____ Certified correct: _____

ABC-257-A

STATE OF CALIFORNIA, DEPARTMENT OF ALCOHOLIC BEVERAGE CONTROL

DECLARATION OF PREMISES USAGE IN SUPPORT OF APPLICATION FOR ON-SALE LICENSE

My planned operation of the premises can best be described as:

1. ☐ Cocktail Lounge   5. ☐ Hotel/Motel   9. ☐ Private Club

2. ☐ Bar: beer or beer & wine   6. ☐ Cafe/Coffee Shop   10. ☐ Other (Describe)___

3. ☐ Complete Restaurant   7. ☐ Bowling Alley

4. ☐ Speciality Restaurant   8. ☐ Discotheque

Do you intend to employ a manager? ☐ Yes ☐ No

Hours of Operation:		Patron Capacity:
to	Fixed Bar? ☐ Yes ☐ No	
Do premises have off-street parking? ☐ Yes ☐ No		Number of cars:

EXPLAIN FOOD SERVICE	ENTERTAINMENT
☐ No Food ☐ Minimal Food (sandwiches, snacks, etc.)	☐ Juke box or recorded music
☐ Restaurant:	☐ Pool tables/coin operated game machines
☐ Full course meals	☐ Card room
☐ Specialty Restaurant Describe (pizza, fish & chips, etc.) _____	☐ Movies
	☐ Band/combo/singer(s), etc.
	☐ Patron dancing
Hours of Meal Service) Breakfast:_____	☐ Bikini/topless dancers
) Lunch:_____	☐ Floor Show
) Dinner:_____	☐ Other (Explain)_____
Estimate what percentage of your total sales will be alcoholic beverages: _____ %	

Are the premises currently operating? ☐ Yes ☐ No

Will your planned operation be substantially the same as recent or present operation of the premises? ☐ Yes ☐ No

---

Date	Applicant Signature

STATE OF CALIFORNIA
DEPARTMENT OF ALCOHOLIC BEVERAGE CONTROL

STATEMENT RE CONSIDERATION
DEPOSITED IN ESCROW

TRANSFEROR

TRANSFEROR'S LICENSE NO.

SECTION I: APPLICANT'S STATEMENT THAT CONSIDERATION HAS BEEN DEPOSITED IN ESCROW

NAME AND ADDRESS OF ESCROW HOLDER

NAME OF APPLICANT AND PREMISES ADDRESS

The above designated applicant states that he is the intended transferee of a retail license, and submits the following statement pursuant to the provisions of Section 24074.3 of the Alcoholic Beverage Control Act:

I hereby state that the purchase price or consideration, as set forth in the escrow agreement required by Section 24074 of the Alcoholic Beverage Control Act is deposited with the escrow holder named above.

I declare under penalty of perjury that the foregoing is true and correct.

Executed at _____ , California, this _____ day of

_____ , 19 ____ .

SIGNATURE(S) OF APPLICANT(S)

Applicant(s) hereby instruct(s) the escrow holder to transmit this statement to the Department of Alcoholic Beverage Control when the escrow holder executes Section II of this document. At that time a copy must also be sent to the transferor.

SECTION II: ESCROW HOLDER'S NOTIFICATION TO THE DEPARTMENT THAT LICENSE MAY TRANSFER

To the Department of Alcoholic Beverage Control:

In connection with the transfer of the Alcoholic Beverage license described above, please be advised that the total consideration set forth in the recorded notice has been deposited in escrow and that all cash required by the escrow instructions to be deposited prior to the close of escrow has in fact been deposited, and/or the escrow holder has the unconditional written assurance of a responsible lender that funds will be deposited in escrow forthwith upon issuance of license.

Escrow holder certifies that disbursement of the consideration provided for in escrow instructions will not establish a preference for any creditor of the transferor except as provided for by Section 24074 of the Alcoholic Beverage Control Act.

ESCROW HOLDER: Mail original and one copy to:

SIGNATURE OF ESCROW HOLDER

DATE SIGNED

SECTION III: DEPARTMENT'S NOTICE TO ESCROW HOLDER THAT LICENSE HAS TRANSFERRED (For Department use only)

LICENSE NO.

DATE ISSUED

This notice, submitted in fulfillment of the provisions of Section 24074 of the Alcoholic Beverage Control Act will serve to confirm that the transferor's license was transferred as shown above.

LICENSING SUPERVISOR - DEPARTMENT OF ALCOHOLIC BEVERAGE CONTROL

ABC 226 (10-77)

STATE OF CALIFORNIA
DEPARTMENT OF ALCOHOLIC BEVERAGE CONTROL

NOTICE OF WITHDRAWAL OF APPLICATION

Date _____   File _____

Name(s) of Applicant(s) _____

_____

Location of Premises _____
                            Number   **Street**

_____
                            City   **County**

License(s) applied for _____

Copies mailed
date _____
_____

Reason for withdrawal: _____

_____

The undersigned hereby request the Department of Alcoholic Beverage Control to withdraw the above-described application and to refund the fee in accordance with Section 23959 of the Alcoholic Beverage Control Act (Business and Professions Code, Division 9) and Rule 60 of the Rules and Regulations issued in pursuance of said Act.

or

Apply fee on supplemental application for _____

_____

_____

_____   _____
Signature of Applicant(s)   Signature of Licensee(s)

_____   _____
Mailing Address   Mailing Address

Witnessed by: _____

NOTE:
    Transferor's License:
        Is being held in district office . . . . □
        Is being returned to licensee . . . . □
        Is being surrendered under Rule 65 (ABC-231 Attached) . . . . □
        Headquarters is to continue to hold under Rule 65 . . . . □
        Was application protested? . . . . Yes □ No □

ABC-209 (12-78)

STATE OF CALIFORNIA
DEPARTMENT OF ALCOHOLIC BEVERAGE CONTROL
Request to Surrender or Cancel License

Name .... License No. ....

DBA .... District Office ....

Address .... License Attached: ☐ Yes ☐ No

City .... County ....

CANCELLATION

I voluntarily cancel my license because I am no longer in business. I understand my license cannot be reactivated or reinstated.

_____
Signature   Date:

SURRENDER - Rule 65

I voluntarily surrender my license for a period of not more than one year. I intend to ☐ Transfer/ ☐ Reactivate the license. I understand that the license must be renewed at the time renewal fees are due or the license will be automatically revoked. I further understand that the Department will proceed to automatically cancel at the expiration of the one-year period if not transferred or reactivated.

Date Closed ....

_____
Signature

Home Phone: _____ Date: _____   _____
                                                      Mailing Address

REQUEST FOR SURRENDER OF RETAIL LICENSE
UNDER SECTION 24045.5(b) OF THE ALCOHOLIC BEVERAGE CONTROL ACT

Surrender Date .... Temporary Permit No. .... issued.

Transferee .... Effective Date ....

.... Expiration Date ....

Important Notice to Licensee

All licenses surrendered will be automatically revoked if the renewal fees are not paid. Any change of mailing address shall be reported to the District Administrator. The surrendered license will be automatically cancelled upon transfer to the temporary permittee.

If the transfer application is denied or withdrawn:

(a) If the transferor intends to resume operation of the licensed business he must request the return of the surrendered license and establish that there has been no change in the ownership or the qualifications of the licensed premises.

(b) If the transferor does not intend to resume operation of the licensed business and does not request return of the surrendered license then the Department will proceed to hold the license under the provisions of Rule 65. The effective date of Rule 65 surrender will be the date of application, denial, or withdrawal.

I/We have read the foregoing and know the contents thereof. Signature ....

Mailing Address .... Telephone No. .... Date ....

Department Use Only: ☐ Premises abandoned ☐ Letter attached requesting surrender or cancellation ☐ Other explanation

ABC–231 (7–74)

DEPARTMENT OF ALCOHOLIC BEVERAGE CONTROL

Rules and Regulations

Rule 65

65. Surrender of License on Closing of Business. (a) Every licensee who surrenders, abandons or quits his licensed premises, or who closes his licensed business for a period exceeding 15 consecutive calendar days, shall, within 15 days after closing, surrendering, quitting, or abandoning his licensed premises, surrender his license or licenses to the Department. The Department may seize the license certificate or certificates of any licensee who fails to comply with the surrender provisions of this rule, and may proceed to revoke his license or licenses.

(b) Upon the voluntary request by any licensee, on such form as the Department may prescribe, the Department may cancel his license or licenses.

(c) A surrendered license may be reinstated upon request made at least 10 days prior to the date of reinstatement upon certification by the licensee that there has been no change of ownership of the licensed business, and that the premises possess the same qualifications required for the original issuance of the license.

(d) Any license voluntarily surrendered under paragraph (a) of this rule shall be revoked if it is not transferred to another person or for use at another premises, or redelivered and the licensed activity resumed, within one year from the date of such surrender. There shall be no extension of such surrender period except when the Department finds good cause exists where: (1) an application is pending for transfer of the surrendered license; or (2) litigation other than that involving disciplinary action by the Department is pending; or (3) the premises for which the license had been issued and for which the license is sought to be redelivered were destroyed due to circumstances beyond the control of the licensee by fire, flood, or other natural catastrophe, or as part of an urban renewal program, and the licensee makes an affirmative showing of good faith efforts that he is attempting to obtain reconstruction of such destroyed premises; or (4) the Director in his judgment finds a case of undue hardship exists which would warrant an extension.

A	MAIL CERTIFIED COPIES TO:	B	PUBLISH IN

NAME _____

ADDRESS _____

CITY _____

COUNTY CLERK'S FILING STAMP

FICTITIOUS BUSINESS NAME STATEMENT

THE FOLLOWING PERSON(S) IS (ARE) DOING BUSINESS AS:

1. •   Fictitious Business Name(s)

2. ••   Street Address, City & State of Principal place of Business in California   Zip Code

3. •••

Full Name of Registrant

(if corporation, show state of incorporation)

Residence Address

City   State   Zip

Full Name of Registrant

(if corporation, show state of incorporation)

Residence Address

City   State   Zip

Full Name of Registrant

(if corporation, show state of incorporation)

Residence Address

City   State   Zip

Full Name of Registrant

(if corporation, show state of incorporation)

Residence Address

City   State   Zip

4. ••••   This business is conducted by ( ) an individual ( ) individuals (Husband & Wife) ( ) a general partnership ( ) a limited partnership ( ) an unincorporated association other than a partnership ( ) a corporation ( ) a business trust (CHECK ONE ONLY)

5.A

Signed_____

Typed or Printed_____

5.B   If Registrant a corporation sign below:

Corporation Name _____

Signature & Title _____

Type or Print
Officer's Name & Title _____

This statement was filed with the County Clerk of _____ County on date indicated by file stamp above.

6. New Fictitious Business Name Statement	
7. Refile — Statement expires December 31.	

File No. _____

I HEREBY CERTIFY THAT THIS COPY IS A CORRECT COPY OF THE ORIGINAL STATEMENT ON FILE IN MY OFFICE.

_____
COUNTY CLERK

BY _____ DEPUTY

File No._____

Original Copy for Filing with County Clerk of _____County

STATEMENT OF ABANDONMENT OF USE OF FICTITIOUS BUSINESS NAME

The following person (persons) have abandoned the use of the fictitious business name _____

at _____
(STREET ADDRESS OF PRINCIPAL PLACE OF BUSINESS)

The fictitious business name referred to above was filed in County on _____

(*)   1. _____   2. _____
             (FULL NAME - TYPE/PRINT)   (FULL NAME - TYPE/PRINT)

      _____   _____
             (ADDRESS)   (ADDRESS)

      _____   _____
             (CITY)   (CITY)

    3. _____   4. _____
             (FULL NAME - TYPE/PRINT)   (FULL NAME - TYPE/PRINT)

      _____   _____
             (ADDRESS)   (ADDRESS)

      _____   _____
             (CITY)   (CITY)

(**) This business was conducted by _____

              Signed _____

This statement was filed with the County Clerk of_____County on date indicated by file stamp above.

File No. _____
Statutory Filing Fee — $5.00

AFFIDAVIT AND LIST OF CREDITORS AND UNPAID TAXES

Under Bulk Sales Law
(to be made in triplicate)

Following is a true, full and correct list of the names and addresses of all the creditors of _____ hereinafter called "vendor" doing business at No. _____ Street, in the Town or City of _____ County of _____ in the State of _____, on this_____ day of _____, 19_____, to whom said vendor is indebted for or on account of services, commodities, goods, wares, or merchandise, or fixtures and equipment used in or about or furnished to the business of the vendor, or for or on account of money borrowed to carry on the business of the vendor or for or on account of labor employed in the course of the business of the vendor, of which the goods, wares, and merchandise, or fixtures and equipment, bargained for or purchased, are a part, together with the amount of indebtedness due and owing and to become due and owing, by the vendor to each of the creditors, and the amount of unpaid taxes with respect to the operation of the business of the vendor, at the time _____

_____

was sold to _____
whose address is No. _____ _____Street, in the Town or City of _____, County of _____, in the State of _____ for a consideration of $ _____

CREDITORS

Name	Address	Amount

TAXES

Nature of Tax	Name of Taxing Body	Amount

X _____Date_____19____.   X _____ Date_____19____.
  Seller   Seller

_____   _____
Address   Address

ESCROW HOLDER CHECK LIST

Escrow No. _____

Date of Closing _____ , 19_____ .

In	Completed	
_____	_____	Listing Agreement
_____	_____	Salesman follow-up check list
_____	_____	Buyer's Agreement
_____	_____	Purchase (Deposit/Receipt) Agreement
_____	_____	Estimated closing cost work sheet
_____	_____	Satisfaction or waiver of contingency
_____	_____	Buyers and Sellers check list
_____	_____	Addendums
_____	_____	Covenant not to compete
_____	_____	Monies for Sales Tax from Buyers $_____
_____	_____	Monies to open Escrow $_____
_____	_____	Monies for escrow fees from buyers $_____
_____	_____	Monies for escrow fees from sellers $_____
_____	_____	Monies to increase deposit $_____
_____	_____	Others (specify) _____
_____	_____	Others (specify) _____
_____	_____	Others (specify) _____
_____	_____	Others (specify) _____
_____	_____	Commission authorization
_____	_____	Bill of sale
_____	_____	Security Agreement
_____	_____	Straight note
_____	_____	Assignment of Note
_____	_____	Affidavit and List of Creditors and Unpaid Taxes
_____	_____	Notice to creditors of bulk transfer (no ABC)
_____	_____	Notice to creditors of bulk transfer with ABC License transfer
_____	_____	Complete set of ABC forms (ABC will supply)
_____	_____	ABC Form #226
_____	_____	Financial statement to Secretary of State UCC-1
_____	_____	Financial statement to Secretary of State UCC-2
_____	_____	Financial statement to Secretary of State UCC-3, 1st notice
_____	_____	Financial statement to Secretary of State UCC-3, 2nd notice
_____	_____	Recording of notice – Date_____19____
_____	_____	Notice to Department of Benefit Payments

213

	Com-
In	*pleted*

Notice to Board of Equalization

Publication – Bulk transfer – Newspaper _____

Publication – Intend to sell alcoholic beverages (ABC)

Publication – ☐ Buyer(s) Fictitious Name   ☐ Seller(s) to withdraw name

Copy of Escrow Instructions ☐ Seller   ☐ Buyer   ☐ Broker

Appointment of attorneys

Creditors claims ☐ approve by seller

Closing monies from Buyer $_____

Closing monies from Seller $_____

Inventory list approved

Fixture and Equipment List approved

Customers List approved

Releases

Clearance receipt – Department of Benefit Payments

Clearance receipt – Board of Equalization

Closing statement – Buyer

Closing statement – Seller

Disbursement taxes _____, $ _____

Disbursement – Commission $_____

Disbursement – Department of Benefit Payments $ _____

Disbursement – Board of Equalization $_____

Disbursement – Creditors claims $_____

Disbursement – ☐ Seller $_____   ☐ Buyer $_____

Others (specify) _____

Others (specify) _____

Delivery of a complete set of escrow instructions
☐ Buyer   ☐ Seller   ☐ Broker

The information is provided solely as a guide and estimate of some of the more common requirements involved in transferring a business. The information above has not been verified by the Broker, its agents, attorneys, CPA or Escrow Holder, and they are not responsible for its accuracy or completeness.

BUYERS AND SELLERS CHECK LIST
Selected highlights of Escrow (San Jose, CA., Santa Clara County only)

Escrow Number_____

In	Complete

1. Alcoholic Beverage License transfer: ABC, 1150 S. Bascom, San Jose (Buyer(s) pays if required) 277-1200 (8–3 pm).
   A. Buyer(s) get application, fill out, bring to opening of Escrow for Seller(s) signature.
   B. Before Buyer(s) returns to ABC, file at County Court House, 70 W. Hedding St., San Jose, 95110, County Recorder Dept., 299-2481.
   C. Seller(s) must bring license to ABC.
   D. Buyer(s) A.S.A.P. Get copy of signed lease or assignment of lease to ABC.
   E. Buyer(s) is to publish "Intent to Sell" ABC Form #207A in local newspaper.
   F. Post ABC Form #207 on door (inside, but visible to outside) within 5 days.
   G. Return ABC Form #293.
   H. Newspapers: Sunnyvale-Valley Journal 736-9090, Santa Clara Sun, 246-5480 (255-7500 Legal Dept.), San Jose-San Jose Post, 287-4866.

2. Bulk Sale only—buyer(s) pays cashier check for purchase price or at least downpayment to open Escrow, Split Escrow Fee 50/50?
   A. P. Brien Wilson, Attorney-at-Law, 20401 Stevens Creek Blvd., Cupertino, CA., 95014. 257-2000.
   B. William H. Dunn, Attorney-at-Law, 170 Park Center Plaza, Suite 202, San Jose, CA., 95113. 286-4850.
   C. Bank of America, 2905 Stevens Creek Blvd., San Jose, CA., 95128. Joanne Okazaki, 277-7658.
   D. Wells Fargo Bank, 121 S. Market St., San Jose, CA., 95113. Joyce Tafoya, 277-6261.
   E. Other Escrow Holder. _____
   G. 6.5% Sales Tax on Fixtures and Equipment, must be paid by Buyer(s).

3. Seller(s) must make declaration of County Tax—(if not filed) 70 W. Hedding, 299-4061.

4. Landlord—Buyer(s) to get new lease assignment (Seller(s) goes first).
   A. Prorate rent.
   B. Replace security on lease, plus most landlords ask for 1st and last month rent in advance.

In	Complete

5. Public Utilities—Buyer(s) should check if deposit is required on telephone, water, PG&E, etc.
   A. Start and cancel as of day of closing escrow together.

6. Insurance—prorate as of day of closing of Escrow, or cancel.
   A. Buyer(s) gets new one. (Buyer(s) should cover when loan is on Seller(s) property): Includes fire, theft and liability, crime, motor vehicles, fidelity bonds on employees, interruptions, health and life, key person, workmen's compensation insurance, buy and sell agreement, group, medical, and other insurances (See Chapter 12 for complete list).

7. Buyer(s) to get new Business License (city) 801 N. 1st Street, Room 217, San Jose, CA., 95110. 277-4985.
   A. Buyer(s) should also check City Hall for special licenses for particular businesses such as dry cleaners, motorcycles, DMV dealer permit, service stations, contractors etc. All departments; police, fire, zoning, redevelopment, planning department, assessors, highway, etc., for any restrictions or violations.

8. Health Dept. License (County)
   A. Buyer(s) check inspection reports for violations.
   B. Seller(s) must cancel license, 2220 Moorpark, San Jose, 95128, 297-1636.

9. Buyer(s) to file for "Fictitious Name" (county), 191 N. 1st St., San Jose, 95113, or DBA (doing business as) 299-2968.
   A. Buyer(s) to publish in local newspaper (Seller(s) must file abandonment).

10. State Board of Equalization—1550 The Alameda, Suite 220, San Jose, 95129. 277-1231.
    Seller(s):
    A. Form BT 401, copies for last three months if paid monthly or copies for last two quarters if paid quarterly plus the cancelled checks or money order receipts. You can pay by cashiers check or money order. You must have cash if you want the clearance receipt immediately. You have a couple of choices: Close out your account or you can transfer to another business account. A couple of days before closing, get the clearance receipt and get it to the Escrow Officer (You cannot get your money before this time).
    The Board of Equalization will usually allow a new owner two weeks or more to open the sales tax impound account.

In | Complete

Buyer(s):

A. Get a new resale number.

B. Estimate your gross sales and expenses for your first month of business.

C. Buyer(s) pays 6.5% sales tax (approximately 3 months) must be on deposit 2 years, 3 ways to do it: 1) Bond; 2) S&L certificates; 3) cash.

11. Department of Benefit Payments. 906 Ruff (Hedding) San Jose, 95110, 277-1475 (if have employees).

Seller(s):

A. For the two most recent calendar quarters preceding date of sale, file copies of Form DE 3 with evidence of payment such as cancelled checks. If photocopies are submitted, please show reverse side of checks as well as front. This gives the date received in Sacramento and the batch number.

B. A closing form DE 3 payment for a current quarter.

C. Form DE 3 (reconciliation of income tax withheld together with state copies of W2's and totaled listing.)

D. Payment of all amounts due and owing the Employment Development Dept. can be by cashiers check, certified check or money order. You must pay cash if you want the clearance receipt immediately. A couple of days before closing, get the clearance receipt (even if no employees). Must bring to Escrow holder before Seller gets his money.

Buyer(s):

A. Complete Form DE 1.

B. Gather the various pamphlets and other valuable information pertaining to your privileges and obligations as an employer.

Note:

Escrow Officer cannot close Escrow, until Certificate of Clearance from Employment Development Department and Certificate from State Board of Equalization are in his hands.

12. Buyer(s) to go to Internal Revenue Service, 123 E. Gish Road, San Jose, CA., 95112, 998-2300, for Federal Employees Tax No. (file form SS-4) if have employees.

A. Check for special tax for bars and cocktails lounges, (for games, etc.). Income, employee(s), Social Security and Federal taxes.

13. Labor Commission Office, State Dept. of Industrial Relations, 880 N. First St., San Jose, CA., 95112. 277-1265. (Workmen's Compensation Insurance).

217

In	Complete

14. Franchise Tax Board, 1570 The Alameda, San Jose, CA. 95129 (800) 852-7050.

15. Department of Consumer Affairs, 30 Van Ness St., San Francisco, CA, 94102

16. Inventory fixture and equipment (included and not included) list signed by both parties.

17. Closing Statement: All Escrow needs is the following:

   a) We hereby agree that the inventory is $ _____, at physical possession.
   b) Keys are accepted by Buyer(s).
   c) All equipment is in working condition at the date of physical possession by Buyer(s).
   d) We hereby agree that all assets: furniture, fixtures and equipment on itemized list in Escrow is here on the day of physical possession.

X_____.   Date _____19_____.
  Seller

_____
Print name and title

X_____.   Date _____19_____.
  Seller

_____
Print name and title

X_____.   Date _____19_____.
  Buyer

_____
Print name and title

X_____.   Date _____19_____.
  Buyer

_____
Print name and title

X_____.   Date _____19_____.
  Broker/agent

The information is provided solely as a guide and estimate of some of the more common requirements involved in starting a business. The information above has not been verified by the Broker, its agents, attorneys, CPA or Escrow Holder and are not responsible for their accuracy or completeness.

SALESPERSON/MANAGER CHECK LIST

Recheck together and against each other to determine if completed before you close escrow:

1. Listing Agreement.

2. Buyer(s) Agreement.

3. Purchase (Deposit/Receipt) Agreements.

4. Escrow Instructions.

    a. Salesperson check list.

    b. Estimated Closing Cost Work Sheet.

    c. Escrow Holders Check List.

    d. Buyer(s) and Seller(s) Check List.

_____   _____
Salesperson (agent)   Date   Broker (manager)   Date

CLOSING STATEMENT

To: _____   Date_____

_____   Escrow No.: _____

_____   Office _____

_____   Address _____

Telephone _____

	Debits	Credits
Selling Price – Business	$	$
Selling Price – Real Property		
Deposits in Escrow		
Deposit paid outside of escrow		
PRO-RATIONS AND REIMBURSEMENTS		
Sales tax on fixtures		
Personal property taxes		
Current Rent		
Lease Deposit		
Insurance		
County Taxes		
Personal Property Taxes		
Real Property Taxes		
ENCUMBRANCES		
Assumed note on Fixtures & Equipment		
Assumed deed of Trust		
New deed of Trust		
CREDITORS CLAIMS		
Broker's Commission		
EXPENSES INCURRED		
Recording & publication notice of Bulk Transfers		
UCC Certifications		
UCC-1 filing fees		
UCC-2 filing fees		
UCC-3 filing fees		
Revenue stamps		
TITLE POLICY		
ESCROW SERVICE CHARGES & FEES		

Completing documents		
Added amendments		
Notary fees		
Messenger Service		
Processing Claims		
Notices, Prorate Funds		
Balance of Funds Due (cashiers check only)		
Total	$	$

We are pleased to enclose herewith the following:

Escrow check $_____ in favor of _____representing your sale proceeds.

Certificate of Payment of Sales & Use Tax.

Certificate of Release of Buyer.

Letter from _____ County Tax Collector regarding Taxes _____

_____.

Buyer in possession.

Letter from _____ County Tax Collector indicated Taxes _____

_____ were/were not paid.

Copy of Promissory note, estimated inventory/cancelled.

Copy of Bill of Sale.

Fixture & Equipment list attached.

Recorded copy of Notice of Bulk Transfer.

Possession Date and True Inventory Valuation.

UCC-2

The undersigned hereby acknowledges receipt of a copy of this statement and certifies the same to be true and correct, and authorizes and ratifies the disbursement of the funds as stated herein, and does further release and discharge the Broker, its agents and the escrow holder from further duties or obligations concerning said escrow.

X_____ Date_____, 19_____   X_____ Date_____, 19_____
  Buyer   Seller

_____   _____
Print name and title   Print name and title

X_____ Date_____, 19_____   X_____ Date_____, 19_____
  Buyer   Seller

_____   _____
Print name and title   Print name and title

221

Glossary

TITLE IN BUSINESS OPPORTUNITIES MAY BE HELD IN FIVE WAYS:

Severalty: Single.

Co-ownership: Two or more persons.

Tenancy in Common: Two or more persons holding an undivided interest in the same property.

Joint Tenancy: Same as tenancy in common, but if one party dies, his or her title passes to the surviving party or parties by operation of law; each must have an equal share.

Community Property: Shared ownership acquired by husband and wife.

FORMS OF BUSINESS ENTITY IN BUSINESS OPPORTUNITIES:

Sole Proprietorship: The sole owner of a business (one individual). The owner is personally liable for the debts of the business.

Partnership: A business owned by two or more persons. Each partner is personally liable for the debts of the partnership.

Limited Partnership: Consists of one or more general partners who run the business and incur personal liability for partnership debts, and one or more limited partners who incur no personal liability for partnership debts. However, a limited partner cannot take part in managing the partnership.

Joint Venture: Two or more persons. Same as partnership except that it exists to undertake a single project.

223

Corporation: A legal entity separate from the persons who own, control, manage, and operate it. Liability of the owner(s) or shareholder(s) is limited to the assets of the corporation.

MORE COMMON DEFINITIONS IN BUSINESS OPPORTUNITIES:

Agent: One acting under authority of a principal to do the principal's business. The agent must use his or her best efforts and keep the principal fully informed of all material facts.

Arbitration: The submission of a disputed matter for resolution outside the normal judicial system. It is often speedier and less costly than courtroom procedures. An arbitration award can be enforced legally in court; if one or more parties cannot agree on a single arbitrator, they can select arbitrators under the rules of the American Arbitration Association.

Bulk-Sale Law: Provisions of the Uniform Commercial Code that regulate the sale of inventory of a business for the protection of the seller's creditors.

Capital Gain: The gain received on the sale of real or personal property (good will, stocks, bonds, etc.), other than property sold as stock-in-trade.

Capitalization: Determination of the value of property by considering its net income and return on investment.

Cash Flow: Income remaining after deducting from gross income, all operating expenses, including loan payments and an allowance for the income tax attributable to net income.

Contract: An agreement freely reached to do or not to do a certain thing, for the breach of which the law provides a remedy. It may be written or oral, but whenever possible should be written, especially where real property is involved. To be enforceable, the contract should contain all essential terms and conditions and should convey the same meaning to each party.

Defamation: Injury to a person's business or personal character or reputation resulting from libelous or slanderous conduct.

Depreciation/Appreciation: Depreciation is a loss in value due to any cause. Appreciation is the opposite, a gain in value due to any cause.

Fiduciary Relationship: A relationship of trust and responsibility existing between two people as from financial matters. The principal may legally trust and depend upon his or her agent to be honest and faithful. The principal may call upon the agent at any time to render an accounting of any funds handled by the agent.

Fraud, Deceit, and Misrepresentation: Intentional or negligent misrepresentation or concealment of a material fact, with justifiable reliance thereon by another party, who is thereby damaged.

Names: Ordinarily, unless done to escape punishment or to defraud others, a person has the right to adopt any name he or she chooses. The adopted name is said to become the real name by reputation. Names can also be changed by court proceedings. When the business name is not the name of the individual or individuals who own it, it is usually necessary to register the name so that the public will have a means of associating the trade name with the individual. This is the reason for filing a fictitious name statement (dba—Doing Business As).

Notice of Intention to Engage in Sale of Alcoholic Beverages: Document that must be posted on premises 30 days prior to issuance or transfer of license and must be published once in newspaper of general circulation if on-sale license is required.

Notice of Intention to Sell (Notice to Creditors of Bulk Transfer): Document that should be recorded and published prior to the sale of a business opportunity in order to give notice of the impending sale to the seller's creditors.

Notice of Intention to Transfer Business Premises: Document that must be recorded in county where business premise is located, and filed with the Department of ABC prior to transfer of a liquor license.

Notice to Pay Rent or Quit: A three-day notice required by law before a tenant, delinquent in rental payments or other obligations may be evicted by suit.

Options: An agreement to hold an offer open for a specified period of time, usually in consideration for the payment of a certain sum of money. The person granting the option is the optioner. The person receiving the option is the optionee. The optioner cannot withdraw the option before its expiration date. The consideration for an option is not normally returnable to the optionee if he or she fails to exercise the option. If the optionee does exercise the option, the consideration is often applied to the purchase price.

Real-Estate Exchange: When certain kinds of "like" property are exchanged, Section 1031 of the Internal Revenue Code provides that part or all of the taxes may be deferred. Real estate held for business or as an investment is considered "like" property. For instance, lakefront lots may be exchanged for apartments, retail stores for office buildings, etc., or a combination of income-producing real estate may be exchanged.

Uniform Commercial Code: The law that establishes a uniform and comprehensive scheme for the regulation of secured transactions in personal property and bulk-sale transfer. This law is designed to protect Buyer, Seller, and Creditors alike in personal property transactions. Division 6 covers Bulk Transfers. Division 9 covers Secured Transactions.

Zoning: Division of a county, city, or other entity into zones or districts according to permitted uses, heights, setback lines, development, and other factors.

	Legal Status	**Decision Maker**	**Public Hearing**	**Grounds for Approval**	**Chances for Approval**
A. Rezoning	Area given new zoning classification; Zoning map redrawn.	Town or County usually empowers planning or zoning board to make recommendations or decision. Board's decision can be appealed to Council.	Yes. May require 2 or 3 hearings for board recommendation and one for Town or Council approval.	Zoning will be more advantageous to community. (Existing zoning is inappropriate)	Most difficult form of zoning relief to achieve.
B. Variance	Particular project exempted from zoning requirements (e.g., height, setback or density.)	Subordinate authorities: Planning, Zoning or Zoning Appeals Board or Hearing Examiner. (Appeals to Council may be permitted.)	Yes. A second public hearing required if board's decision is appealed to Council.	Zoning restrictions create hardship for landowner and prevent reasonable use of land.	Easier than rezoning, but varies with current government policies in area.
C. Conditional Use (Special Exception)	Use is lawful if approved by public agency or local council.	Usually subordinate public agencies— sometimes Town or County Council.	Yes.	At discretion of specified board.	Depending on use, may be easier or harder than getting a variance approved.

Note: It is imperative that local, county, and state zoning regulations and ordinances be thoroughly checked for each situation. The above table is for reference only.

Business Opportunities, General Resources, and References

Business

Business: Its Nature and Environment. By R. Glos. 1972.
Introduction to Business. By T. Sielaff. 1966.
Your Future in Your Own Business. By E. Winter. 1971.

Business — Bibliography

Business Student's Guide to Selected Library Sources. By W. Barker. 1971.

Business — Forms, Blanks, Etc.

Business Forms. By J. Kish. 1971.
Handbook of Business Form Letters and Forms. By J. Elfenbein. 1972.

Business — Handbooks, Manuals, Etc.

How To Start A Small Business. By L. Lackey. 1971.

Business Crimes

Computer Crime. By Walker. 1974.
Crime Pays. By T. G. Plate. 1975.
The Crime That No One Talks About. By Harold Cohen. 1974.
Dirty Money. By Thurston Clark. 1975.
Illegal But Not Criminal. By John Conklin. 1977.
Stealing. By Mark Lipman. 1973.
The Thief in the White Collar. By Norman Jaspan. 1960.

Business Cycles

Money and Markets. By Beryl W. Sprinkel. 1971.

Business Forecasting

Art of Forecasting. By L. Bean. 1969.
Planning and Forecasting in the Smaller Company. By J. Bacon. 1971.
Pragmatic Forecasting. By J. Cantor. 1971.

Business Mathematics

Applied Business Statistics. By E. McElroy. 1971.
Business Mathematics. By R. Thorn. 1971.
Essential Business Mathematics. By L. Snyder. 1972.
Mathematics of Retail Merchandising. By B. Corbman. 1972.

227

Business Periodicals — Directories	*Ayer Directory of Publications.* Annual.
Business Periodicals — Indexes	*Business Periodicals Index.* Monthly; Quarterly, Annuals.
California — Information Services	*California Handbook.* By T. Trzyna. 1971.
California — Manufacturers Directories	*California International Business Directory.* Annual. *California Manufacturers Register.* Annual.
Employment Interviewing	*Training in Depth Interviewing.* By W. Banaka. 1971.
Franchises (Retail Trade) — United States	*Franchise Handbook.* By J. Cameron. 1970.
Franchises (Retail Trade) — United States — Directories	*Directory of Franchising Organizations.* Annual. *Franchise Opportunities Handbook.* By U.S. Office of Minority Business Enterprise. 1973.
Income — United States	*Statistics of Income: Business Income Tax Returns.* By U.S. Internal Revenue Service. Annual. *Survey of Buying Power.* By Sales Management. Annual. Includes estimates of population, effective buying income, retail sales.
Insurance	*Best's Reports*: Property, Liability, Health and Life Insurers. *Risk and Insurance.* By Mark R. Greene, 1977.
Labor	*Directory of National and International Labor Unions in the U.S.* Biennial. *Employment and Earnings, States and Areas, Based on the Standard Industrial Classification.* G.P.O. Annual. Each vol. cumulative from 1939. (Bulletin No. 1370) *Handbook of Labor Statistics.* G.P.O. Annual. *Occupational Outlook Handbook: Employment Information on Occupations For Use in Guidance.* G.P.O. Biennially.
Management	*Art of Getting Your Own Sweet Way.* By P. Crosby. 1972. *Business: Its Nature and Environment.* By R. Glos. 1972. *Management.* By P. Drucker. 1974. *Management and the Activity Trap.* By G. Odiorne. 1974. *Management of Organizations.* By H. Hicks. 1972. *Management-Minded Supervision.* By B. Boyd. 1968. *Management: The Basic Concepts.* By H. Albers. 1972. *Managing: A Contemporary Introduction.* By J. Massic. 1973. *Managing Change.* By J. Morgan. 1972. *So You Want To Be A Manager.* By E. Reeves. 1971. *Taking the Guesswork Out Of Long Range Planning.* By S. Goodman. 1971.
Management — Anecdotes, Satire, Etc.	*Peter Prescription.* By L. Peter. 1972.
Market Surveys	*Market Guide.* Editor & Publisher. Annual. *Survey of Buying Power.* By Sales Management. Annual. Includes estimates of population, effective buying income, retail sales.

Marketing	*Attitude Measurement of Marketing Strategies.* By G. Hughes. 1971. *Life-Styled Marketing.* By M. Hanan. 1972. *Marketing a New Product.* By J. Zif. 1971. *Marketing and Society.* By R. Gist. 1971. *Marketing Handbook.* Ed. by A. Frey. 1965. *People Motivators.* By H. Turner. 1973.
Marketing — Case Studies — Indexes	*Case Studies in Marketing.* By L. Berman. 1971.
Marketing — Information Services	*Handbook of International Business and Investment Facts and Information Sources.* By Juvenal Angel. 1967.
Marketing Management	*Decision Making in Marketing.* 1971. *Marketing Management: Analysis, Planning & Control.* By P. Kotler. 1967. *Marketing Research: Management and Methods.* By W. Wentz. 1972.
Merchandising	*Mathematics of Retail Merchandising.* By B. Corbman. 1972.
Personnel Management	*Employee Drug Abuse.* By C. Chambers. 1972. *Personnel: The Human Problems of Management.* By G. Strauss. 1972. *Twenty-two Biggest Mistakes Managers Make & How To Correct Them.* By J. Van Fleet. 1973.
Real Estate	*Real Estate Principles.* By H. C. Davey. 1976.
Restaurant Management	*So You Want to Start a Restaurant?* By D. Dyer. 1971. *Planning and Operating a Successful Food Service Operation.* By W. Kahr. 1973. *Selected Readings For an Introduction to Hotel and Restaurant Management.* Comp. by D. Keister. 1971.
Retail Trade — United States	*Survey of Buying Power.* By Sales Management. Annual. Includes estimates of population, effective buying income, retail sales.
Retail Trade — United States — Statistics	*Retail Trade.* By U.S. Bureau of the Census. Census of Business. 1967. *Selected Services: Area Statistics.* By United States Bureau of the Census. Census of Business, 1967.
Sales Forecasting	*Pragmatic Forecasting.* By J. Cantor. 1971.
Sales Promotion	*Dartnell Sales Promotion Handbook.* By Dartnell Corporation. 1965.
Salesmen and Salesmanship	*Manufacturers Representative.* By F. Lebell. 1971. *Salesmanship.* By C. Kirkpatrick. 1971. *Secrets of Closing Sales.* By C. Roth. 1970. *Successful Low Pressure Salesmanship.* By E. Berman. 1957.
Salesmen and Salesmanship — Anecdotes, Satire, Etc.	*Handbook of Sales For All Situations.* By H. Saint-Laurent. 1971.
San Jose, California — Directories	*Contacts Influential Reference Book.* Annual. Peninsula ed. 1973 *Haines San Jose City & Suburban Criss Cross Directory* *San Jose, Calif.: Suburban City Directory.*

229

San Jose, California — Population	*Census Tracts: San Jose, Calif.* By United States Bureau of the Census of population and housing.
Santa Clara County, California — Manufacturers — Directories	*Directory of Manufacturers.* By Santa Clara County Chamber of Commerce, Inc. Frequently Revised.
Small Business	*A Reference Manual of Practical information on buying and selling a business.* By Dr. W. Jurek and Associates.
	Ethnic Enterprise in America. By I. Light. 1972
	One Hundred and One Businesses You Can Start and Run With Less Than 1,000 Dollars. By H. Kahm. 1968.
	How To Organize and Operate a Small Business. By P. C. Kelly. 1973.
	How to Run A Small Business. By J. K. Lasser. 1974.
	White Collar Crime. By U.S. Chamber of Commerce. 1974.
	Starting and Succeeding In Your Own Small Business . By Louis Allen. 1968.
Small Business — Finance	*Banker's Handbook of Federal Aids to Financing.* By H. Spolen. 1971. Looseleaf.
	Complete Guide to Financial Management. By D. S. Brightly. 1970.
	How to Negotiate a Business Loan. By R. C. Belew. 1973.
	How to Start, Finance and Manage Your Own Business. By J. R. Mancuso.
	Local Economic Development Corporation: Legal and Financial Guideline, 1970. By New York (City) Practicing Law Institute. 1971.
	University Dictionary of Business and Finance. By T. V. Crowell.
Small Business — Management	*Doing Business in California.* By California Div. of Business & Industry Development. 1973. Three separately published pamphlets bound into one vol.: No. 1, "A Guide for Establishing A Business", No. 2, Principle Business Taxes, No. 3, "Labor Laws Affecting Business."
	How To Start a Typing Service in Your Own Home. By P. Wilbanks. 1972.
	How to Succeed in Business When The Chips Are Down. By W. Wayne. 1972.
	Manage More by Doing Less. By R. D. Loin, 1971.
	Managing the Small Business. By L. L. Sleinmatz.
	Mind Your Own Business. By T. L. Weber. 1973.
	Small Business Management. By J. Petrof. 1972.
	Small Business Management. By H. N. Broom. 1975.
	Up Your Own Organization. By D. Dibble. 1971.
	What You Should Know About Small Business Management. By D. Grunewald. 1966.
	Winning The Money Game. By D. Dibble
Small Business Investment Companies — Directories	*Guide to Venture Capital Sources.* 1972-1973. By S. Rubel.
United States — Commerce — Addresses, Essays, Lectures	*Challenges For Business in the 1970's.* 1972. Based on a series of eight articles in Fortune.
United States — Commerce — Directories	*Directory of American Importers and Exporters.* Published by World Wide Trade Service. Annual.
	Middle Market Directory. By Dun & Bradstreet.
	Verified Directory of Manufacturer's Representatives (Agents) Biannual.

230

United States — Commerce — Handbooks, Manuals, Etc.	*Introduction to Doing Import and Export Business.* By Chamber of Commerce of the U.S. 1962. Supplements the Foreign Commerce Handbook.
United States — Economic Conditions	*Business Statistics.* By U.S. Office of Business Economics. Biannual. *Economic Report of the President. Together with the Annual Report of the Council of Economic Advisors.* By U.S. President. Annual. *Forecast.* By United California Bank. Research and Planning Div. Annual. *New York Times Guide to Business and Finance.* By A. Kraus. 1972.
United States — Taxes	*Federal Tax Course* by Commerce Clearing House, Inc., N.Y. *Tax Guide for Buying and Selling a Business.* By Stanley Hagendorf. 1976. *Tax Guide for Small Business.* By U.S. Internal Revenue Service. *Tax Reform Act of 1976.* By Morton Myerson. 1976. *Your Income Tax.* By J. K. Lasser.
Employment of Women	*How To Go To Work When Your Husband Is Against It.* 1972. *Matching College Women to Jobs.* By J. Angel, 1970. *One Hundred Ways To Make Money at Home.* By Good Housekeeping. 1971.
Employment of Women — Congresses	*Second Careers for Women: Reports of Workshops Held at Stanford University.* May 2, 1970. 1971.
Woman Employment — United States — Case Studies	*Women At Work.* Comp. By. W. O'Neill 1972.

OTHER RESOURCES AND REFERENCES

Business Associations	*American Management Association.* 135 W. 50th Street, N.Y., N.Y. 10020
Business-Opportunity Listing Service	*Western Investment Listing Service.* 375 S. Mayfair Ave., Daly City, CA., 94015 (95 cities in Calif. and Nevada)
Business Reports	*Small Business Reporter.* By Bank of America. 1979. Free. *Statement of Determination of Geologic Hazard Zones and/or Flood Hazard Zones.* By JCP-Engineers & Geologists, Inc., 7246 Sharon Drive, San Jose, CA 95129
Business References	*Reference Book.* By the Department of Real Estate.
Business Seminars	*"How to Buy and Sell Business Opportunities"* and *"Business Opportunity Appraiser"* by American Business Consultants, Inc., 1540 Nuthatch Lane, Sunnyvale, California 94087 (Telephone: 408-732-8931).
Consumer Information Center — Pubelo, CO 81009	*Consumer Information Catalog.* 1979. Free.
Small Business Administration — Washington, D.C. 20416	*Buying and Selling a Small Business.* $2.30. *Cash Planning in Small Mfg. Co.* SBA 1-20. Free. *Directory of Operating Small Business Investment Co's. For Sale Booklets.* SBA 115-B. Free. *How to Find a Likely Successor.* SBA 198 *Management Aids.* SBA 115-A. Free.

Protect Your Business Against Crime. 1974.
Small Business Bibliography. SBA 18, 85, & 86. Free.
Small Marketers Aids. SBA 71. Free.

Superintendent of Documents — United States Government Printing Office Washington, DC 20402 (30,000 Subjects)

Consumers Guide to Federal Publications. Free.
Government Periodicals and Subscription Services. Free.
Ratio Analysis for Small Business. Management Series 20.
Subject Bibliography. SB-004. Free.